MINDFUL POLITICS

MINDFUL POLITICS

A BUDDHIST GUIDE TO MAKING
THE WORLD A BETTER PLACE

edited by MELVIN McLEOD

WISDOM PUBLICATIONS • BOSTON

Wisdom Publications, Inc.
199 Elm Street
Somerville MA 02144 USA
www.wisdompubs.org

Library of Congress Cataloging-in-Publication Data

Mindful politics : a Buddhist guide to making the world a better place / edited by Melvin McLeod.
    p. cm.
  Includes index.
  ISBN 0-86171-298-6 (pbk. : alk. paper)
  1. Buddhism and politics. 2. Buddhists—Political activity. I. McLeod, Melvin.
  BQ4570.S7M56 2006
  294.3'372—dc22

                                    2006009979

ISBN 0-86171-298-6

First Printing
10 09 08 07 06
5   4   3   2   1

Cover design by Laura Shaw. Interior by Gopa & Ted2, Inc.
Set in Weiss 10.75pt/15pt.

Wisdom Publications' books are printed on acid-free paper and meet the guidelines for permanence and durability of the Production Guidelines for Book Longevity set by the Council on Library Resources.

Printed in the United States of America.

♻ This book was produced with environmental mindfulness. We have elected to print this title on 50% PCW recycled paper. As a result, we have saved the following resources: 111 trees, 77 million BTUs of energy, 9,715 lbs. of greenhouse gases, 40,325 gallons of water, and 5,178 lbs. of solid waste. For more information, please visit our web site, www.wisdompubs.org

TABLE OF CONTENTS

SECTION THREE: ACTION

INTRODUCTION

IF THE BUDDHA ever ran for political office, he might offer this four-point platform:

- ✦ May all beings enjoy happiness and the root of happiness.
- ✦ May they be free from suffering and the root of suffering.
- ✦ May they not be separated from the great happiness devoid of suffering.
- ✦ May they dwell in the great equanimity free of passion, aggression, and ignorance.

What kind of political platform is that?, you may ask, *it's ridiculous.* Possibly. *It's just bleeding-heart idealism.* Yes, in a way. *That's the not way the world works.* No it isn't. *It's too radical, it would change everything.* Yes it would, and a good thing, too. *That's what all politicians believe anyway.* No it isn't; look closely at what they really say and do. *No government or political party could ever espouse a program like that.* Not for the foreseeable future. But maybe you and I could start by making it the basis for our own lives as citizens. I hope this book can help.

I have spent my life studying politics. I took a degree in political science, including a period of study in Washington, D.C. As a journalist I often covered political stories. I graduated from the National Defense College of Canada, the country's highest institution for the study of domestic and international affairs. Yet I have learned more about politics from editing this book than from any of that.

What I have learned is what really matters in politics. Normally when we think about politics, we think about issues, policies, programs—the stuff of day-to-day government. Or we think of the contest of politics—the parties, the polls, the candidates, the strategies.

These are all important questions, of course, but they are only the surface manifestation of deeper political issues, issues which are moral, psychological, and, ultimately, spiritual. Politics is really about how we live together as human beings, and all spiritual practices point to one simple but profound truth about human life—that only love leads to peace, hatred never does. This is as true for nations as it is for individuals.

Take, for example, the four-line "platform" I quoted above, which is known as the *four limitless ones*. The key word in this prayer is *all*. This benevolent wish extends not just to some people but to all people. Not just to people of a particular party, nation, class, race, region, religion, gender, or ideology with which we identify and whose interests we promote, but to all people, without bias or discrimination. Think how different our societies, our governments, our policies, and our world would be if this view were at the heart of our politics.

Even at a more conventional level, we can see that emotion is far more important in politics than intellect. Around the world, long-standing wars are driven by the terrible cycle of revenge, of wrongs committed in response to previous wrongs. Elsewhere, conflict and alienation are fueled by fear, insecurity, jealousy, hatred, and greed. And everywhere, people are divided from their fellow human beings by the fundamental dualistic split between self and other, the split that Buddhism says is the root of all our suffering.

These emotions and attitudes are the real substance of politics, and they are the province of spirituality. What does Buddhism—what does any religion—have to offer to politics? Buddhism doesn't tell us much about what we normally think of as politics; it doesn't tell us anything specific about what policies are best or what parties to support. But it does offer us ways to work with our hearts and minds to address the deeper issues of our lives together as human beings. It's not treaties that will really bring peace in the Middle East. It's not legislation that will really change the lives of those who live in poverty and misery. It is only forgiveness, generosity, awareness, kindness, and selflessness that will really make a difference.

I believe that Buddhism is unique in the range of its meditation practices that can transform the way we live together, which is to say, the way we live politically. I see *Mindful Politics* as a practice book, an offering of Buddhist wisdom, insight, and meditations to help us on our path as responsible and caring citizens.

More than that, I think you will find that the insights and practices found in this book can be applied in all your relationships. All relationships involve questions of power and conflicting interests; all are, to some degree or another, political. I believe you will find this book helpful at work, in your marriage, with your family and friends, in all the places and all the ways that people relate to each other. Whether it's intimate affairs or international affairs, human relationships all operate on the same basic principles; it's only the scale that changes.

We have to recognize that we can't really change the world. We can't really change who others are and what they think. We can only work with our own heart and mind. But the transformative power of that is extraordinary.

So this is not what you might expect in a book on politics. The words *Republican* and *Democrat* appear only a few times and there is little in the way of ideology or specific policy. I have defined "politics" very broadly, as describing all the important ways in which we live together as human beings. So while there's no discussion of transient electoral politics or legislation, we look seriously at the issues that will determine in the long term the direction of human society, issues of peace, gender, race, economics, and the environment.

Nor is this book even what you might expect in a book on Buddhism and politics. It is not a book specifically about the Engaged Buddhism movement, although important voices from that movement are heard here. This is not a scholarly or an academic book, nor does it delve into the long history of Buddhism's political role in Asia. This is a handbook, a guide, a practice book, for people who want to draw on Buddhism's insights and practices to help them contribute to making the world a better place. I have intentionally avoided topical or passing issues in the hope that this book, like the timeless wisdom it offers, will be as helpful in the future as it is now.

I have divided this book into three sections, View, Practice, and Action, following a traditional Buddhist description of the spiritual path.

In the section on View, we begin with the Buddhist philosophy and understanding of the world that will inform our practice and action. We look at this view from a variety of angles, from Charles Johnson's summary of important Buddhist tenets and how they relate to politics, to bell hooks' pointed commentary on dominator culture both inside and outside of Buddhism; from the Dalai Lama's call to the world for a sense of universal responsibility, to Thich Nhat Hahn's heartfelt poem "Call Me By My True Names"; from David Loy's groundbreaking analysis of ego operating at the collective level, to Chögyam Trungpa's breathtaking vision of an enlightened society.

In the Practice section, we learn a variety of practices from Buddhism's cornucopia of meditation techniques. Here are ways to work with our own hearts and minds to change the ways that individuals and communities relate to each other: Pema Chödrön's teaching on how to remain steady in the face of our own fear and anger, and Thich Nhat Hahn's advice on how to listen openly and speak lovingly; Gehlek Rinpoche's instruction on compassion meditation, and Ezra Bayda's essay on the importance and practice of forgiveness; Thanissaro Bhikkhu's look at the Buddha's instructions on how to heal a wounded community, and Margaret Wheatley's sentiments on not losing heart in a suffering world.

These practices are the heart of the book; they are the heart of mindful politics. They are not goals to achieve, but tools we can work with moment to moment in our relationships—both personal and collective.

Informed by the view, softened yet strengthened by the practice, we must apply ourselves to the great questions before us as citizens. In the final section of the book, Action, some of contemporary Buddhism's best thinkers examine specific areas of political concern. Even here the discussion must be quite broad—Buddhism doesn't have much to say about the details of politics, about debates, laws, or treaties. But I think you'll find their insights helpful and to the point. Whether it's Rita Gross' advice on how to be a more effective feminist or the Home Minister of Bhutan's discussion of Gross National Happiness; Sueng Sahn's stern "Letter to a Dictator" or Gaylon Ferguson's surprising phone conversation about racism, their analysis is powerfully effective precisely because it is spiritually based. It is one of Buddhism's central tenets that skillful means flow naturally from wisdom. That point is proven here.

I would like to thank Tim McNeill and Josh Bartok of Wisdom Publications for inviting me to edit this anthology. I have gotten more from it than I ever could have imagined. I would also like to thank my colleagues at the *Shambhala Sun* and *Buddhadharma* magazines, where we study and discuss and try to practice the dharma together. I would like to thank my wife Pam Rubin, whose work in feminism and the law I greatly admire. And I express my profound appreciation to my teachers, Khenpo Tsultrim Gyamtso Rinpoche and the late Chögyam Trungpa Rinpoche, whose compassion and teachings encompass all humanity.

I do not live the life this book describes. I do not love all beings equally, without aversion or attachment. But like parents do, I love my young daughter completely (and if only I could love all beings like I love her). Because of her life ahead in the twenty-first century, and all those who will share that century with her, I pray that all beings be happy, that suffering diminish, and that this century be better than the last, or at least no worse. For that to happen, we will all have to exert ourselves and open our hearts as never before in history. May this book make even the slightest contribution to our lives together in the twenty-first century.

Melvin McLeod

SECTION ONE:
VIEW

MONKS, whatsoever states are unwholesome, partake of the unwholesome, pertain to the unwholesome—all these have the mind as their forerunner. Mind arises as the first of them, followed by the unwholesome states.

Monks, whatsoever states are wholesome, partake of the wholesome, pertain to the wholesome—all these have the mind as their forerunner. Mind arises as the first of them, followed by the wholesome states.

No other thing do I know, O monks, which is so responsible for causing unarisen unwholesome states to arise and arisen wholesome states to wane as negligence. In one who is negligent, unarisen unwholesome states will arise and arisen wholesome states will wane.

No other thing do I know, O monks, which is so responsible for causing unarisen wholesome states to arise and arisen unwholesome states to wane as diligence. In one who is diligent, wholesome states not yet arisen will arise and unwholesome states that have arisen will wane.

—Buddha, from *Numerical Discourses of the Buddha,* Chapter of the Ones

We are all equal, says the Dalai Lama, in seeking happiness and peace. Yet as individuals and as nations, we value our own happiness over all others'. This is called "ego" in Buddhism and it is the root of our suffering, both personal and collective. He proposes a new approach to global politics based on taking responsibility for the happiness of all people.

★ ★ ★

A NEW APPROACH
TO GLOBAL PROBLEMS

by the Dalai Lama

OF THE MANY PROBLEMS we face today, some are natural calamities, which must be accepted and faced with equanimity. Others, however, are of our own making, created by misunderstanding, and can be corrected. One such type arises from the conflict of ideologies, political or religious, when people fight each other for petty ends, losing sight of the basic humanity that binds us all together as a single human family. We must remember that the different religions, ideologies, and political systems of the world are meant for human beings to achieve happiness. We must not lose sight of this fundamental goal and at no time should we place means above ends; the supremacy of humanity over matter and ideology must always be maintained.

Whether they belong to more evolved species like humans or to simpler ones such as animals, all beings primarily seek peace, comfort, and security. Life is as dear to the mute animal as it is to any human being; even the simplest insect strives for protection from dangers that threaten its life. Just as each one of us wants to live and does not wish to die, so it is with all other creatures in the universe, though their power to effect this is a different matter.

Broadly speaking there are two types of happiness and suffering, mental and physical, and of the two, I believe that *mental* suffering and happiness are the more acute. Hence, I stress the training of the mind to endure suffering and attain a more lasting state of happiness. However, I also have a more general and concrete idea of happiness: a combination of inner peace, economic development, and, above all, world peace. To achieve such goals I feel it is necessary to develop a sense of *universal responsibility*, a deep concern for all, irrespective of creed, color, sex, or nationality.

The premise behind this idea of universal responsibility is the simple fact that, in general terms, all others' desires are the same as mine. Every being wants happiness and does not want suffering. If we, as intelligent human beings, do not accept this fact, there will be more and more suffering on this planet. If we adopt a self-centered approach to life and constantly try to use others for our own self-interest, we may gain temporary benefits, but in the long run we will not succeed in achieving even personal happiness, and world peace will be completely out of the question.

In their quest for happiness, humans have used different methods, which all too often have been cruel and repellent. Behaving in ways utterly unbecoming to their status as humans, they inflict suffering upon fellow humans and other living beings for their own selfish gains. In the end, such short-sighted actions bring suffering to oneself as well as to others. To be born a human being is a rare event in itself, and it is wise to use this opportunity as effectively and skillfully as possible. We must have the proper perspective, that of the universal life process, so that the happiness or glory of one person or group is not sought at the expense of others.

All this calls for a new approach to global problems. The world is becoming smaller and smaller—and more and more interdependent—as a result of rapid technological advances and international trade as well as increasing trans-national relations. We now depend very much on each other. In ancient times problems were mostly family-size, and they were naturally tackled at the family level, but the situation has changed. Today we are so interdependent, so closely interconnected with each other, that without a sense of universal responsibility, a feeling of universal brotherhood and sisterhood, and an understanding and belief that we really are part of one big human family, we cannot hope to overcome the dangers to our very existence—let alone bring about peace and happiness.

No nation can any longer satisfactorily solve its problems alone; too much depends on the interest, attitude, and cooperation of other nations.

A universal humanitarian approach to world problems seems the only sound basis for world peace. What does this mean? We begin from the recognition mentioned previously that all beings cherish happiness and do not want suffering. It then becomes both morally wrong and pragmatically unwise to pursue only one's own happiness oblivious to the feelings and aspirations of all others who surround us as members of the same human family. The wiser course is to think of others also when pursuing our own happiness. This will lead to what I call "wise self-interest," which hopefully will transform itself into "compromised self-interest," or better still, "mutual interest."

Although the increasing interdependence among nations might be expected to generate more sympathetic cooperation, it is difficult to achieve a spirit of genuine cooperation as long as people remain indifferent to the feelings and happiness of others. When people are motivated mostly by greed and jealousy, it is not possible for them to live in harmony. A spiritual approach may not solve all the political problems that have been caused by the existing self-centered approach, but in the long run it will overcome the very basis of the problems that we face today.

On the other hand, if humankind continues to approach its problems considering only temporary expediency, future generations will have to face tremendous difficulties. The global population is increasing, and our resources are being rapidly depleted. Look at the trees, for example. No one knows exactly what adverse effects massive deforestation will have on the climate, the soil, and global ecology as a whole. We are facing problems because people are concentrating only on their short-term, selfish interests, not thinking of the entire human family. They are not thinking of the Earth and the long-term effects on universal life as a whole. If we of the present generation do not think about these now, future generations may not be able to cope with them.

According to Buddhist psychology, most of our troubles are due to our passionate desire for and attachment to things that we misapprehend as enduring entities. The pursuit of the objects of our desire and attachment involves the use of aggression and competitiveness as supposedly efficacious instruments. These mental processes easily translate into actions, breeding belligerence as an obvious effect. Such processes have been going on in the human mind since time immemorial, but their execution has become more effective under modern conditions. What can we do to control and regulate these "poisons"—delusion, greed, and aggression? For it is these poisons that are behind almost every trouble in the world.

As one brought up in the Mahayana Buddhist tradition, I feel that love and compassion are the moral fabric of world peace. Let me first define what I mean by compassion. When you have pity or compassion for a very poor person, you are showing sympathy because he or she is poor; your compassion is based on altruistic considerations. On the other hand, love toward your wife, your husband, your children, or a close friend is usually based on attachment. When your attachment changes, your kindness also changes; it may disappear. This is not true love. Real love is not based on attachment, but on altruism. In this case your compassion will remain as a humane response to suffering as long as beings continue to suffer.

This type of compassion is what we must strive to cultivate in ourselves, and we must develop it from a limited amount to the limitless. Undiscriminating, spontaneous, and unlimited compassion for all sentient beings is obviously not the usual love that one has for friends or family, which is alloyed with ignorance, desire, and attachment. The kind of love we should advocate is this wider love that you can have even for someone who has done harm to you: your enemy.

The rationale for compassion is that every one of us wants to avoid suffering and gain happiness. This, in turn, is based on the valid feeling of "I," which determines the universal desire for happiness. Indeed, all beings are born with similar desires and should have an equal right to fulfill them. If I compare myself with others, who are countless, I feel that others are more important because I am just one person, whereas others are many. Further, the Tibetan Buddhist tradition teaches us to view all sentient beings as our dear mothers and to show our gratitude by loving them all. In this way we see that all beings in the universe share a family relationship.

Whether one believes in religion or not, there is no one who does not appreciate love and compassion. Right from the moment of our birth, we are under the care and kindness of our parents; later in life, when facing the sufferings of disease and old age, we are again dependent on the kindness of others. If at the beginning and end of our lives we depend upon others' kindness, why then in the middle should we not act kindly towards others?

The development of a kind heart (a feeling of closeness for all human beings) does not involve the religiosity we normally associate with conventional religious practice. It is not only for people who believe in religion, but is for everyone regardless of race, religion, or political affiliation. It is for anyone who considers himself or herself, above all, a member of the human family and who sees things from this larger and longer perspective. This is a powerful feeling that we should develop and apply; instead, we often neglect it, particularly in our prime years when we experience a false sense of security.

When we take into account a longer perspective, the fact that all wish to gain happiness and avoid suffering, and keep in mind our relative unimportance in relation to countless others, we can conclude that it is worthwhile to share our possessions with others. When you train in this sort of outlook, a true sense of compassion—a true sense of love and respect for others—becomes possible. Individual happiness ceases to be a conscious self-seeking effort; it becomes an automatic and far superior by-product of the whole process of loving and serving others.

Another result of spiritual development, most useful in day-to-day life, is that it gives a calmness and presence of mind. Our lives are in constant flux, bringing many difficulties. When faced with a calm and clear mind, problems can be successfully resolved. When, instead, we lose control over our minds through hatred, selfishness, jealousy, and anger, we lose our sense of judgment. Our minds are blinded and at those wild moments anything can happen, including war. Thus, the practice of compassion and wisdom is useful to all, especially to those responsible for running national affairs, in whose hands lie the power and opportunity to create the structure of world peace.

The principles I have discussed so far are in accordance with the ethical teachings of all world religions. I maintain that every major religion of the world—Buddhism, Christianity, Confucianism, Hinduism, Islam, Jainism, Judaism, Sikhism, Taoism, Zoroastrianism—has similar ideals of love, the same goal of benefiting humanity through spiritual practice, and the same effect of making its followers into better human beings. All religions teach moral precepts for perfecting the functions of mind, body, and speech. All teach us not to lie or steal or take others' lives, and so on. The common goal of all moral precepts laid down by the great teachers of humanity is unselfishness. The great teachers wanted to lead their followers away from the paths of negative deeds caused by ignorance and to introduce them to paths of goodness.

All religions agree upon the necessity to control the undisciplined mind that harbors selfishness and other roots of trouble, and each teaches a path leading to a spiritual state that is peaceful, disciplined, ethical, and wise. It is in this sense that I believe all religions have essentially the same message. Differences of dogma may be ascribed to differences of time and circumstance as well as cultural influences; indeed, there is no end to scholastic argument when we consider the purely metaphysical side of religion. However, it is much more beneficial to try to implement in daily life the shared precepts for goodness taught by all religions rather than to argue about minor differences in approach.

There are two primary tasks facing religious practitioners who are concerned with world peace. First, we must promote better interfaith understanding so as to create a workable degree of unity among all religions. This may be achieved in part by respecting each other's beliefs and by emphasizing our common concern for human well-being. Second, we must bring about a viable consensus on basic spiritual values that touch every human heart and enhance general human happiness. This means we must emphasize the common denominator of all world religions— humanitarian ideals. These two steps will enable us to act both individually and together to create the necessary spiritual conditions for world peace.

Practitioners of different faiths can work together for world peace when we view different religions as essentially instruments to develop a good heart—love and respect for others, a true sense of community. The most important thing is to look at the purpose of religion and not at the details of theology or metaphysics, which can lead to mere intellectualism. I believe that all the major religions of the world can contribute to world peace and work together for the benefit of humanity, if we put aside subtle metaphysical differences, which are really the internal business of each religion.

Despite the progressive secularization brought about by worldwide modernization and despite systematic attempts in some parts of the world to destroy spiritual values, the vast majority of humanity continues to believe in one religion or another. The undying faith in religion, evident even under irreligious political systems, clearly demonstrates the potency of religion as such. This spiritual energy and power can be purposefully used to bring about the spiritual conditions necessary for world peace. Religious leaders and humanitarians all over the world have a special role to play in this respect.

Whether we will be able to achieve world peace or not, we have no choice but to work toward that goal. If our minds are dominated by anger, we will lose the best part of human intelligence—wisdom, the ability to decide between right and wrong. Anger is one of the most serious problems facing the world today.

Anger plays no small role in current conflicts. These conflicts arise from a failure to understand one another's humanness. The answer is not the development and use of greater military force, nor an arms race. Nor is it purely political or purely technological. Basically it is spiritual, in the sense that what is required is a sensitive understanding of our common human situation. Hatred and fighting cannot bring happiness to anyone, even to the winners of battles. Violence always produces misery and is essentially counter-productive. It is, therefore, time for world leaders to learn to transcend the differences of race, culture, and ideology and to regard one another through eyes that see the common human situation. To do so would benefit individuals, communities, nations, and the world at large.

I suggest that world leaders meet about once a year in a beautiful place without any business, just to get to know each other as human beings.

Then, later, they could meet to discuss mutual and global problems. I am sure many others share my wish that world leaders meet at the conference table in such an atmosphere of mutual respect and understanding of each other's humanness.

To improve person-to-person contact in the world at large, I would like to see greater encouragement of international tourism. Also, mass media, particularly in democratic societies, can make a considerable contribution to world peace by giving greater coverage to human interest items that reflect the ultimate oneness of humanity. With the rise of a few big powers in the international arena, the humanitarian role of international organizations is being bypassed and neglected. I hope that this will be corrected and that all international organizations, especially the United Nations, will be more active and effective in ensuring maximum benefit to humanity and promoting international understanding. It will indeed be tragic if the few powerful members continue to misuse world bodies like the U.N. for their one-sided interests. The U.N. must become the instrument of world peace. This world body must be respected by all, for the U.N. is the only source of hope for small oppressed nations and hence for the planet as a whole.

As all nations are economically dependent upon one another more than ever before, human understanding must go beyond national boundaries and embrace the international community at large. Indeed, unless we can create an atmosphere of genuine cooperation, gained not by threatened or actual use of force but by heartfelt understanding, world problems will only increase. If people in poorer countries are denied the happiness they desire and deserve, they will naturally be dissatisfied and pose problems for the rich. If unwanted social, political, and cultural forms continue to be imposed upon unwilling people, the attainment of world peace is doubtful. However, if we satisfy people at a heart-to-heart level, peace will surely come.

Within each nation, the individual ought to be given the right to happiness, and among nations, there must be equal concern for the welfare of even the smallest nations. I am not suggesting that one system is better than another and all should adopt it. On the contrary, a variety of political systems and ideologies is desirable and accords with the variety of dispositions within the human community. This variety enhances the ceaseless human quest for happiness. Thus each community should be free to evolve its own political and socioeconomic system, based on the principle of self-determination.

The achievement of justice, harmony, and peace depends on many factors. We should think about them in terms of human benefit in the long run rather than the short term. I realize the enormity of the task before us, but I see no other alternative than the one I am proposing, which is based on our common humanity. Nations have no choice but to be concerned about the welfare of others, not so much because of their belief in humanity, but because it is in the mutual and long-term interest of all concerned.

Under present conditions, there is definitely a growing need for human understanding and a sense of universal responsibility. In order to achieve such ideas, we must generate a good and kind heart, for without this, we can achieve neither universal happiness nor lasting world peace. We cannot create peace on paper. While advocating universal responsibility and universal brotherhood and sisterhood, the facts are that humanity is organized in separate entities in the form of national societies. Thus, in a realistic sense, I feel it is these societies that must act as the building-blocks for world peace.

Attempts have been made in the past to create societies more just and equal. Institutions have been established with noble charters to combat anti-social forces. Unfortunately, such ideas have been cheated by selfishness. More than ever before, we witness today how ethics and noble principles are obscured by the shadow of self-interest, particularly in the political sphere. There is a school of thought that warns us to refrain from politics altogether, as politics has become synonymous with amorality. Politics devoid of ethics does not further human welfare, and life without morality reduces humans to the level of beasts.

However, politics is not axiomatically "dirty." I question the popular assumption that religion and ethics have no place in politics and that religious persons should seclude themselves as hermits. Such a view of religion is one-sided; it lacks a proper perspective on the individual's relation to society and the role of religion in our lives. Ethics is as crucial to a politician as it is to a religious practitioner. Dangerous consequences will follow when politicians and rulers forget moral principles. Whether we believe in God or karma, ethics is the foundation of every religion.

Such human qualities as morality, compassion, decency, wisdom, and so forth have been the foundations of all civilizations. These qualities must be cultivated and sustained through systematic moral education in a conducive social environment so that a more humane world may emerge. The qualities required to create such a world must be inculcated right from the beginning, from childhood. We cannot wait for the next generation to make this change; the present generation must attempt a renewal of basic human values. If there is any hope, it is in the future generations, but not unless we institute major change on a worldwide scale in our present educational system. We need a revolution in our commitment to and practice of universal humanitarian values.

Living in society, we should share the sufferings of our fellow citizens and practice compassion and tolerance not only toward our loved ones but also toward our enemies. This is the test of our moral strength. We must set an example by our own practice, for we cannot hope to convince others of the value of religion by mere words. We must live up to the same high standards of integrity and sacrifice that we ask of others. The ultimate purpose of all religions is to serve and benefit humanity. This is why it is so important that religion always be used to effect the happiness and peace of all beings and not merely to convert others.

In this regard there are two things important to keep in mind: self-examination and self-correction. We should constantly check our attitude toward others, examining ourselves carefully, and we should correct ourselves immediately when we find we are in the wrong.

Finally, a few words about material progress. I have heard a great deal of complaint against material progress from Westerners, and yet, paradoxically, it has been the very pride of the Western world. I see nothing wrong with material progress per se, provided people are always given precedence. It is my firm belief that in order to solve human problems in all their dimensions, we must combine and harmonize economic development with spiritual growth.

However, we must know its limitations. Although materialistic knowledge in the form of science and technology has contributed enormously to human welfare, it is not capable of creating lasting happiness. In America, for example, where technological development is perhaps more advanced than in any other country, there is still a great deal of mental suffering. This is because materialistic knowledge can only provide a type of happiness that is dependent upon physical conditions. It cannot provide happiness that springs from inner development independent of external factors.

For renewal of human values and attainment of lasting happiness, we need to look to the common humanitarian heritage of all nations the world over. May this essay serve as an urgent reminder lest we forget the human values that unite us all as a single family on this planet.

I have written the above lines
To tell my constant feeling.
Whenever I meet even a "foreigner,"
I have always the same feeling:
"I am meeting another member of the human family."
This attitude has deepened
My affection and respect for all beings.
May this natural wish be
My small contribution to world peace.
I pray for a more friendly,
More caring, and more understanding
Human family on this planet.
To all who dislike suffering,
Who cherish lasting happiness—
This is my heartfelt appeal.

In the following essay, the award-winning novelist and essayist Charles Johnson reflects on some of Buddhism's most important principles—impermanence, suffering, emptiness, and compassion—and how they can inform a politics of mindfulness and "beloved community."

★ ★ ★

— BE PEACE EMBODIED: PRINCIPLES —
— OF MINDFUL POLITICS —

by Charles R. Johnson

TO MY EYE, elections are the most glorious of civilization's regular trials, defining the nature of a democratic republic. For when the framers of the American Constitution declared that the nation's president "shall hold his office during the term of four years," they ingeniously guaranteed that a healthy degree of quadrennial change, suspense, tumult, renewal, and spirited debate would be inscribed into our political and social lives. Put another way, American voters, if they take their civic duty seriously, can never rest. Every four years they must decide on the direction of their collective destiny. Twenty-five times in each century they must define for themselves their understanding of the "good life," and vote for candidates and proposals that embody their vision of what this country and its influence on the world should be.

Yet for all its virtues, this necessary process, which the media frequently presents as a highly competitive "battle" or "war," can fuel the most ugly partisan passions, fears, frustrations, incivility, and forms of dualism we are likely to find in the realm of samsara. If perceived through the distorting lens of conflict-laden language and concepts that deliberately pit one citizen against another ("Speech has something in it like a spider's web," Thomas Hobbes once remarked), politics divides people on election night into "winners" and "losers," and creates bitterness and attachment that can cloud consciousness and cripple spiritual development—though one of our greatest American leaders, Dr. Martin Luther King, Jr., proved time and again that this need not be so.

On December 20, 1956, the day the Montgomery bus boycott ended, King—whose model for nonviolent civil disobedience in Alabama drew inspiration from Gandhi's struggle with the British—said, "We must seek an integration based on mutual respect. As we go back to the buses, let us be loving enough to turn an enemy into a friend." Though his home was bombed and his wife and baby endangered during the campaign to end segregation in the "Cradle of the Confederacy," the twenty-six-year-old Reverend King never forgot that "all life is interrelated," nor that we are all "caught in an inescapable network of mutuality, tied in a single garment of destiny. Whatever affects one directly, affects all indirectly." He called this the "beloved community," which in my view is simply sangha by another name.

If we can, through the kind of mindfulness exhibited by Dr. King during one of the most revolutionary moments in American history, remember that politics is merely the skin of social life beneath which we find a more profound experience of ourselves and others, then our Constitution-mandated sea change every four years can potentially be an uplifting experience rather than a spiritually debilitating one. For as the Chan Buddhist nun Jingnuo wrote four centuries ago, "If you bring to everything an illumined mind, you won't get lost."

The buddhadharma captures such course-correcting illumination in the terse Pali description of existence known as "the three marks": *anicca, dukkha, anatta*, often translated as, "Life is transient, sorrowful, and selfless." In this eidetic formulation about the marks that stain all phenomena, anatta reminds us that the belief in a substantive, enduring self is an illusion, while dukkha emphasizes the first noble truth of universal suffering based on selfish desire and clinging to the things of this world (including our thoughts and feelings about those things). Both the latter terms are experientially and logically grounded in the first mark, anicca, which means "impermanent," and speaks to Shakyamuni Buddha's insight that "whatever is subject to arising must also be subject to ceasing."

With that general statement, the Buddha is referring to everything in our experience—all material and immaterial objects, men and women, societies and states of mind, legislation and governments. Any physicist would add that even the thirteen-billion-year-old universe itself will one day be reduced to black holes that will eventually disintegrate into stray particles, and these, too, will decay. From the moment of our so-called "birth" we have been dying. "Changing all the time," says Thich Nhat Hanh, "not a single element remains the same for two consecutive moments." In essence, we are processes, not products. Therefore, the *Diamond Sutra* ends with this memorable verse:

> *Thus shall you think of all this fleeting world:*
> *A star at dawn, a bubble in a stream;*
> *A flash of lightning in a summer cloud,*
> *A flickering lamp, a phantom, and a dream.*

We can all understand this. There is nothing particularly mystical about the fundamental nature of reality being change, process, and transformation. Nor is there anything esoteric in the wisdom that we err if we desire or try to cling to evanescent phenomena that change faster than we can chase them. In the buddhadharma, the true nature of things is *shunyata*, Sanskrit for "emptiness." But we would be wrong if we interpreted this emptiness as a lack, or as vacuous. In his outstanding book *Nonduality*, scholar (and contributor to the present volume) David Loy provides a concise account of shunyata:

> It comes from the root *shunya*, which means "to swell" in two senses: hollow or empty, and also like the womb of a pregnant woman. Both are implied in the Mahayana usage: the first denies any fixed self-nature to anything; the second implies that this is also fullness and limitless possibility, for lack of any fixed characteristics allows the infinite diversity of impermanent phenomena.

Those who experience shunyata know that all things have eternally been in a perfect state of tranquillity, and that as Buddhaghosa says in the Visuddhimagga:

Suffering alone exists, none who suffers;
The deed there is, but no doer thereof;
Nirvana is, but no one seeking it;
The Path there is, but none who travel it.

In *The Buddhist Vision,* Alex Kennedy points out that the recognition of impermanence or emptiness necessarily leads to the nonconceptual intuition that all perceived conditioned and transitory things are interdependent. Thich Nhat Hanh's word for this is "interbeing," a neologism he coined to express the traditional Buddhist understanding of the concatenated links in dependent origination. Kennedy says,

> When we analyze any object, we can never come to a substance beyond which our analysis cannot penetrate. We can never find anything conditioned which has an underlying substantial reality.... All things, whether subject or object, are processes linked together in an intricate network of mutual conditions.... The ordinary man is distracted by the bright surface of the world and mistakes this for reality.

All things are empty in themselves, only existing—as Dr. King said—in a delicate "network of mutuality" where, as we are told in the Visuddhimagga, "it is not easy to find a being who has not formerly been your mother, your father, your brother, your sister, your son, your daughter." After awakening, or the experience of *nirvana,* which in Sanskrit literally means to "blow out" selfish desire and the illusory belief in a separate sense of one's life, the student of the Way experiences ultimate reality as a "we-relation." "Perfect peace," said Shakyamuni, "can dwell only where all vanity has disappeared."

However, in Buddhism we must acknowledge two levels of truth. First, there is ultimate, ontological truth. In *The Long Discourses of the Buddha,* Maurice Walshe explains that on this level, existence is experienced as "a mere process or physical and mental phenomena within which, or beyond which, no real ego-entity nor any abiding substance can be found." Secondly, there is conventional or relative truth, described by Walshe as the samsaric world "according to which people and things exist just as they appear to the naïve understanding." For myself, I enjoy thinking of these two truths in terms of our knowing the subatomic realm of electrons and positrons exists, but in our everyday lives we necessarily conduct ourselves in terms of Newtonian physics, because if we step out a tenth floor window or in front of a fast-moving truck, we will go *splat*.

The great Indian dialectician Nagarjuna, founder of the Madhyamaka school, demonstrated that these two truths are not in conflict, because samsara is nirvana. The sacred is the profane. The everyday is the holy. The dream world of samsara, which is the world of so much suffering and the world of relative truth, is the projection of our delusions and selfish desires onto nirvana. Yet samsara is logically prior to and necessary for the awakening to nirvana. The important point here, says John Blofeld in *The Zen Teachings of Huang Po*, is that "the enlightened man is capable of perceiving both unity and multiplicity without the least contradiction between them." His words echo in the lambent verse of Jingnuo, which appears in a wonderful book edited by Beata Grant, *Daughters of Emptiness: Poems by Buddhist Nuns of China*: "Everything is in the ordinary affairs of the everyday world." That is, if one is guided by mindfulness, the transcendent is found no less in quotidian tasks such as serving tea, motorcycle maintenance, or the arranging of rock gardens than in the recitation of mantras; no less in washing the dishes, writing this article, or actively participating in mercurial political affairs than in the oldest monastic rituals.

Insofar as Buddhist practitioners grasp reality as a we-relation, they are unshakeable in the experience of the Other as themselves. Thus, in the social and political world of samsara, there can be but a single proper response to all sentient beings, regardless of their political affiliations or views: compassion and loving-kindness. That ethical posture is codified in the bodhisattva vows and Shantideva's *A Guide to the Bodhisattva's Way of Life*:

> *First of all I should make an effort*
> *To meditate upon the equality between self and others:*

I should protect all beings as I do myself
Because we are all equal in (wanting) pleasure and
*   (not wanting) pain.*
Hence I should dispel the misery of others
Because it is suffering, just like my own,
And I should benefit others
Because they are sentient beings, just like myself.
When both myself and others
Are similar in that we wish to be happy,
What is so special about me?
Why do I strive for my happiness alone?

For those following the Way, individual salvation is never enough; they work tirelessly for the liberation not just of men and women, but of all sentient beings. Politics, therefore, offers the opportunity to use samsaric means for nirvanic ends—or what Shakyamuni might call "skillful means," which adapt the dharma to those imperfect tools we are obliged to work with in the relative-phenomenal world. The step on the eightfold path called "right conduct" demands such conscientious involvement in the relative-phenomenal realm, for we ourselves are inseparable from that world and can live here and now, nowhere else. But it is how the dharma student works in the world that is of all importance.

He or she will, I believe, bring one dimension of "right view" to the political arena—that is, the understanding that our perspectives and views on a particular issue are not the only veridical or possible ones. The follower of the Way will practice civility and "right speech," which the *Mahasatipatthana Sutra* says involves "refraining from lying, refraining from slander, refraining from harsh speech, refraining from frivolous speech." This person will listen with full empathy to the political Other, listening as carefully as when following his or her own breaths and thoughts in meditation, for egoless listening is one of the attributes of love.

They will dispassionately examine evidence, tame their minds, know where their thoughts have come from, and be able to distinguish what in the mind is the product of past conditioning and received opinion (political ads, propaganda), what thoughts are genuinely their own, and what their desires may be projecting on reality.

And if peace is their goal, they will in the field of politics be themselves peace embodied. They will work indefatigably in the present moment, but without the beggarly attachment to reward, recognition, or future results. And when disappointment comes, as it must—as it did so often to those unsung heroes of the Civil Rights movement—Buddhists doing political work would do well not to despair, thinking, "I have lost, they have won," but remember that no victory won for the sangha, or "beloved community," can last forever (nor any defeat), because every worldly thing is stained by anicca. In "defeat," if it comes, they might find solace in the judicious distinction that "Pain is something that comes in life, but suffering is voluntary or optional." (Or on their refrigerator door they might tape this quote from Chan master Sheng Yen: "I follow four dictates: face it, accept it, deal with it, then let it go.")

Finally, they will take as a reliable guide for spiritually informed political action the statement Dr. King made in his stirring Nobel Prize acceptance speech exactly forty years ago:

> Civilization and violence are antithetical concepts. Nonviolence is the answer to the crucial and moral question of our time.... The foundation of such a method is love.... I have the audacity to believe that peoples everywhere can have three meals a day for their bodies, education and culture for their minds, and dignity, equality, and freedom for their spirits.

Dr. King's political objectives in 1964 were, at bottom, of a piece with bodhisattva goals, and they complement nicely the ones Buddhists in the countries of the Far East have traditionally worked to achieve. In *Inner Revolution*, Robert Thurman informs us that Nagarjuna was the mentor of a great king of a dynasty in southern India, King Udayi Shatavahana, sometime between the first century B.C.E. and the second century C.E. Nagarjuna first instructed the king on what he needed to know for the king's own liberation, then he advised him on how a ruler should oversee an enlightened society. He said, "O King! Just as you love to consider what to do to help yourself, so should you love to consider what to do to help others!" According to Thurman, Nagarjuna "taught his friend the king how to care for every being in the kingdom: by building schools every-where and endowing honest, kind, and brilliant teachers; by providing for all his subjects' needs, opening free restaurants and inns for travelers; by tempering justice with mercy, sending barbers, doctors, and teachers to the prisons to serve the inmates; by thinking of each prisoner as his own wayward child, to be corrected in order to return to free society and use his or her precious human life to attain enlightenment."

Thurman says, "This activism is implicit in the earlier teachings of the Buddha, and in his actions, though his focus at that time was on individ-ual transformation, the prerequisite of social transformation." In our brief passage through this life, we must have both inner and outer revolutions, since the former is essential for deepening the latter. When we no longer divide the great emptiness, shunyata, into "this" and "that," we are empow-ered to reduce without discrimination the suffering of all sentient beings in the six realms of existence, as Thich Nhat Hanh and his monks demon-strated so beautifully during the Vietnam War, coming to the aid of orphans, widows, and the wounded on both sides of the civil war that devastated their country.

Naturally, lay Buddhists will need the support of their sangha as they engage in political action. No one understands better the importance of taking refuge in the community of dharma followers than Buddhist monk and Vietnam veteran Claude Anshin Thomas. He understands suffering as a teacher and "sangha as the entire spectrum of the universe." In his memoir, At Hell's Gate: A Soldier's Journey from War to Peace, he says, "As a Buddhist, I cannot think myself into a new way of living, I have to live myself into a new way of thinking." That wisdom is captured concisely in his reflections on how dharma followers approach the goal of peace:

Peace is not an idea. Peace is not a political movement, not a theory or a dogma. Peace is a way of life: living mindfully in the present moment.... It is not a question of politics, but of actions. It is not a matter of improving a political system or even taking care of homeless people alone. These are valuable but will not alone end war and suffering. We must simply stop the endless wars that rage within.... Imagine, if everyone stopped the war in themselves—there would be no seeds from which war could grow.

Politics starts in the heart, for it is there that we discover our deep connection to all other beings. Joined with awareness, this feeling of unity and sympathy is the first and most important step in transforming society. But it cannot be selective, for we are one with both our friends and our enemies, with those who suffer and those who cause suffering. This is not easy for us. Even Thich Nhat Hanh, an accomplished Buddhist teacher and founder of the Engaged Buddhism movement, had to reach deep into his heart to make this discovery.

★ ★ ★

— CALL ME BY MY TRUE NAMES —

by Thich Nhat Hanh

IN 1976, I wrote a poem about three people—a twelve-year-old girl, one of the boat people crossing the Gulf of Siam, who was raped by a sea pirate and threw herself into the sea; the sea pirate, who was born in a remote village along the coast in Thailand; and me. I was not on the boat—in fact, I was many thousands of miles away—but because I was mindful, I knew what was going on in the Gulf.

I was angry when I received the news of her death, but I found out after many hours of meditating after I heard the news that I could not just take sides against the sea pirate. I saw that if I had been born in his village and had been brought up under the same conditions, I would have been exactly like him. Taking sides is too easy. Out of my suffering, I wrote this poem, entitled "Please Call Me By My True Names." I have many names, and when you call me by any of them, I have to say, "Yes."

Do not say that I'll depart tomorrow
because even today I still arrive.

Look deeply: I arrive in every second
to be a bud on a spring branch,
to be a tiny bird, whose wings are still fragile,
learning to sing in my new nest,
to be a caterpillar in the heart of a flower,
to be a jewel hiding itself in a stone.

I still arrive, in order to laugh and to cry,
in order to fear and to hope,
the rhythm of my heart is the birth and death
of all that are alive.

I am the mayfly
metamorphosing on the surface of the river.
And I am the bird which, when spring comes,
arrives in time to eat the mayfly.

I am the frog swimming happily
in the clear water of a pond,
and I am also the grass-snake who,
approaching in silence, feeds itself on the frog.

I am the child in Uganda, all skin and bones,
my legs as thin as bamboo sticks.
And I am the arms merchant,
selling deadly weapons to Uganda.

I am the twelve-year-old girl, refugee on a small boat,
who throws herself into the ocean
after being raped by a sea pirate,
and I am the pirate,
my heart not yet capable of seeing and loving.

I am a member of the politburo,
with plenty of power in my hands.
And I am the man
who has to pay his "debt of blood" to my people,
dying slowly in a forced labor camp.

My joy is like Spring, so warm it makes flowers bloom.
my pain is like a river of tears,
so full it fills up the four oceans.

Please call me by my true names,
so I can hear all my cries and my laughs at once,
so I can see that my joy and pain are but one.

Please call me by my true names,
so I can wake up,
and so the door of my heart can be left open,
the door of compassion.

Many people think they need an enemy. Governments work hard to get us to be afraid and to hate so we will rally behind them. If they do not have a real enemy, they will invent one in order to mobilize us. Recently I went to Russia with some American and European friends, and we found that the Russian people are wonderful. For so many years the American government told their people that the Russians were "an evil empire."

It is not correct to believe that the world's situation is in the hands of the government and that if the presidents would only have the correct policies, there would be peace. Our daily lives have the most to do with the situation of the world. If we can change our daily lives, we can change our governments and we can change the world. Our presidents and our governments are us. They reflect our lifestyle and our way of thinking. The way we hold a cup of tea, pick up a newspaper, and even use toilet paper have to do with peace.

As a novice in a Buddhist monastery, I was taught to be aware of each thing I did throughout the day. For more than fifty years since, I have been practicing mindfulness like this. When I started, I thought that this kind of practice was only for beginners, that advanced people did more important things, but now I know that the practice of mindfulness is for everyone. Meditation is to see into our own nature and wake up. If we are not aware of what is going on in ourselves and in the world, how can we see into our own nature and wake up? Are we really awake when we drink our tea, read our newspaper, or use the toilet?

Our society makes it difficult for us to be awake. There are so many distractions. We know that 40,000 children die of hunger every day in the Third World, yet we keep forgetting. The kind of society we live in makes us forgetful. That is why we need practice to help us be mindful. For example, I know a number of friends who refrain from eating dinner two times each week in order to remember the situation in the Third World.

One day I asked a young Vietnamese refugee who was eating a bowl of rice whether children in his country ate rice of such high quality. He said, "No," because he knows the situation. He experienced hunger in Vietnam—there were times when he ate only dried potatoes, while he longed for a bowl of rice. In France, he has been eating rice for a year, and he is already beginning to forget. But when I asked him, he remembered. I could not ask the same question of a French or an American child, because they have not had the experience of hunger. It is difficult for people in the West to understand the situation in the Third World. It seems to have nothing to do with their situation. I told the Vietnamese boy that the rice he was eating in France came from Thailand, and that most Thai children do not have rice of such high quality, because the best rice is set aside for export to Japan and the West in exchange for foreign currency. In Vietnam we have a delicious banana called *chuôi già*, but the children and adults in Vietnam do not have the right to eat these bananas because they too are all for export. In return, Vietnam gets guns in order to kill ourselves and our brothers. Some of us practice this exercise of mindfulness: We sponsor a child in the Third World and get news from him or her, thus keeping in touch with the reality outside. We try many ways to be awake, but our society still keeps us forgetful. Meditation is to help us remember.

There are other ways for us to nourish awareness. One thirteen-year-old Dutch boy visited our retreat center and joined us for a silent lunch. It was the first time he had eaten in silence, and he was embarrassed. Afterwards, I asked him if he had felt uncomfortable, and he said, "Yes." I explained that the reason we eat in silence is to be in touch with the food and the presence of each other. If we talk a lot, we cannot enjoy these things. I asked him if there was some time when he turned off the TV in order to enjoy his dinner more, and he said, "Yes."

Later in the day, I invited him to join us for another silent meal, and he enjoyed it very much. Society destroys us with so many noises and distractions that we have lost our taste for silence. Every time we have a few minutes, we turn on the TV or make a phone call. We do not know how to be ourselves without something to distract us. So, the first thing we need to do is to return to ourselves and reorganize our daily lives so that we are not just victims of society and other people.

Many peace organizations do not have the spirit of peace themselves, and they even find it difficult working with other peace organizations. If peace workers are really happy, they will radiate peace themselves. To educate people for peace, we can use words, or we can speak with our lives. If we are not peaceful, if we are not feeling well in our skin, we cannot demonstrate real peace, and we cannot raise our children well either. To take good care of our children means to take good care of ourselves, to be aware of our situation. Please sit with your child and, together, contemplate the little flowers that grow among the grasses. Breathing in and out, smiling together—that is real peace education. When we can learn to appreciate these small, beautiful things, we will not have to search for anything else. We can be peace ourselves, and we can make peace with our friends and even with our so-called enemies.

One of the most important insights of contemporary Buddhist thought is that the causes of suffering are not just personal; they are also social and political. Here, the provocative and original Buddhist thinker David Loy analyzes how the three poisons of greed, ill will, and delusion drive our political and economic systems.

★ ★ ★

WEGO: THE SOCIAL ROOTS OF SUFFERING

by David Loy

SHAKYAMUNI BUDDHA, the historical Buddha, lived in ancient India at least 2,400 years ago. Buddhism is an Iron Age religion. So how could it help us to understand and address modern issues such as the war on terrorism, economic globalization, and biotechnology?

What the Buddha did know about was human suffering: how it works, what causes it, and how to end it. But the word "suffering" is not a good translation of the Pali term *dukkha*. The Pali term is meant to convey that even those who are wealthy and healthy nonetheless experience a basic dissatisfaction that continually festers. The fact that we find life dissatisfactory, one damned problem after another, is not accidental or coincidental. It is the very nature of the unawakened mind to be bothered about something, because at the core of our being there is a free-floating anxiety that has no particular object but can be plugged into any problematic situation.

In order to understand why that anxiety exists, we must relate dukkha to another crucial Buddhist term, *anatta*, or "non-self." Our basic frustration is due most of all to the fact that our sense of being a separate self, set apart from the world we are in, is an illusion. Another way to express this is that the ego-self is ungrounded, and we experience this ungroundedness as an uncomfortable emptiness or hole at the very core of our being. We feel this problem as a sense of *lack*, of inadequacy, of unreality, and in compensation we usually spend our lives trying to accomplish things that we think will make us more real.

But what does this have to do with social challenges? Doesn't it imply that social problems are just projections of our own dissatisfaction? Unfortunately, it's not that simple. Being social beings, we tend to group our sense of lack, even as we strive to compensate by creating collective senses of self.

In fact, many of our social problems can be traced back to this deluded sense of collective self, this "wego," or group ego. It can be defined as one's own race, class, gender, nation (the primary secular god of the modern world), religion, or some combination thereof. In each case, a collective identity is created by discriminating one's own group from another. As in the personal ego, the "inside" is opposed to the other "outside," and this makes conflict inevitable, not just because of competition with other groups, but because the socially constructed nature of group identity means that one's own group can never feel secure *enough*. For example, our GNP is not big enough, our nation is not powerful ("secure") enough, we are not technologically developed enough. And if these are instances of group-lack or group-dukkha, our GNP can *never* be big enough, our military can *never* be powerful enough, and we can *never* have enough technology. This means that trying to solve our economic, political, and ecological problems with more of the same is a deluded response.

Religion at its best encourages us to understand and subvert the destructive dualism between self and other, and between collective self and collective other. This kind of self-less universalism—or, better, nondiscrimination that does not place *us* over *them*—provides the basis for Buddhist social action. In some ways, however, our situation today is quite different from that of Shakyamuni Buddha's. Today we have not only more powerful scientific technologies, but also much more powerful institutions.

The problem with institutions is that they tend to take on a life of their own as new types of wego. Consider, for example, how a big corporation works. To survive in a competitive market, it must adapt to the constraints built into that market. Even if the CEO of a multinational company wants to be socially responsible, he or she is limited by the expectations of stockholders and Wall Street analysts; if profits are threatened by his sensitivity to social concerns, he is likely to lose his job. Such corporations are new forms of impersonal, collective self, which are very good at preserving themselves and increasing their power, quite apart from the personal motivations of the individuals who serve them. This suggests that the response of a socially Engaged Buddhism must become somewhat different too. We are challenged to find new ways to address the new forms of dukkha that institutions now create and reinforce.

There is another Buddhist principle that can help us explain this connection between dukkha and collective selves: the three roots of evil, also known as the three poisons. Instead of emphasizing the duality between good and evil, Buddhism distinguishes between wholesome and unwholesome (kusala/akusala) tendencies. The main sources of unwholesome behavior—the three roots of evil—are greed, ill will, and delusion. To end dukkha, these three need to be transformed into their positive counterparts: greed into generosity, ill will into loving-kindness, delusion into wisdom.

An important question is this: Do the three roots of evil also work impersonally and structurally in modern institutions? Let's look at how greed, ill will, and delusion are embedded in our economic, political, and social systems.

INSTITUTIONALIZED GREED

In our economic system corporations are never profitable enough and people never consume enough. It's a circular process in which we all participate, whether as workers, employers, consumers, investors, or pensioners, but we usually have little or no personal sense of moral responsibility for what happens. Awareness has been diffused so completely that it is lost in the impersonal anonymity of the corporate economic system.

Contrary to what we are repeatedly told, however, such an economic system is neither natural nor inevitable. It is based on an historically-conditioned worldview that views the earth as resources, human beings as labor, and money as capital to be used for producing more capital. Everything else becomes a means to the goal of profit, which can have no end except more and more of the same thing. Greed has taken on a life of its own.

INSTITUTIONALIZED ILL WILL

In Buddhist terms, much of the world's suffering has been a result of our way of thinking about good and evil. The basic problem with a simplistic good-versus-evil way of understanding conflict is that, because it tends to preclude further thought, it keeps us from looking deeper. Once something has been identified as evil, there is no more need to explain it; it is time to focus on fighting against it.

Here one could point to the criminal justice system in the United States, which incarcerates a larger proportion of its population than any other nation. Why do we lock up so many people? One reason is that the incarcerated have become for us a kind of socially repressed "shadow" in the Jungian sense: Together, they represent what is wrong with modern U.S. society, so we vent our collective ill will on them by expelling and confining them out of sight. That way we do not need to think about them and what all those prisons imply about the kind of society we have become today.

However, the best example of institutionalized ill will is, of course, collective aggression: the institutionalization of militarism. After World War II, the U.S. did not de-militarize, but decided to maintain a permanent war-economy to fight communism. The collapse of communism at the end of the 1980s created a problem for the military-industrial complex, but now an open-ended "war against terrorism" has conveniently taken its place.

INSTITUTIONALIZED DELUSION

The most fundamental delusion, both individually and collectively, is our sense of a self/other duality—that "I" am inside and the rest of the world is outside. Nationalism is a powerful institutional version of such a wego. For that matter, so is the basic species duality between *Homo sapiens* and the rest of the biosphere, which is why we feel free to use and abuse nature technologically, with almost no regard for the consequences for other species.

There are many aspects to institutionalized delusion. One of them is an extraordinary level of simple ignorance in the United States regarding basic history, geography, and science. Is there any other "advanced" nation where three times as many people believe in Satan and the virgin birth as in evolution? It is difficult to avoid the conclusion that the function of schools is no longer education, in any broad sense of the word, but job training and indoctrination into consumerist values, accompanied by patriotic myths of superior American virtues. Since the major media are profit-making institutions whose bottom-line is advertising revenue, their concern is to do what maximizes those profits: "infotainment" instead of news, and molding public opinion into a very narrow band of acceptable views. It is never in their own interest to question the grip of consumerism.

If we understand this third collective problem as *institutionalized ignoring*, it helps us to see that modern life in developed nations is organized in a way that works to conceal the dukkha it causes. The system inflicts dukkha on all of us, but most of all on people whom we do not see and therefore do not need to think about, like those incarcerated in prisons. Thanks to clever advertising and peer pressure, my son can learn to crave Nike shoes and Gap shirts without ever wondering about how they are made. I can satisfy my coffee and chocolate cravings without any awareness of the social conditions of the farmers who grow those commodities for me. In fact, without some serious effort on my part, I may never face the relationship between my addictions and the often destructive mono-cultural agriculture that makes them possible. My son and I are encouraged to live in a self-enclosed cocoon of hedonistic consumption.

This ignorance is also perpetuated on the production side. The stock market functions as a black hole of ethical responsibility: On one side are personal and institutional stockholders, who together create a generalized pressure for greater return on investment. On the other side are corporate CEOs, who are judged by how well they respond to that pressure, regardless of the social or ecological consequences. Investors can pour over the financial data provided by stock analysts without ever reflecting on the non-economic impact of the companies they invest in.

The cumulative effect of this ignorance is a wego largely unaware of, and indifferent to, what is going on in the rest of the world. This self-preoccupation is complicit with much social dukkha, because our consumerist lifestyle depends on a global web of unjust social relationships and destructive ecological impacts. The ultimate irony of it all is the uncomfortable fact that, no matter how much money one may have, consumerism is ultimately boring and dispiriting.

Realizing the nature of these three institutional poisons is just as spiritual and just as important as any personal realization that may result from Buddhist practice. In fact, any individual awakening we may have on our meditation cushions remains incomplete until it is supplemented by such a "social awakening." In both cases, what is needed is a greater awareness that goes beyond the limitations of ego- and wego-consciousness. Usually we think of expanded consciousness in individual terms, but today we must penetrate through the veils of social delusion to attain greater understanding of dualistic social, economic, and ecological realities.

If the parallel between individual ego and collective wego holds, it is difficult to avoid the conclusion that the great social, economic, and ecological crises of our day are, first and foremost, *spiritual* challenges, which therefore call for a response that is (at least in part) also spiritual.

So what can Buddhism say about the solution to these problems? It is not enough to stop with the first and second noble truths: social dukkha and its social causes. We need the third and fourth truths as well: an alternative vision of society, and a path to *realize*, make real, that vision.

The early Buddhist sutras usually define enlightenment in negative terms, as the *end* of craving and dukkha. In a similar fashion, we can envision the solution to social dukkha as a society that does not institutionalize greed, ill will, or delusion. In their place, what might be called a dharmic society would have institutions encouraging their positive counterparts: generosity and compassion, grounded in a wisdom that recognizes our interconnectedness.

So far, so good, but that approach does not take us very far. Is a reformed capitalism consistent with a dharmic society, or do we need altogether different kinds of economic institutions? Can representative democracy be revitalized by stricter controls on campaigns and lobbying, or do we require a more participatory and decentralized political system? Can the United Nations be transformed into the kind of international organization the world needs, or does an emerging global community call for something different?

I do not think that Buddhism has the answers to these types of questions. That is not because Buddhism is lacking something it should have, and indeed I do not see that any other religion or ideology has the answers either. It is hardly surprising, then, that many of those most committed to social transformation are dubious about the role of religion. At this critical point in history, the challenge for a socially Engaged Buddhism is not to persuade citizens that religion can play a positive role, but to show them.

However, I think this is *not* demonstrated by trying to develop a distinct Buddhist social movement. Rather, Buddhism has a role to play within the burgeoning "anti-globalization" movement (or perhaps better: "peace and social justice" movement). Although it crystallized into self-consciousness during the 1999 anti-WTO demonstrations in Seattle, and many representatives have been gathering at annual World Social Forums in Porto Alegre, Brazil, and Mumbai, India, this movement remains largely unstructured. That is its strength as well as its weakness. Like most Buddhist social theory, it has so far been stronger on diagnosis than solutions.

Globalization involves many things—interacting economic, technological, cultural, and political developments—but in its present form it is most of all about commodifying all the natural "resources" (including labor) in every corner of the globe, and converting all the world's peoples to the "Gospel" of Produce/Consume, in ways that are accelerating the ecological destruction of the biosphere. Since many aspects of this process are politically embarrassing to those who benefit from it, the World Bank and IMF promote it with the euphemistic phrase "poverty reduction," despite the uncomfortable fact that it is actually aggravating the worldwide gap between rich and poor. As this suggests, such globalization serves the self-interest of economic and political elites (there is no

significant difference between them), who when necessary do not hesi-
tate to use police and military force to overcome resistance. In short, globalization as presently practiced can be seen as working to extend the
institutionalized greed, ill will, and delusion already discussed.

The two principles of socially Engaged Buddhism presented above—the
connection between wego and social dukkha, and the three institutionalized "roots of evil"—add an important dimension to the anti-
globalization critique. But what can Buddhism contribute to the
development of solutions? I suggest three Buddhist implications.

THE IMPORTANCE OF A PERSONAL SPIRITUAL PRACTICE

The basis of Buddhist social praxis is the obvious need to work on oneself as well as on the social system. If we have not begun to transform our
own greed, ill-will, and delusion, our efforts to address their institutionalized forms are likely to be useless or worse. We may have some success
in challenging the socio-political order, but that will not lead to an awakened society. Recent history provides us with many examples of revolutionary leaders, often well intentioned, who eventually reproduced the
evils they fought against. In the end, one gang of thugs has been replaced
by another.

From a spiritual perspective, there is nothing surprising about that. If I
do not struggle with the greed inside myself, it is quite likely that, once
in power, I too will be inclined to take advantage of the situation to serve
my own interests. If I do not acknowledge the ill will in my own heart, I
am likely to project my anger onto those who obstruct my purposes. If
unaware that my own sense of duality is a dangerous delusion, I will
understand the problem of social change as the need for me to dominate
the sociopolitical order. Add a conviction of my good intentions, along
with my superior understanding of the situation, and one has a recipe for
social as well as personal disaster.

COMMITMENT TO NONVIOLENCE

Struggling first of all with ourselves leads naturally to this second social principle. A nonviolent approach is implied by our nonduality with all "others," including those we find ourselves struggling against. The Buddhist emphasis on impermanence implies another way to express that nonduality—the inseparability of means and ends. Peace is not only the goal, it must also be the way; or as Thich Nhat Hanh has put it, peace is every step. We ourselves must be the peace we want to create. A deeper understanding reduces our sense of duality from other people, including those in positions of power relative to us. Gandhi, for example, always treated the British authorities in India with respect. He never tried to dehumanize them, which is one reason why he was so successful. Buddhist emphasis on delusion provides an important guideline here: the nastier another person may be to us, the more he or she is acting out of delusion and dukkha. It makes no difference whether he or she has any inkling of this truth. For Buddhism such ignorance is never bliss. The basic problem is not evil, but delusion.

Gandhi reminds us of another good reason to avoid violence: nonviolence is more likely to be effective. The struggle for social change is not so much a power struggle as a spiritual one, a clash of worldviews and moral visions. The successful nonviolent revolutions against communism in Eastern Europe show us that elites fall when they lose the hearts and minds of the people.

AWAKENING TOGETHER

A third basic principle, from a Buddhist perspective, is that our social engagement is not about sacrificing our own happiness to help unfortunate others who are suffering. That just reinforces a self-defeating (and self-exhausting) dualism between us and them. Rather, we join together to improve the situation for all of us. A recent email included the remark of a First Peoples woman that makes this point perfectly: "If you have come here to help me, you are wasting your time. But if you have come

because your liberation is tied up with mine, then let us work together."
This point needs to be emphasized, because the bodhisattva path is often
misunderstood. A bodhisattva does not sacrifice or delay his/her own
awakening to help others. Rather, bodhisattvas are deepening and inte-
grating their awakening by learning to live in a more selfless way. They
devote themselves to relieving the world's dukkha because spiritual liberation includes realizing that each of us is nondual with the world. This
means that none of us can be fully awakened until everyone "else" is too.
From a Buddhist perspective, then, the critical world situation means that
today we need new types of bodhisattvas; or, more precisely, that bodhisattvas sometimes need to manifest their compassion in more socially
engaged ways. "Bodhisattvas" means you and me.

Although these Buddhist principles encourage what Stephen Batche-
lor has called a "culture of awakening," they do not amount to a distinct
social program. Together, however, they add a more spiritual dimension
to the peace and justice movement that has sprung up worldwide in recent
years. Present social elites and power structures have shown themselves
incapable of addressing the various crises that already threaten humanity
and the future of the biosphere. It has become obvious that those elites
are themselves a large part of the problem, and that the solutions will
need to come from somewhere else. The global peace and justice movement has an increasingly important role to play, and a socially-awakened
Buddhism can help to make that movement more spiritually aware.

Imperialism, racism, capitalism, and patriarchy—bell hooks believes the best response to the politics of domination is Buddhism. Developed by people of color living in cultures of domination, addressing issues of survival and suffering, Buddhism is the ideal spiritual path for those experiencing oppression. But first, says this renowned feminist and political thinker, Western Buddhism must address its own culture of domination.

★ ★ ★

BUDDHISM AND THE
POLITICS OF DOMINATION
by bell hooks

DURING MY TWENTIES I turned toward Buddhism to fulfill my long-ing to walk a spiritual path yet also be mindful of the world of politics. As a prophetic spiritual practice, Engaged Buddhism offered a vision of the spiritual practitioner at work in the world, being an example of loving-kindness, compassion, embodied peace, and mindfulness.

The book that guided me toward an understanding of the myriad ways Buddhism might help concerned seekers eager to participate in creating a just world was *The Raft Is Not The Shore: Conversions Toward A Buddhist Chris-tian Awareness*, by Thich Nhat Hanh and Daniel Berrigan. These two ded-icated spiritual teachers were involved in the messy world of anti-war politics. Yet they both were clear that the foundation informing their actions was spiritual practice. It was spiritual belief and not any allegiance to political parties or ideology that was guiding their work for peace.

In *The Soul of Politics* Jim Wallis explains: "At the core of prophetic reli-gion is transformation—a change of heart, a revolution of the spirit, a con-version of the soul that issues forth in new personal and social behavior." With profound insight Wallis shares the way spiritual and religious values can lead to a renewed vision of politics during times of grave social crisis. Now, after more than thirty years of engagement with Buddhist thinking and practice, I find myself turning again and again to Buddhism to find ways to end the suffering caused by a global politics of domination.

In the United States, where imperialist, racist, and patriarchal politics shapes so much of our daily life, only those citizens who are in denial can act as though there is some utopian realm of spiritual practice where religion and politics never meet. Even so, when I share that I am thinking about the issue of Buddhism and politics, colleagues and friends repeatedly express their conviction that these two issues are utterly separate. While I agree that it is possible to engage in Buddhist practice without engagement in politics, I know from experience that politics always seems to find its way into every sphere of our life.

For example, there has never been a time during my more than thirty years of engaged Buddhist practice when there has not been some white person somewhere asking me what "attracts a black person to Buddhism." At that moment it does not matter whether I came to a Buddhist gathering to focus on spiritual practice—I cannot escape the politics of race. And even though I think this is a question that directly reflects unenlightened mind and the politics of white supremacy, it is unlikely that the questioner sees her or his inquiry in the same light.

Still, I assume that if the questioners sat with the question, working through it from the ground of spiritual practice rather than racial bias, they would see that the roots of Buddhism were formed among people of color globally, within a world of domination, addressing the issue of suffering and survival. This makes it a spiritual path uniquely suited for any black person in the Diaspora wanting to find a way out of the Western metaphysical dualism that is the ideological basis for much group oppression in our society, and the ideology most of us learn early in the Christian church. Indeed, Buddhism has yet to capture the attention of masses of black folks in the United States precisely because of the way in which a politics of race and class exclusion permeates the dissemination of Buddhist thought in the West.

Often in Buddhist settings black people are treated as though we were the guests of white hosts, who perceive themselves to be infinitely more enlightened, the "real" Buddhists because they have read the right texts, traveled to the right countries, and been anointed by the right teachers. Those of us (most of us black folks) who have no stories to tell of our sojourn in the right place with the right teachers are always treated as though we do not really have the right to front row seats under the

Bodhi tree. We are treated as though we can never reach the heart of Buddhism because we just are not pure enough. Only those special few who have been at the right place with the right teacher have the good fortune to be seen as the "real" black Buddhists. No matter our lineage or the direction of our spiritual path, our very presence (visibly black) in predominately white Western Buddhist settings triggers thoughts about race and/or racism in those who observe us, whether we want it to or not.

White Buddhists' inability to move beyond race and just be with us as fellow practitioners is a form of race and class elitism. No wonder, then, that there are growing numbers of black practitioners who prefer settings that mainly focus on folks like themselves. While such settings may be temporarily useful, we are all still suffering if we can never come together in settings where racism does not shape the nature of interactions.

Concurrently, when individual black folks who are Buddhist practitioners come to Buddhist discussions and speak overtly against domination, we are often seen as not spiritual enough, as bringing the messy, conflict-laden world of politics to Buddhism. In this past year I have attended several conferences where it was clear that individual black folks had permission to speak on race and racism at particular panels. But if we raised these issues at other panels, the ones deemed to be on the "real" subject of Buddhism, our comments were either ignored or dismissed as irrelevant.

In many ways this reminds me of the challenges we faced years ago within the feminist movement, when black women/women of color began to challenge the ways that white supremacist thought and action had shaped the theory and practice of the movement. We demanded change, rethinking, and growth in critical consciousness, a practice grounded in unlearning racism prior to engagement with difference. The white women (mostly highly educated, mostly from privileged class backgrounds) who saw the movement as their territory were more often than not angry and resisted change. However, the theory and practice of feminism did change, and the door was opened to allow for an inclusive, visionary feminism to emerge.

A similar door has opened in Buddhist settings, especially among practitioners who have taken to heart the practice of compassion in a culture
of domination. A prophetic aspect of Buddhist practice is the challenge
to move past dualism, the binary *either/or* thinking that dominator culture
socializes everyone to see as normal. In *World as Lover, World as Self,* Joanna
Macy expressed the nature of this movement beyond dualism when
describing how we are all transformed by cultivating compassion and
insight: "You have to have compassion because it gives you the juice, the
power to move. When you open to the pain of the world you move, you
act. But...it can burn you out so you need the other—you need insight
into the radical interdependence of all phenomena. With that wisdom
you know that it is not a battle between good guys and bad guys, but that
the line between good and evil runs through the landscape of every
human heart."

Thich Nhat Hanh and the Dalai Lama are such powerful presences in
the United States in part because of the ways they teach us to forgive, to
move past blame. For people of color, or any victims of dominator culture,
the movement past blame can allow for a profound release of rage. For
unenlightened white folk, trapped by guilt or the fear of being blamed, it
can be the release that allows an understanding of accountability to
emerge. The concept of not having an enemy is one that many citizens
of our nation cannot accept, because so much of our political organiz-
ing—whether by the radical right or the radical left—has been galva-
nized less by a love of justice and more by a hatred of enemies. Most folk
I know would rather denounce George Bush than examine the ways we
all participate in the perpetuation of domination culture, of imperialist
white supremacist capitalist patriarchy.

More than ever, as our nation begins to project a politics that has all the
ingredients of twentieth-century fascism (religious, patriarchal, fear-
based, nationalist, and racist, supported by ruling-class right-wing ideology, much of which is expressed via fundamentalist Christianity) engaged
Buddhist practice offers both a place of refuge and a place of alternative
possibility. All that we do to break away from the idea of the separate ego
and to acknowledge our interdependence is already a radical step away

from race, nationality, religious affiliation, sexual preference, class posi-
tionality, and educational status as fixed markers in life.

Explaining the work of Thich Nhat Hanh, Sister Annabel Laity shares
that "our true home is not the safety of a particular belief or ideology. Nor
is it the safety of a bank account, a house, car, family, or employment.
Our true home is the solidity and freedom of our mind cultivated in the
context of a community." When we are truly awake we are able to
embrace diversity, to move past artificially-constructed dominator thinking that promotes fear of what is different, fear of the stranger. And ultimately, though hierarchies of power within Buddhism might seek to make
us think otherwise, practice is liberation; it is not being in the right place
at the right time with the right teacher.

How liberated I felt when Thich Nhat Hanh, writing about the inter-
section of Buddhism and politics during the Vietnam War in *The Raft Is
Not the Shore,* explained that "it was quite plain that if you have to choose
between Buddhism and peace, then you must choose peace. Because if
you choose Buddhism you sacrifice peace and Buddhism does not accept
that. Furthermore, Buddhism is not a number of temples and organizations. Buddhism is in your heart. Even if you don't have any temple or any
monks, you can still be a Buddhist in your heart and life." Just as Thich
Nhat Hanh teaches that killing destroys the work of Buddhism, allegiance to dominator culture does not allow us to cultivate the mind of
compassion.

When we bring to politics a prophetic and inclusive spirituality, we
have prepared the ground of our being so that we can act mindfully. For
Buddhist practitioners, mindful awareness is the skillful means by which
we release the attachment to dominator thinking and practice. Living
within a culture of white supremacy, many white people resist the notion
that they have nothing to learn from people of color. Although they allow
themselves to be guided by teachers of color who come from all over the
world, they may not use mindful awareness to link their acceptance of
such teachers with their continued fear and non-acceptance of people of
color who may live and work in their own communities. How is it that
white people seeking enlightenment can see past the color of the Dalai

Lama or Thich Nhat Hanh, but not see in the faces of these two men the faces of all the brown and black people of the world who are suffering?

A child in my neighborhood who cannot yet read comes to my house and sees the face of the Dalai Lama on the cover of a magazine. Innocently she asks, "Is that your cousin? His face looks like your face." We laugh together as I share that the first time I saw the Dalai Lama in a small setting, I thought, "He looks like the men in my family." And I contemplated why the open-hearted embrace of this colored stranger in a world of whiteness does not extend to the unknown men of color who daily suffer dehumanization in a world that is not seen. Fortunately, in the world of dependent co-arising, of Interbeing, we manifest our interdependence by seeing the links that connect us, by recognizing that everywhere in the world the politics of domination estranges people. The path of the bodhisattva is one that leads us to move into this estrangement with the strength and power of loving community, bringing with us a concern for justice and a steadfast mind of compassion.

Some have argued that Buddhism is not a religion but a collection of religions, and Buddhism's many schools differ widely on both philosophical and practical questions, including ethics and politics. Some schools forbid killing, for instance, while others feel it can be justified in certain circumstances. Using the Tibetan system that organizes the schools into a single, progressive path, Buddhist scholar and teacher Reginald Ray examines different Buddhist approaches to political action.

★ ★ ★

THE BUDDHA'S POLITICS

by Reginald A. Ray

THE BUDDHA'S ENLIGHTENMENT had several important "political implications." First, the Buddha understood that all action within samsara is necessarily political. Let us define "politics" as "taking the side of an individual or group and engaging in activities that further the goals of oneself and those one is aligned with." In this sense, even the attempt to maintain a self—the definition of samsara—is political, because it involves efforts to promote, aggrandize, and protect oneself and the group or groups that are always part of ego's identity.

Second, in his decision to teach and form a community, the Buddha was also acting in a political way. He was working to further his own agenda as an enlightened person, and to influence those he was training toward the same realization. But since the Buddha had stepped beyond samsara, his way of being political was different from the ordinary conception and practice of politics. Politics usually assumes the valuing of some persons or groups over others. When politics is understood in this way, it assumes that wealth, status, power, and privilege can lead to satisfying results and are worth pursuing. The Buddha's realization obviously left little room for politics in this conventional sense. Having realized the illusory nature of his "self," there was no person on his side for him to favor. The Buddha took the side of all sentient beings, including humans of whatever race, social station, or karmic situation. For him, there could be no question of advancing one group against another; he engaged in activities to further the goals of all beings, without exception or discrimination. Third, what the Buddha sought for all beings was the same freedom and fulfillment that he himself had found. But this could only be achieved through attention to the world, for as Buddhism throughout its history affirms, the health, safety, wellbeing, and sanity of one's life situation often determines one's ability to follow the path. Thus, the Buddha spent much of his time establishing stable and well-functioning renunciant communities; assisting lay people to live with intelligence, practicality, and kindness; and advising rulers how to govern wisely and with compassion.

Finally, just as the Buddha was political, so too were his disciples. They also struggled with the politics of ego and were called upon to support and further the goals of the Buddhist community. From this viewpoint, we can understand the spiritual program the Buddha offered his followers as political training, but from a completely non-territorial, enlightened perspective.

The training the Buddha developed for his students recapitulated the journey that he himself had taken. This training can be summarized according to the Tibetan understanding of the three stages, or "vehicles" (yanas) of the Buddhist path. They were trained, first, in the Hinayana, the Immediate Vehicle which involves the discovery of non-self within oneself; second, the Mahayana, or Great Vehicle, in which one learns how to act from the experience of non-self to benefit others; and, finally, the Vajrayana, or Indestructible Vehicle, in which realization becomes entirely non-conceptual and action becomes spontaneous. In the following, I interpret the practices and viewpoints of these three yanas in political terms, making explicit what is often implicit within the traditional Asian formulations. Thus I read the Buddha as providing instruction to political activists and would-be activists.

HINAYANA: REVISING OUR OWN STANDPOINT

Each of the three major phases of the path has its own political theme. The primary Hinayana message is that in order to change the world, we have to change ourselves first. Before we try to engage in external politics, we have to gain some maturation in discovering the experience of non-self within. This is something that Buddhist teachers and engaged Buddhists emphasize repeatedly. In the 1970s, one of the primary aspirations of my generation was to transform society from the ground up. But we heard our teachers say over and over, "The desire to change the world is a very good thing. However, if you don't work on yourself first, you'll bring all of your personal paranoia, arrogance, aggression, and preconceptions along, and you'll just get in a fight with whomever you're trying to change."

According to the Buddha, there are four ways in which we need to work on and change ourselves—four ways to approach the space of non-self—before we can attempt external political action.

+ First, we need to be realistic about what's possible in life. The Buddha said that there are no ideal situations; every situation in human life, without exception, is conflicted, distressed, and filled with suffering. This means that if we are going to engage in political action, we need to be clear from the beginning that we are not striving to create an ideal situation. If we really believe that the ideal is possible, we are going to be continually upset, angry, confused, and resentful. And we'll be engaged in a losing battle. Thus, right at the beginning of one's political training, there needs to be a recognition of the necessary imperfections and distress involved in all human activities. This is, of course, the first noble truth.

+ The second point is that dharmic political action requires much understanding of karmic conditions. In order to work with a problematic situation, whether we're talking about cutting down redwoods in California or polluting rivers or the destructive power of consumerism or militarism, the first thing we have to do is understand the major causes and conditions behind the situation. It's not good enough to march in and say, "This is screwed up and we're going to provide an alternative." That kind of approach is based on ignorance (we don't know what we're dealing with), aggression (we don't appreciate that if we were experiencing the same conditions as those involved we'd probably be doing the same thing), and arrogance (we think that we have all the answers).

The Dalai Lama often says, "All human beings just want to be happy." If people are doing things that are making them unhappy, there are reasons why they're doing it. It's not that they want to be unhappy. It's that their life has come to a point where they are doing things that are making themselves and other people miserable. The more that we understand that fact and see exactly why it is so in each situation, the more we can intervene in a constructive and effective way. This is the second noble truth, the cause of suffering.

✦ The next point, corresponding to the third noble truth, is that ultimate freedom is not based on external conditions. The freedom we long for is already within us. This does not mean that external circumstances do not have an important impact on our ability to realize inner freedom, for they do. But the freedom itself is independent from all causes and conditions, and is available to anyone in any situation.

It is interesting to think of the leaders of the Indian independence movement, who were thrown into prison by the British during the occupation. When the British imprisoned Nehru, Gandhi, and others like them, it was the biggest mistake, because in prison these leaders practiced, they meditated, and they gained some experience of inner freedom. When they came out they were a force that could not be stopped. Pretty soon India was independent and the British Empire had been dealt a fatal blow—because of these few people in prison, meditating. Gandhi exemplified just how powerful inner freedom can be in the political arena.

While inner freedom is free from any conditioned circumstances, our ability to achieve it is often bound up with our life circumstances. For example, when people are enslaved, their states of mind are deeply reinforced in negative and often destructive ways, and they are often unable to locate their own sense of human dignity, power, and creativity. Once we realize that true freedom is within, and once we ourselves have some taste of it through meditation, then we can look in a very intelligent way at the things that enslave people and make it so difficult for them to realize inner freedom. This allows us to avoid confusing inner with outer freedom. Thus, we don't think that simply getting rid of a regime or changing a political structure, in and of itself, is going to give people the fundamental inner freedom we all seek.

✦ The fourth point, corresponding to the fourth noble truth of the path, includes several items. First, when we feel called to engage in external political activity, our primary commitment must always be to work on ourselves. That must remain the foundation of all our attempts to transform external situations.

Second, we must understand that meditation, the centerpiece of the Buddhist path, is itself the most radical kind of political action. Why? In meditation, we step out of the value system of the conventional world and start to look at things from a fresh viewpoint. We don't know what we are going to come up with, but we do know we are not likely to remain an uncritical supporter of the status quo. Meditation tends to bring out our own intelligence and insight; it encourages our individuality, our sense of outrage, and our sense of compassion. Meditation is not activism as we usually think of it, yet it fulfills the definition in a radical way, because it is activity that fundamentally aims to change the world.

Finally, there is always the knowledge that our political activities themselves are a way of working on ourselves. As we engage politically, our own arrogance, aggression, small-mindedness, and self-centeredness are going to be exposed. We should take these as golden opportunities, offering us a more informed, more humble, and less self-preoccupied way of working with others.

MAHAYANA: TURNING ORDINARY POLITICS INSIDE OUT

The Hinayana provides a necessary precursor and foundation for engaging in external political action. It enables us to be free of ego politics and approach situations in an open, free, and non-territorial way. The resulting

relieved, peaceful, and self-contained state of mind naturally gives birth
to loving-kindness and compassion for others. So now, in the Mahayana,
we can seek to operate from the realization of non-ego in our attempts to
be helpful to others. The Mahayana offers six practices to help us work
politically, corresponding to the classical practices of the six *paramitas*, or
transcendent actions.

+ The first is *generosity*. When we engage the world based on our
  Hinayana discovery of non-self, we can cultivate an attitude of openness, respect, impartiality, and universal altruism, not trying to benefit one group of people over another. This is where those of us invested
  in political activism may have a problem, because we may see one
  group as good and another as bad. While one group may indeed be
  victims and another perpetrators, all are confused, lost, and afflicted,
  and our action to redress imbalances will benefit both sides.

    In addressing people who are causing problems for others, we
  can't be helpful if we don't respect them and if we don't appreciate
  their situation, experience, and point of view. We have to see them
  and know them; only and then does communication become possible. Now, of course, all of us slide off the point constantly and we're
  always misjudging people. That's understood. But we always have
  to return to this idea of this practice of unlimited, unconditional
  generosity.

+ Next is *discipline*. This means that we are unwavering in our commitment to political action as a way to help other people and not primarily to benefit ourselves. At a certain point in our political work,
  the going can become very difficult. We find that the anticipated
  results are not materializing as expected, the people we are working
  with are frustrating, and we find ourselves losing our original inspiration. In this situation—which is the rule rather than the exception—the willingness to continue on, regardless of our own feeling
  of fulfillment or frustration, is critical. Without that, nothing of benefit is ever going to be possible.

✦ The next one, *patience*, also emerges from our Hinayana discovery of non-self. Letting go of our own preconceptions and ambitions, seeing more of the totality of the situation, we can look with respect, understanding, and evenness at other people and what they are going through. Without reacting, we provide psychological room for them to see themselves, as if in a mirror. More than that, we can abide patiently, looking for the moment when genuine communication becomes possible and we can address the situation in a precise and effective way.

✦ Flowing directly from patience is *energy*, or exertion. People trying to help others typically experience exhaustion and depression, what we call burnout. But rather than feeling that we have to generate our own energy to overpower the suffering, we realize that every situation we meet has its own texture, energy, and dynamics. When we open our minds and hearts to what is going on, we often find possibilities and openings we did not notice. We may even find the situation itself, which had seemed so negative, unworkable, or even hostile, softening and opening toward us. To do this, of course, we have to be incredibly patient, letting go of all preconceptions.

✦ The fifth Mahayana practice is *meditation*. In contrast to the Hinayana practice, here meditation is not done primarily to develop oneself, but for political reasons. In the Mahayana, we develop and deepen the mind of non-self for the benefit of others. Here we are not talking about meditation done for a normal political reason, but meditation as a way of opening to one's own depths. Underneath the superficial personality are resources such as inspiration, compassion, generosity, love, sympathy, and bravery. Meditation is the way to open up to these depths of our own being. If you want to be an effective person in the world, you need to know how to draw on something deeper than your own immediate, self-conscious sense of "me." In the Mahayana, meditation is the way to do that.

✦ The last Mahayana practice is that of *transcendental wisdom*. The more
one looks into situations and fathoms their causes and conditions,
the more groundless and mysterious they become. The more you
look, the more things begin to appear with a kind of endless, unfath-
omable quality. Rather than causing confusion, this leads to greater
clarity toward the innumerable and finally ineffable elements that
compose the infinite complex of all that is. This understanding frees
us from having to judge or pin things down in any solid sense. It
enables us to engage situations with complete openness, freshness,
and accuracy.

We might summarize these Mahayana practices by saying that they
"turn ordinary politics inside out." When we are in a situation and are
tempted to manipulate somebody, we just boycott that impulse. Something comes up and we feel the familiar urge to control or attack somebody. But we turn the whole thing inside out, and maybe we say
something kind instead. Turning politics inside out can be so powerful. It
is powerful for us, because all the six Mahayana practices become not
only possible but the order of the day. And it is powerful for other people because it also has the power to shock them into that same open, generous, expansive space. Then they may find the warmth and connection
to completely change the situation.

In the Mahayana we don't go along with our own expectations. In
fact, we do the opposite of even what we ourselves expect, which turns
out also to be the opposite of what others expect. Of course, to do so
can be quite frightening; when we act in this outrageous way it is as if
we were looking down a vast, empty, black well. Yet leaping into that
open space can be so interesting, humorous, and liberating. At a certain
point, acting with unreserved altruism toward others is the only way
we can truly and completely free ourselves and become who we most
deeply are.

VAJRAYANA: ACTION BEYOND CONCEPTUAL THOUGHT

The ten practices of the Hinayana and Mahayana involve conscious intention, technique, and exertion. In the Vajrayana, we enter an entirely new arena where political action passes beyond conscious intention and effort, and indeed beyond conceptual thinking altogether.

The kind of engagement articulated in the Vajrayana is not fully possible without a significant amount of meditative and even retreat training. Nevertheless, it is important to include in the present discussion because it shows where "Buddhism and politics" eventually ends up.

In the Vajrayana, one learns how open one's awareness fully, so that it becomes an impartial and all-inclusive mirror in which all situations are reflected at once. This awareness brings to fruition the Hinayana and the Mahayana training: it is utterly realistic because it is based on reality as it is; it is all-understanding, because karmic causes and conditions are accommodated without exclusion; and it is awakening itself, because in that state of mind there is no room for any self, or any limiting preconception at all.

The nature of this mirror-like awareness is, according to the Vajrayana, joyful and blissful. The joy is the inner experience of complete freedom, and the bliss is seeing things exactly as they are, without any restraint, reservation, or distortion. The awakened state is also constantly giving birth, and so within it there is always movement and motion: out of the infinite inner space of the unborn mind, inspiration toward the suffering world arises in a spontaneous and completely selfless way.

This inspiration does not arise abstractly. It appears as the specific response of unfabricated awareness (we cannot talk, at this point, of a self or actor in any sense) to the situation reflected in the mirror of mind. Strangely enough, when the totality of political situations becomes the object of response, and when this response does not originate with a self-conscious subject, then each aspect of the situation is addressed in the most fitting and effective way possible.

This makes clear the Vajrayana way of viewing renunciation. Once ego vacates the scene—even if momentarily—we come upon an inner "mind" that is immense, fearless, and astounding in its resourcefulness. The mind that acts, then, is not "us," but buddhanature, and the resultant activity is what is called buddha activity. Like the Buddha before us, in utterly renouncing "the world," we free our own innermost wisdom to engage the suffering world fully and completely, and the beings in our lives are the beneficiaries of this political engagement.

The Vajrayana gradually leads us to a view of the world that is quite different from any encountered before. We have our job to do as human beings. We have a lot of problems and this is the arena of our activity, and should be, even in terms of dharmic politics. But there is a bigger picture, always. The bigger picture is that there's a kind of perfection in the universe that includes all the happiness and suffering, all the pain and pleasure, all our successes and failures, and even our death. At a certain point, we begin to experience everything that goes on as part of a perfect, seamless, impeachable unfolding of things as they are.

We might ask, "What does this have to do with politics?" I think it has something very important to do with politics, because when you realize this about life, it helps you to relax; it helps you let go of your "me" all that more readily. You do engage, but less neurotically, less invested in the success and failure or what you do. To relax in this way doesn't mean that you stop trying. You might even try harder and be willing to take more risks.

We can do this because we sense that there's this bigger picture—that somehow we're all being held by something larger than ourselves. It is all rather a mystery: in one sense we become less invested in what happens; but we are also more invested, because something is coming through us that we can only observe with awe and devotion. We feel irresistibly called to serve this "other," which is somehow at the same time our deepest self, with every breath and heartbeat of our life, and with our death as well. In this process, we begin to see that our often degraded human politics is just a confused and twisted reflection of

something else: that reality itself is "political" and "its" politics is inseparable from an impartial, continually unfolding, and never-ending love
for all that is.

Jerry Brown, the Zen-influenced former governor of California and now mayor of Oakland, remains one of the most interesting politicians in America. Roshi Bernie Glassman is a Zen teacher who has founded a series of successful social service and peace-making organizations. James Gimian is an expert on *The Art of War* who studied the Buddhist approach to politics and conflict under Chögyam Trungpa Rinpoche. I had the chance to discuss the collision of Buddhist ideals and political realities with these three interesting and very different political people.

★ ★ ★

— JOINING HEAVEN AND EARTH: —
———— LOFTY IDEALS VERSUS ————
HARD REALITIES

A discussion with Jerry Brown, Bernie Glassman, and James Gimian

MELVIN MCLEOD: Perhaps the best place to begin this conversation is to look for a fundamental definition of the word *politics*.

JERRY BROWN: The political is about the collectivity—the nation, the state, the city, the community. It refers not to personal choice—*I want to do this* or *I want to do that*—but to working with other people to arrive at some operating agreement about an issue that is important.

Politics is different from contemplation, and it's different from personal friendship, although the political implies like-minded people sharing certain beliefs and certain understandings of what the good is and what the bad is. Politics is about working through divisive issues, because by definition in a democratic society there is lots of disagreement. Politics refers to a process of struggle, of competition, of discussion, and ultimately of agreeing on certain actions by certain methods. Politics requires people listening to each other and finding some accommodation that will allow them to live peacefully in the same place.

BERNIE GLASSMAN: A lot of people talk about three sectors in society: the government, the major corporations, and the nongovernmental organizations and religious groups, which is the sector our organization is working in. The politics within each of these sectors may look very different. And among these three it's hard to know who's really in control.

JAMES GIMIAN: When you ask for a fundamental definition of *politics*, my mind goes to the basic experience of duality. From a Buddhist point of view, duality arises whenever you experience separation from the so-called external world. In a society, that means that whenever you relate to another person, they will have needs or desires or aspirations that will not necessarily coincide with your own. And the process of working that out so you can both occupy the same space is essentially politics.

It is helpful to start from that point of view because for Buddhists the question is this: How does working in the political realm become an extension of my practice? Mayor Brown said that politics is different from contemplation. I would say that if politics is about resolving issues arising from duality—which essentially means contention and conflict—then anybody who undertakes a deep contemplative process to overcome the false belief in ego is doing deeply political work. That's because they are addressing the root cause of the basic duality, which is what leads to conflict and gives rise to the need for politics. Now, that may seem theoretical, but I think it's the basis of the political work that Mayor Brown and Roshi Glassman are deeply involved in and are very articulate about.

MELVIN MCLEOD: The involvement of religion in politics can have a positive effect or, as we are seeing in many parts of the world, it can have terribly negative consequences. What can make the entrance of spiritual principles into politics helpful as opposed to destructive?

BERNIE GLASSMAN: In our work we have three basic tenets that come right out of Buddhist training. First, when we enter into the political world, we enter from a standpoint of *not knowing*. We don't enter with a solution in mind; we enter with a deep listening and an open space. The second tenet is *bearing witness*, fully knowing the situation we are in. And the third tenet is *taking action*. We are not just contemplating what is going on; we put a lot of energy into taking action, but based on not knowing and bearing witness. This is quite different from coming into a situation and saying, "I've got the answer, this is the way it has to be." To me, this makes it a spiritual approach.

JERRY BROWN: Certainly, starting from a position of not knowing is open, whereas starting from a position of conviction leaves less space for any listening or learning from people who are different from you. So not knowing and openness are very important principles. Of course, in politics one is not easily received as a "not-knower." People expect the people they elect to know where they are going, even if they don't, even if they have a lot of doubts. But as a general principle, I think not knowing would be a good starting point.

I think what religion and spirituality should bring to politics is a rootedness in perennial wisdom, as it is called in some quarters—a rootedness in the traditions people have. Based on where people live and what their upbringing is, there are principles that are passed on from one generation to the next, and these are the bedrock of who people are. At the heart of these traditions are understandings about the way we need to treat each other and the way we need to live. These understandings are more fundamental than campaign principles, which are tactical ideas, and economic principles, which are based on limited premises like scarcity and maximizing utility. Economics dominates politics, but I believe the direct spiritual experience and the basic axioms of religious tradition are a more inclusive and fundamental set of reference points. That's what is needed today because the cost-benefit analysis—the reduction to efficiency—becomes inhuman, hostile, and destructive of the environment when taken beyond a certain point. I see our direct spiritual experience and the traditional wisdom people have been brought up with as a counterpoint to the hegemony of economic thinking.

MELVIN MCLEOD: Which is a fundamental nihilism really, a mechanistic view of human relations...

JERRY BROWN: I thought it was significant that when the chicken pox vaccine was being introduced, the analysis went like this: mothers in the workforce lose X numbers of days a year because their children have chicken pox, and that costs Y amount of money. The vaccine costs considerably less, so we should introduce it. There was no real commentary on the reduction in suffering, or the human dimension, but only the very abstract proposition of its impact on the gross national product. That is what I am talking about.

JAMES GIMIAN: One way to approach this question is to distinguish between *religion* and *spirituality*. If by religion you mean some established organization or belief system that a person uses to substantiate their existence, then they are just using it to create more territory. That makes it difficult to work effectively in politics, because if you are trying to solidify your sense of personal identity that creates more duality and conflict, as opposed to what we could call spirituality, which tries to create openness. Then you are willing to look for a solution that transcends your own objectives and includes the goals of all sides. Then the resolution can go beyond what you may have thought possible.

There is an interesting dynamic between the initial open space and the first moment you begin creating action. While openness and not knowing are fundamental to creating a ground where you can resolve conflict, you also do that with some kind of basic direction or vision. But as soon as you take some action, people start sorting themselves out in relationship to that and asking, "What's their agenda?" So how do you present a vision and have openness at the same time?

BERNIE GLASSMAN: I use the metaphor of a carpenter. The carpenter has a bag of tools that he has accumulated over his lifetime. Somebody calls and says there is something wrong with their door. Coming in from a standpoint of knowing would be like having your hand stuck to a particular tool. Maybe it's stuck to the hammer, so you come and start banging away at the door. The not-knowing stance is that you come with all these tools, and you bear witness to this door. Where is it sticking, what is the problem? Then you pull out the right tool.

It is very important to have lots of tools—to have the vision and ideas you talk about—but not to the point where you are stuck on anything in particular as you approach the situation. You are coming with deep listening, with deep openness—and then you use the right tools.

JAMES GIMIAN: Doesn't conflict arise if you are not willing to fix the door the way the owner wants you to? If you have a basic difference, are you then willing to repair that door however the homeowner wants it, whether or not that's the best way to fix it?

BERNIE GLASSMAN: First of all, I don't believe in a utopia of non-conflict. Whatever you do is going to create conflict in some ways and peace in other ways. We are looking at the overall reduction of suffering, but there is no way that what you do will not cause conflict somewhere. You can't come from a position of saying you will eliminate all conflict. I think the approach of not-knowing and bearing witness is the most effective way to reduce suffering. But as soon as you take action, you create all kinds of conflict. Whatever action you take is going to create some conflict—with your spouse, with your community, with your whatever.

JERRY BROWN: Oliver Wendell Holmes, in his great book on the common law, said, "Men must act and whenever they act, there are consequences." I do think there are some reference points we can use in choosing how to act. One is the well-being of each individual. There is a certain level of material well-being and intellectual and imaginative possibilities that each child brings into the world, and that's a reference point we can use to measure how our communities or our country or our world is doing.

Second, we have the environment—the oceans, the rivers, the soil, the air, these interconnected systems that are being disrupted to a greater or lesser degree. The environment can be a reference point for what we should be doing about manufacturing, about jobs, about how we move around and how we collect things. So there are two reference points we can use to judge our actions: their impact on each individual and their impact on other forms of life and the larger ecology.

MELVIN MCLEOD: Here is one of the most difficult problems of political action from a spiritual point of view. Politics is an inherently conflictual, dualistic arena and to act politically you have to take some sort of position. But how do you do that without contributing to the conflict and division that lies at the heart of the problem? How do you take sides without taking sides?

BERNIE GLASSMAN: In my book *Instructions to the Cook*, based on the thirteenth-century Zen master Dogen's classic work, the main theme is that we have to see the ingredients as clearly as possible and then make the best meal with those ingredients—not with the ingredients we don't have but with the ones we do. We make the best meal we can and then we offer it. It may be yucky or it may be good. We don't know beforehand, and that's not our role.

I must not wait until I have some right ingredient, whether it is money or enlightenment or a chef's knowledge or any of that. I have to work with the ingredients I have, knowing that some people may hate that meal and some may love it. My job is to take those ingredients, and do the best I can with them, and offer the meal. I don't have any sense of a utopia, or waiting around for a nondual world, or an enlightened world, or for me to be fully enlightened, or any of those things. During each moment stuff is coming up and I have to do the best I can.

JAMES GIMIAN: What connects personal practice to this question of how to work in the world without perpetuating the basic confusion of duality is including yourself in the process. You have to work on yourself, as opposed to thinking you are just working on an external reality. When we talk about the bodhisattva vow and putting other people before ourselves, that's based on an experience of emptiness. You realize that these actions you take are not to fulfill your own grasping and fixation. At the same time, you realize you are working to help the bigger situation. If those two understandings go hand in hand, then you don't have to wait for some perfect situation. You start right where you are.

MELVIN MCLEOD: Mayor Brown, you are the one person in this discussion who is a clearly identified member of a political party. You are known to represent a certain pole in the political spectrum, a certain territory or position. Why do you feel that joining a political party is the best way to act politically?

JERRY BROWN: Well, it is the best way because it happens to be what fits with the conditions in America. Some 75 percent of the voters vote for one major party or the other. That leaves only a small amount of space for an independent. The party is a frame that simplifies issues, but neither party can serve as any major repository of truth. Nietzsche said, "A thinking man is not a party man." I think that is probably true. If you are a member of a political party, all it does is give some indication of what you generally prefer. The Republicans tend to want to keep taxes down and protect wealth and property. Democrats tend to try to equalize things through the instrumentality of government. But both approaches have plenty of negative consequences when pushed too far or pushed in the wrong way. So it's really a collision of imperfect approximations.

Many of the things that are done in politics are very small adjustments in the ongoing flow of economic and political activity. It isn't like we can look into our toolbox and reshape the world. Human beings can't be engineered, and shouldn't be engineered in that way. In politics we show up in a situation and make relatively limited choices.

So I would say that we have to have a certain level of modesty about what is possible in politics, and recognize that the parties are not profoundly different. If you look at the differences among people, the party is only one part of it. Ethnicity is another part, geography is another part, and maybe gender is another part. We have all these categories we find ourselves in, with a lot of collision among them. Even though you have to be in a category—you are male, you are female, you are over 65 or under, you are a Democrat, you are a conservative—these are just approximations. They say some important things, but being human transcends all of that. And that is where we should be looking when we have to make the really important decisions.

MELVIN MCLEOD: The American Buddhist world, or at least its prominent adherents, is generally skewed toward the liberal end of the spectrum. Is this a reflection of inherent Buddhist values or simply of the type of Westerners who have been attracted to Buddhism over recent decades?

JAMES GIMIAN: A lot of what we are seeing in North America is because of the particular generation, what we might broadly call the Boomers, who have largely populated and been leading the North American Buddhist communities. Also, Buddhism is still a new and fringy phenomenon in the West. It is not enfranchised in the society like it is in Asia. Perhaps in a couple of generations, if it grows and survives, if it becomes propertied and enfranchised, you might well see different values reflected in the Buddhist community, conservative values having to do with maintaining a tradition. But right now, Buddhists are generally people who reacted to a certain time in history and sought spiritual solutions for problems which were deeply political, deeply societal.

MELVIN MCLEOD: Roshi Glassman, do you feel Buddhist values call for any particular political position, such as liberalism?

BERNIE GLASSMAN: I don't think they do. If you look through history—Japanese history, for instance—Buddhism did not play such a liberal role. I don't think you could say about Buddhism in general what you said about Buddhism in the West. In the 1960s, Buddhism attracted a certain kind of Westerner who was coming from the liberal side. But I agree with Jim that with time, as it gets more vested, Buddhism won't be just liberal anymore; it will include the whole spectrum of people.

JERRY BROWN: There are a lot of transitory arrangements and ideas in politics; they are fashionable for a while and then they pass out of practice. I don't think we can escape being positioned in some temporary arrangement—that's just part of what it is to be human—but I can't see that Buddhism is going to align itself with some category that will keep changing over time. It seems to me we have to get beyond these things, although each way of being Buddhist—from Tibet to Japan to Berkeley,

California—will develop its own rituals and liturgies and folkways to manifest the basic experience.

BERNIE GLASSMAN: Yes, the difference between Texas Buddhism and Berkeley Buddhism is going to be huge.

MELVIN MCLEOD: Beyond questions of policy, there are profound problems with the political process—the parties practice a take-no-prisoners partisanship and the voters feel a corrosive cynicism about it all. What can we do to bring some dignity and civility and respectfulness to the political process?

JERRY BROWN: One reason why politics seems so disreputable is that politicians, in order to stay in their profession, have to keep very divergent interests somewhat mollified. People with very different opinions all have to feel that they are being represented. Therefore, politicians can't always be totally precise, and they get the reputation for speaking dishonestly. The people they represent can't agree and yet they only have one representative, so that builds into the process a certain footwork on the part of the politician that leads to cynical interpretations.

I think the basics of nonviolence and treating people and things with more care is a powerful idea that has to be brought to bear in the hurly-burly of politics. The conflictual nature of political competition is always in need of the corrective of interconnectedness, of nonviolence.

BERNIE GLASSMAN: The practices of not-knowing and deep listening have led me to try to bring all of the voices to the table. This is not unique to Buddhism, but I think if you are coming from a deep Buddhist viewpoint and you really acknowledge the interconnectedness of life, you must listen to all the voices, all the aspects of yourself. That changes the political process dramatically. When I built the Greyston community development and social service mandala, I brought in Democrats and Republicans. People told me, "Don't deal with the churches, they're going to screw everything up." I brought in the churches. They said, "Don't deal with the government." I brought in the government. I tried to bring every voice into the discussion. It's not always easy to get people to sit down at the same table, but it's something extremely helpful that Buddhism brings to the process.

JAMES GIMIAN: If you're asking what a unique Buddhist contribution to politics could be, I think it would be about maintaining a radical perspective throughout the process. By radical I mean always coming back to the roots. From a Buddhist perspective, basic reality has to do with the truth of suffering. We accept that there is going to be a certain kind of dissatisfaction. We don't try to ignore it or cover it over, because it is often the covering-over that perpetuates conflict.

Along with suffering, we have egolessness and impermanence, which are the other two of the three marks of existence. Things are constantly changing, and that scares a lot of people. In a political arena, people don't like change. But it's a fundamental truth of human existence that things are constantly in flux—changing from an inner point of view and from an outer point of view—and if we acknowledge that it will help people become comfortable with it.

All of these things lead to a more natural gentleness, and I think that's what it comes down to in the end. The result of this kind of radical perspective is a natural gentleness that makes it possible to work with groups of people and come to resolutions that they can't even imagine initially.

MELVIN MCLEOD: Buddhism says that the real answer to human suffering is spiritual. So what are the limits of what can be achieved in politics? The converse might be: If we want to really change things, would we have to present a spiritual view? For instance, Roshi Glassman, can you have a powerful effect on the situation in the Middle East by purely political means, or do you have to act as a spiritual teacher in some way?

BERNIE GLASSMAN: I don't think I have to act as a spiritual teacher to do that. My feeling is that to have real effect you have to be dealing in all of the spheres. You can't leave any of them out. In the Middle East, we are involved in the political world, the social action world, the religious world, the cultural world. I think you have to deal with each of those. Whichever one you leave out, that's the one that will destroy your progress.

JERRY BROWN: I have to say two things. First, I think the idea that we can have some big impact on this complicated thing called the world—all these billions of people and all these complicated systems that we form a small part of—is a bit fatuous. I don't know what to say about it. However, at the same time, I do operate with the idea that I am doing something that has some impact that can be positive. So that right there is a rather paradoxical stance of both impotence and empowerment.

Second, presenting people with spiritual teachings is no easy matter if you are a politician and hold an elected office. It would be difficult to be heard unless one spoke very carefully. I still recall Ko'un Yamada Roshi saying when I lived in Kamakura, "You yourself are completely empty." But I don't think I'm going to bring that up at a city council meeting, much less on the campaign trail or on "Hardball."

The more we can talk in common sense, the more we can utter simple and straightforward truths, the more people will listen. We can't get caught up in the latest language. There's a lot of cant in the political process. The important thing is to speak in words that you use when you are speaking to a friend or another person. Words at the most basic level have a certain power because they are not so abstracted and distorted. Common sense is so rare, and it has a power that constantly has to be brought to bear on the politics of our time.

JAMES GIMIAN: I think what Mayor Brown has articulated is a very Buddhist perspective—that it comes down not to a religion but to our basic human experience. If you can communicate that from the depths of your being, that's a very powerful contribution in a political context.

Unique among modern Buddhist teachers, the late Chögyam Trungpa Rinpoche offered the world a comprehensive political and social vision based on the wisdom of meditative practice. His vision of an enlightened human society was based on a body of teachings named for Shambhala, a legendary kingdom where spirituality, politics, and culture were perfectly joined. Chögyam Trungpa's biographer, Fabrice Midal, summarizes Trungpa's teachings on how enlightened society can become a reality.

★ ★ ★

CREATING ENLIGHTENED SOCIETY: THE SHAMBHALA TEACHINGS OF CHÖGYAM TRUNGPA

by Fabrice Midal

ON THE SILK ROUTE of Central Asia, there are many legends and mythical or historic tales concerning the existence of a peaceful, prosperous kingdom, called Shambhala. Its inhabitants lived in dignity and in profound harmony with one another. This land has been a source of inspiration for the cultural, artistic, political, and military traditions throughout much of Asia.

Shambhala is supposed to be located to the north of India and the Himalayas, beyond the river Sita in what is now eastern Turkestan. But fundamentally, as Chögyam Trungpa Rinpoche explained, it is to be found "in the middle of Asia, in the middle, or the heart, of the Orient." It is the physical and spiritual axis of this region of the world. The people enjoy excellent harvests, great wealth, happiness, and freedom from illness. All the inhabitants devote their time to meditation. The path leading to Shambhala is above all a spiritual one.

The Shambhala vision taught by Chögyam Trungpa displays the basic unity that exists between the spiritual perspective and social life. In his words: "The kingdom of Shambhala could be said to be a mythical kingdom or a real kingdom.... Spirituality was secularized, meaning that day-to-day living situations were handled properly. Life was not based on the worship of a deity or on vigorous religious practice, as such. Rather, that wonderful world of Shambhala was based on actually relating with your life, your body, your food, your household, your marital situation, your breath, your environment, your atmosphere."

While many Buddhist teachings emphasize the need for renunciation from civil society—as in the example of the Buddha himself, who reached enlightenment after giving up his throne and leaving home—the Shambhala vision invites all of us to work at building such a kingdom. "Many religions have encouraged individuals to become monks or nuns," Rinpoche notes. "Although monasticism is very natural, in some sense, it's also a heightened or rarefied level of existence. In the Shambhala teachings our main concern is working with society. We want to develop an enlightened society that will be based on the idea of pure letting go."

By asking his own students to marry and get jobs, Trungpa Rinpoche was not renouncing part of the authentic Buddhist tradition. He was not watering it down, nor was he adapting it. Instead he was bringing out its ultimate purpose. He was asking his students to see all appearances, everything that we perceive, from a viewpoint of wisdom, and so to develop a sacred vision that would allow them to understand the primordial purity of all phenomena. The Shambhala teachings do not ask us to abandon the world of relative truth for that of ultimate truth, because they are intrinsically one.

THE SPIRITUAL CRISIS OF THE WEST

In this era, we are totally alienated from ourselves, and we have lost the connection with initiation, or the transmission of spiritual influence or traditional teachings. This is what is generally called the spiritual crisis of the West.

The various forms of transmission no longer touch us. They seem so far removed and abstract that no one knows how to incorporate them into their lives. Their capacity to transform the existences of those who receive them has been considerably reduced. The traditional chain of initiation has been broken.

The Shambhala teachings offer the possibility of rediscovering a spiritual path that does not rely on any dogmas, even though it is profoundly rooted in ancient tradition. Although such teachings may be traditional, they are not religious. Instead, they invite all of us to discover the path *in ourselves*. In this way, the statement that the Kingdom of Shambhala really exists in each person's heart is not just a simple image, but describes accurately everybody's deepest aspiration.

In the "holy night" that has fallen on the West, which is spoken of by the German poet Friedrich Hölderlin, genuine spirituality is no longer commonplace. There then exist several possibilities. You can invent new paths to suit yourself by listening to your "inner voice" (while running the risk of reducing this opening to an individual psychological process unsupported by any real discipline); you can adopt the dogmas of a religion and so acquire the reference points you need to be sure you are on the right path; or else, inside yourself, you can discover the path of a totally different tradition.

It is this last possibility that Chögyam Trungpa offered in such a striking way in his Shambhala teachings. Over and above all morality, all norms of behavior, people must find their own intimate path home, which involves rediscovering their own heart. Such a discovery is inseparable from any true discipline, and it can only be done by renouncing our own frivolousness. But this apprenticeship solves no problems. Instead, by opening the way, it pushes us to a deeper exploration of our relationship with ourselves and the world. Thus, such a path does not protect us from the harshness of reality and the distress of our era; it actually draws us inside them more completely.

Trungpa Rinpoche was well aware of the crisis gripping the West, and he sought to understand how its social problems could be solved. His interest in politics was a response to the distress of our era. Things had reached such a point and the confusion of our world was so deeply entrenched, he felt, that it would be a mistake to work only on spiritual practice. Rinpoche discouraged his students from exiling themselves or withdrawing completely from the world, so he did not recommend going into retreat for too long a period of time, although he acknowledged the importance of retreat practice as a means of uncovering confusion and connecting with simplicity as the ground for action.

He saw that contemporary Western culture was not dedicated to encouraging wakefulness or sanity in human beings, but instead that many aspects of Western culture tended to put people to sleep, especially because of the emphasis on more and more material, psychological, and even spiritual comfort. The pursuit of comfort makes human beings incapable of realizing themselves as true human beings, and it makes it impossible to develop genuine discipline, which is the source of true joy.

BASIC GOODNESS

The human heart is the "invariable middle" where the Kingdom of Shambhala can be found. It cannot be sullied or stained. Whenever we encounter it in its fundamental nakedness, we experience what Chögyam Trungpa called *basic goodness*. This expression is one of the central notions of this teaching. We must now try to understand it, because it is the ground in which we can plant the seed of an enlightened society.

Basic goodness is the purity inherent in all experience, the openness that is present in every situation. Thus it cannot be conditioned by the circumstances we find ourselves in. This primordial state is free of any stains, of any doubts or concepts that distance it from spontaneous direct experience. Even if the basic opening has been covered over, like the sky with clouds, it can never be altered, just as clouds never damage the sky. Basic goodness manifests itself in every instant of pure presence. Even if they are fleeting, such instants form a continuity in our experience that puts us in touch with something beyond all measure.

The important word in this expression is *basic*, because it indicates the primordial aspect of experience, independent of any circumstances. As for the word *goodness*, it comes across as surprising, even irritating, given all the evil, deception, cowardice, and hypocrisy we constantly see in ourselves and in the world. But this is not a moral term. It is not the expression of Trungpa Rinpoche's personal opinion to say that we are all good—that would be incredibly naïve. Instead, the point is to make us aware of our tendency not to see the openness, both basic and good, that constitutes us.

The word *goodness* accentuates the term *basic* to make us sense its true resonance. It is an invitation to let the primordial space of our own nature unravel in all its fullness. When we relax into what is basic, its "goodness" appears, even if the tender heart itself is, properly speaking, neither good nor bad. It simply is what it is.

Chögyam Trungpa used the term *goodness* with extraordinary accuracy, for etymologically it means "without fault." Basic goodness is faultless because it is unborn, and so cannot die. It is unconditional; it depends on nothing. In an interview in 1985, he affirmed: "Usually, religion is connected with punishing yourself. People still tend to take original sin seriously. They should let go of that. Maybe basic goodness will replace original sin!" Before any judgment, before any doctrine, it is possible to make contact with our own intelligence, as we can with true reality, and discover the resources it contains.

Another aspect of this state of enlightenment, this opening that constitutes a human being, is gentleness and sensitivity. Whatever our culture, race, or education, humans are born with this basic tenderness, this capacity to be touched by the world, to feel sad and to cry, to feel joyful. These are extremely simple qualities (which we may or may not recognize and cultivate).When we are genuine, we appreciate the world. This can be as simple as a mangy dog biting its tail, clouds crossing the sky and announcing snow, the fact of missing a train that pulls away at the very moment you arrive on the platform, or a particularly well-performed piece of music. Suddenly, we are moved. This is the germ of an opening that can be termed the experience of basic goodness.

So this phrase means a state of presence and naked awareness, the tenderness and gentleness of an open heart, and the ultimate experience of enlightenment with its benevolence toward others. In such moments, the world appears sharper and simpler: "When things become so wretched and so poor, the appreciation of simplicity has completely gone wrong," Chögyam Trungpa wrote. "Therefore we have to introduce some dignity and goodness into the situation. Human beings have lost their strength; they have become feeble." In this way, spontaneously emerging sense perceptions are all opportunities to connect with basic goodness.

Basic goodness is at the heart of the Shambhala teachings. For many people, it is a veritable koan whose true resonance can only be reached in the practice of meditation. It is both the ground of the path and its fruition. After this apprenticeship in learning to recognize, again and again, each moment of our singular experience, we discover the unconditional possibility of trusting our own hearts.

Such is the beginning of what Trungpa Rinpoche calls the "path of the warrior," and it is the ground of creating an enlightened society. Here, enlightened society doesn't necessarily mean a located society. It should first be seen as an inspiration that could enrich every aspect of our relation to the world, an inspiration that has taken on different names at different times in our history. Enlightened society is not something that we have to attain or fight for, but more the source of our inspiration in the present moment.

THE NEED TO UNITE SPIRITUALITY AND POLITICS TO HELP OTHERS

Chögyam Trungpa was aware of the limitations of any teaching that does not penetrate the deepest structures of the mind. Particularly in relationship to his closest students, those he would trust to carry on the tradition he was imparting to them, it was not enough to practice meditation a few minutes a day or follow a few teachings during vacations or weekends. It was not even enough to be driven by an altruistic spirit. He hoped that Buddhism and Shambhala would be incorporated into every aspect of life, transforming not only our minds but also the details of how we live. Such a far-reaching vision, such a prospect that shakes up our usual beliefs, is linked with the idea of founding a human society oriented toward establishing enlightenment.

To understand the foundation of his "political" goals and their intrinsic link with his view of spiritual development, we must examine what motivates the practitioner on the Shambhala path and the Buddhist path of Mahayana. The Mahayana model of a wise and realized practitioner is the bodhisattva, whose motivation is always to help all beings.

From the Mahayana perspective, the point of reducing our own confusion is to enable us to work more coherently and effectively for everyone's benefit. As Rinpoche explains: "The basic Mahayana vision is to work for the benefit of others and create a situation that will benefit others. Therefore, you take the attitude that you are willing to dedicate yourself to others. When you take that attitude, you begin to realize that others are more important than yourself." Thanks to this motivation, the practitioner's path becomes real and alive, and far from theoretical. Chögyam Trungpa's social commitment derived from this principle.

For him, there was a profound unity between the spiritual and political worlds, to such a degree that dividing them meant losing sight of their primary harmony. His "mystical" project, to adopt the term used by the philosopher Charles Péguy, took this primary unity into account. Its aim was to incorporate human dignity in one's life in a way that was not limited to spirituality. "People involved with a spiritual discipline have a tendency to want nothing to do with their ordinary life; they regard politics as something secular and undesirable, dirty," he says. But for Chögyam Trungpa, politics was of fundamental importance. He wanted to invent and create an arena in which spirituality and politics were no longer separate.

As early as 1976–78, he started speaking about the vision he had for society. Beyond presenting the basic teachings of Buddhism and creating the right conditions for the practice and study of Buddhism and Shambhala, he also had the idea to create a genuine community. In that sense, he revealed himself as a social visionary and, in the best sense of the term, a politician. The last great, and perhaps most visionary, project of Trungpa Rinpoche's life was to foster the development of enlightened society, which he described in terms of the Kingdom of Shambhala. He wanted to see this not just realized in metaphorical terms but embodied in human society, on Earth.

This indeed reveals the unique aspect of Chögyam Trungpa's work. So far as I know, no other Buddhist teacher in the West has attempted such a sweeping project, not even to a far lesser degree. He did not just advise people about how to conduct their lives. He certainly did not want to play the sage; he did not invent a new political theory or dream of a new utopia. Instead he showed how to create a true society in concrete terms. He taught that a "universal" or grand project or vision remains a purely intellectual concept if it is not brought down to earth in a concrete and individual way. "Enlightened society comes from the kitchen-sink level, from the bedroom level," he says. "Otherwise there's no enlightened society, and everything is purely a hoax."

In other words, Chögyam Trungpa did not see himself as a political philosopher; he was above all a man of action who wanted to transform the world by transforming people's perception and how they lived. However articulate his critique might have been of our society, its main purpose was to change the way we live, in a way that was itself quite radical for the West.

CREATING AN ENLIGHTENED SOCIETY

How then is it possible to unite the need for a genuine inner transformation, a discipline as rigorous as it is profound, with a desire to act in the world and devote our lives to others?

The Beat poet Allen Ginsberg took an active part in demonstrations against the Vietnam War and was involved in other political movements that aimed at transforming the world. For example, as an active Buddhist, on June 11, 1978, at the Rocky Flats Nuclear Weapons Plant, he was one of the demonstrators who sat down to meditate on the rail track in order to block the delivery of nuclear material to the weapons factory.

Rinpoche thought there were problems with this sort of political action, which he regarded as often ineffective and limited. In a commentary on the Mahayana slogan "When the world is filled with evil, transform all mishaps into the path of bodhi," he remarked: "Whatever occurs in your life—environmental problems, political problems, or psychological problems—should be transformed into a part of your wakefulness, or bodhi.... [Protesters] were purely reacting against the world being filled with evil; they were not able to transform mishaps into the path of bodhi."

For Trungpa Rinpoche, this sort of demonstration often contained an expression of aggression, which cannot lead to true social change. It seemed far more important to him to act on a truly political level.

One of the characteristics of the modern world is that it reinforces individualism. After a few years in the West, he realized that this obsessive individualism, based on the cult of each person's subjectivity, was contributing to the creation of a climate of distress and alienation that made it much more difficult to establish a true society.

How can we really live together if we are constantly driven by competition as a way of affirming ourselves? The basic relaxation that we can experience in meditation practice transforms this struggle for independence. We can stop struggling to affirm subjectivity and begin to trust in the basic nature of what is. This is not a matter of giving up our freedom, but rather of accepting it.

It is on this basis that a genuine society can be established. For Chögyam Trungpa, it would be an "enlightened society." One important aspect of this society that makes it particularly "enlightened" is an ability to live together in a harmonious way. In this situation, the sum—everyone together—surpasses the parts.

Building a genuine society is not possible if we start with aggressive individualism; on the contrary, we must start with some yearning toward egolessness. One of the aims of the Buddhist and Shambhala teachings is to make us more aware so that we can acknowledge that "our particular shells are obviously hard, stuffy and smelly, impure, full of shit," as he says.

Once we acknowledge the problem, there is hope for an end to polluting the world. Chögyam Trungpa Rinpoche was no airy dreamer who thought that the doctrine of basic goodness would make everyone miraculously nice to each other. Enlightened society is not a society composed of individuals who have all reached enlightenment, but instead is made up of those who have the courage to work at developing a society in which everyone works on their own sanity and cares for one another. Even then, it is not a simple matter of devoting oneself to other people. One has to be willing to share one's life with other people, which means giving up a great deal of privacy and self-centered views. One has to actually, personally, make a commitment to do this. By setting aside this commitment and dealing with human, social, economic, or natural resources only on a conceptual level, as tends to be the case today, we give up the possibility of a real society. Everything is our business, and everyone is important and worthy: this is what Chögyam Trungpa taught, which is miles away from our usual situation, in which we are concerned above all with our own existence.

In this writing on the Shambhala teachings, Chögyam Trungpa describes a universal human wisdom that can help solve the world's problems. This basic goodness is available in each moment in our perceptions of the world around us. It is the discovery that our lives, in spite of all our problems, are fundamentally workable and good. Because we can experience our lives in this way—because we are not afraid of who we are—we can create enlightened society.

* * *

THE DISCOVERY OF BASIC GOODNESS

by Chögyam Trungpa Rinpoche

ALTHOUGH the Shambhala tradition is founded on the sanity and gentleness of the Buddhist tradition, at the same time it has its own independent basis, which is directly cultivating who and what we are as human beings. With the great problems now facing human society, it seems increasingly important to find simple and nonsectarian ways to work with ourselves and to share our understanding with others. The Shambhala teachings, or "Shambhala vision," as this approach is more broadly called, is one such attempt to encourage a wholesome existence for ourselves and others.

The current state of world affairs is a source of concern to all of us: the threat of nuclear war, widespread poverty and economic instability, social and political chaos, and psychological upheavals of many kinds. The world is in absolute turmoil. The Shambhala teachings are founded on the premise that there *is* basic human wisdom that can help solve the world's problems. This wisdom does not belong to any one culture or religion, nor does it come only from the West or the East. Rather, it is a tradition of human warriorship that has existed in many cultures at many times throughout history.

Warriorship here does not refer to making war on others. Aggression is the source of our problems, not the solution. Here the word *warrior* is taken from the Tibetan *pawo*, which literally means "he who is brave." Warriorship in this context is the tradition of human bravery, or the tradition of fearlessness, and on our planet Earth there have been many fine examples of warriorship.

The key to warriorship and the first principle of Shambhala vision is not being afraid of who you are. Ultimately, that is the definition of bravery: not being afraid of yourself. The Shambhala vision teaches that, in the face of the world's problems, we can be heroic and kind at the same time. The Shambhala vision is the opposite of selfishness. When we are afraid of ourselves and afraid of the seeming threat that the world presents, then we become extremely selfish. We want to build our own little nests, our own little cocoons, so that we can live by ourselves in a more secure way.

But we can be much more brave than that. We must try to think beyond our homes, beyond the fire burning in the fireplace, beyond sending our children to school or getting to work in the morning. We must try to think how we can help this world. If we don't help, nobody will. It is our turn to help the world. At the same time, helping others does not mean abandoning our individual lives. You don't have to rush out to become the mayor of your city or the president of the United States in order to help others, but you can begin with your relatives and friends and the people around you. In fact, you can start with yourself. The important thing is to realize that you are never off duty. You can never just relax, because the whole world needs help.

While everyone has a responsibility to help the world, we can create additional chaos if we try to impose our ideas or our help upon others. Many people have theories about what the world needs. Some people think the world needs communism; some people think that the world needs democracy; some people think that technology will save the world; some people think that technology will destroy it.

The Shambhala teachings are not based on converting the world to another theory. The premise of the Shambhala vision is that, in order to establish an enlightened society for others, we need to discover what we inherently have to offer the world. So, to begin with, we should make an effort to examine our own experience, in order to see what it contains that is of value in helping ourselves and others to uplift their existence.

If we are willing to take an unbiased look, we will find that, in spite of all our problems and confusion, all our emotional and psychological ups and downs, there is something basically good about our existence as human beings. Unless we can discover that ground of goodness in our own lives, we cannot hope to improve the lives of others. If we are simply miserable and wretched beings, how can we possibly imagine, let alone realize, an enlightened society?

Discovering real goodness comes from appreciating very simple experiences. We are not talking about how good it feels to make a million dollars or finally graduate from college or buy a new house, but we are speaking here of the basic goodness of being alive—which does not depend on our accomplishments or fulfilling our desires. We experience glimpses of goodness all the time, but we often fail to acknowledge them. When we see a bright color, we are witnessing our own inherent goodness. When we hear a beautiful sound, we are hearing our own basic goodness. When we step out of the shower, we feel fresh and clean, and when we walk out of a stuffy room, we appreciate the sudden whiff of fresh air. These events may take only a fraction of a second, but they are real experiences of goodness. They happen to us all the time, but usually we ignore them as mundane or purely coincidental. According to the Shambhala principles, however, it is worthwhile to recognize and take advantage of these moments because they are revealing basic non-aggression and freshness in our lives—basic goodness.

Every human being has a basic nature of goodness, which is undiluted and unconfused. That goodness contains tremendous gentleness and appreciation. As human beings, we can make love. We can stroke someone with a gentle touch; we can kiss someone with gentle understanding. We can appreciate beauty. We can appreciate the best of this world. We can appreciate its vividness: the yellowness of yellow, the redness of red, the greenness of green, the purpleness of purple. Our experience is real. When yellow is yellow, can we say it is red if we don't like the yellowness of it? That would be contradicting reality. When we have sunshine, can we reject it and say that sunshine is terrible? Can we really say that? When we have brilliant sunshine or wonderful snowfall, we appreciate it. And when we appreciate reality, it can actually work on us. We may have to get up in the morning after only a few hours' sleep, but if we look out the window and see the sun shining, it can cheer us up. We can actually cure ourselves of depression if we recognize that the world we have is good.

As human beings, we are basically awake and we *can* understand reality. We are not enslaved by our lives; we are free. Being free, in this case, means simply that we have a body and a mind, and we can uplift ourselves in order to work with reality in a dignified and humorous way. If we begin to perk up, we will find that the whole universe—including the seasons, the snowfall, the ice, and the mud—is also powerfully working with us. Life is a humorous situation, but it is not mocking us. We find that, after all, we can handle our world; we can handle our universe properly and fully in an uplifted fashion.

The discovery of basic goodness is not a religious experience, particularly. Rather it is the realization that we can directly experience and work with reality, the real world that we are in. Experiencing the basic goodness of our lives makes us feel that we are intelligent and decent people and that the world is not a threat. When we feel that our lives are genuine and good, we do not have to deceive ourselves or other people. We can see our shortcomings without feeling guilty or inadequate, and at the same time, we can see our potential for extending goodness to others. We can tell the truth straightforwardly and be absolutely open, but steadfast at the same time.

The essence of warriorship, or the essence of human bravery, is refusing to give up on anyone or anything. We can never say that we are simply falling to pieces or that anyone else is, and we can never say that about the world either. Within our lifetime there will be great problems in the world, but let us make sure that within our lifetime no disasters happen. We can prevent them. It is up to us. We can save the world from destruction to begin with. That is why the Shambhala vision exists. It is a centuries-old idea: By serving this world, we can save it. But saving the world is not enough. We have to work to build an enlightened human society as well.

Here are eight short essays from a diverse group of people who have thought about Buddhism and politics, from the multi-talented actor and writer Peter Coyote, to the African-American professor of Buddhism Jan Willis, to the self-professed "dharma punk" Noah Levine. It's a fascinating reflection of the various ways Buddhists approach political questions and the different styles of thought evolving in Western Buddhism.

★ ★ ★

— NOWHERE TO SPIT: EIGHT VIEWS —
— ON THE PRACTICE OF POLITICS —

THE POLITICS OF INTERDEPENDENCE
by Peter Coyote

NORMALLY the word *politics* means "competition between competing interest groups or individuals for power and leadership." This is actually the fourth of eight definitions for the word listed in *Webster's Third New International Dictionary*. The first definition, which I find more useful, defines politics as "the art of adjusting and ordering relationships between individuals and groups in a political community." The words *adjusting* and *ordering* stress relationship and interdependence, whereas *competition* implies domination and hierarchy.

Relationship and interdependence are "mutually dependent arising"— the core of the Buddha's understanding. This core insight implies some procedures and goals for the practice of politics that might beneficially alter the way it is presently construed. At the very least it affords an opportunity to consider the practice of politics from the perspective of Buddha.

The first principle might be expressed this way: *Political acts and solutions should afford all beings maximal opportunity to fulfill their evolutionary destinies.* (In this context, "beings" should be understood to include insects, plants, animals, and the soil itself.) Practically, this requires considering the needs

Peter Coyote is a writer, actor, Engaged Buddhist, and the author of Sleeping Where I Fall.

of all beings when evaluating political goals and strategies. To say, "There can be no more factories in such and such a place," is a flat denial that creates conflict, because there may be people who need the work and others who need the products. An alternative and inclusive set of statements might be the following: "We may need factories or power plants, but they should be constructed in a way that does no harm. Furthermore, they should be located where the interests of plants, animals, and humans are not negatively affected, and their products should sell at a cost that does not oppress those who require them for survival." This invites higher degrees of complexity and problem-solving, which in turn invites increased participation.

The second principle might be this: *If there is no self, there is no other.* Our "opponent," however disagreeable, is highlighting an aspect of mind we may have difficulty owning, an aspect that must be understood and addressed if we hope to make progress. It can only be accessed by intimacy. Resistance builds strength (as it does in a gym) and hardens the position of one's opponent. Careful evaluation of the first principle will gradually unpack and expose the conflicting "interests" and desires of the proponent. These interests must be pursued to their roots in one's own psyche until they can be faced without the wrath and judgment that diminish one's opponent. Doing so will, at the least, win the respect of those with whom you struggle. This respect increases intimacy and a sense of relationship—the deep goal of all political work.

The third principle might be this: *Procedures or solutions that compromise the dignity ("intrinsic worth") of one's opponent imply domination and hierarchy, not relationship. Consequently, they should be excluded from political discourse.*

It is hard to imagine too much harm arising from a diligent practice of these three principles. Nothing will work in every situation, and a corollary of all political work must be "No one always wins." Since outcomes are beyond our control, what we can control are our intentions and personal behavior. By adhering to these three principles, we model the world we hope to establish through politics. This can never be understood as a defeat.

WHY DEMOCRACY NEEDS DHARMA

by David Kaczynski

ENGAGING in political action today requires attention to suffering, but too often the attention of politicians is absorbed in their own power. Instead of mindfulness, politicians and their professional handlers use extreme care to avoid a campaign-destroying gaffe. There is a prevailing shamelessness as candidates for high office accept campaign contributions from powerful interests and seek to advance themselves by destroying their opponents' reputations and careers. Voters' perceptions are subject to constant manipulation by campaign advertising and the news media. The political game is fueled with money, and its players know that a vote cast in ignorance, fear, or narrow self-interest counts just as much as a vote cast thoughtfully for others' benefit. In this zero-sum game of money, influence, and image, winning is left to the winners.

Is a "progressive" politics even possible in samsara?

Buddhist practice is a unique mixture of patience, pragmatism, idealism, and openness. The life of a Buddhist includes practice and is itself practice as we aspire to reach enlightenment. Dedicating our practice for the benefit of all sentient beings acknowledges a profound connectedness— the karmic connectedness of beings through interdependent arising and the ultimate connectedness of beings through our shared buddhanature. In Buddhist study and practice we discover the limitations of concepts— not only our concepts about people and circumstances, but our concepts regarding how they ought or ought not to be.

Through practice, we place ourselves in open connectedness with others while avoiding the impatient overreaching of concepts toward some imagined outcome. When we work to benefit others, skillful means emerge from the insights of Buddhist practice and from a deep regard for others' buddhanature. This is the kind of "liberation" Buddhists know about.

David Kaczynski is executive director of New Yorkers Against the Death Penalty. He and his wife Linda Patrik received national attention in 1996 when it was revealed that David's brother, Theodore, known as the Unabomber, had been turned in by his own family.

The ideal of democracy in the West, with its emphasis on process, inclusiveness, and human dignity, is imbued with many of the qualities and insights of the dharma. As Buddhists, we also understand that there is no truth or wisdom without compassion. Engaged Buddhism represents an antidote to the politics of fear, hate, violence, and separation. We realize that on the path to enlightenment, no one is left behind. Practice and study help us avoid the traps of polarized thinking. We resist war, yet we honor the soldier's pain and sacrifice. We oppose the death penalty, yet we open our hearts to murder victims' family members. We know that truth and transformation can be realized through listening and paying attention, as well as through speaking and taking action. We are the ones who don't turn our heads away, who abide without discouragement, and who avoid becoming a mirror image of the enemy, because in the end we have no enemies.

Can there be a truly democratic politics without dharma in the broad sense? Is there anything more needed in public life than the dharma?

A PEACEFUL WORLD BEGINS WITH SMALL PEACEFUL ACTIONS
by Jan Willis

SHARING this tiny planet amid a vast universe, we are all interconnected beings, incapable even for the briefest moment of complete independence. Yet we conduct our lives as though we each possessed complete and ultimate control of our individual, isolated universes. We imagine enemies and competitors, and we fight for our share. Though we can sometimes envision a peaceful world, it becomes almost natural to see violence as inevitable and peace as impossible. But it is not.

We know in our hearts that violence does not bring peace, that hatred breeds more hatred, and that only with love and compassion can hatred ever truly be appeased. We seem to know innately, with our hearts, what is right, proper, and just. We recognize that, as human beings, we all wish

Jan Willis is professor of religion at Wesleyan University and author of Dreaming Me: From Baptist to Buddhist, One Woman's Spiritual Journey.

to be happy and to avoid suffering. If we could, we would change the world so that every being enjoyed respect, peace, happiness, and ease. Yet often it seems we don't know how, or where, to start.

I believe we have to start with very small actions. We may not, by ourselves, be able to change the entire world all at once, but we can begin to change a tiny piece of it in our everyday environment.

We have many wise guidelines. The Reverend Dr. Martin Luther King, Jr., for example, that African-American bodhisattva of our time, reminded us that we cannot truly be free until all human beings are free. He once noted that, "As long as there is poverty in the world, I can never be totally rich.... As long as people are afflicted with debilitating diseases, I can never be totally healthy.... I can never be what I ought to be until you are what you ought to be." But Dr. King also knew—and demonstrated— that any war for freedom must be a war waged with love.

In 1963, as a teenager, I had the good fortune of participating in the "Birmingham campaign" for civil rights led by Reverend King. It was a hopeful time. Feeling part of a larger community of like-minded nonviolent protestors, I felt buoyed up by the possibility of triumph over injustice. When, later, after leaders like Malcolm X, King, and the Kennedys had been struck down by violence, a period of hopelessness settled in.

For many of us today that hopelessness still seems to hold sway. And so, before we endeavor to change the world, we need to rekindle hope again. The thing I've learned about hope, however, is that it grows from action, not from thought. If we wish to see an enlightened world of peace and justice for all, we have to move beyond merely imagining it, to nonviolent actions, however small, that will help to usher it in. This goes for politicians as well.

PRACTICE *IS* POLITICS
by Noah Levine

BUDDHIST practice is a political action. Training one's mind, heart, and actions in wisdom and compassion is the ultimate form of political

---

Noah Levine is the author of Dharma Punx.

rebellion. The spiritual path is an engaged act of going against ignorance and oppression. Perhaps this is why the Buddha referred to his path to awakening as having been "against the stream."

From a Buddhist perspective we find ourselves incarnated in the human realm of samsara. This realm is characterized by what are sometimes called the three fires of greed, hatred, and delusion. Through personal effort and training we begin to extinguish the three fires, only to look around and see that although we are no longer engulfed in flames, the whole world is caught in a blazing inferno of suffering.

Even the most superficial assessment of the political situation in this world makes the Buddhist view of samsara ring true. We can easily see the greed, hatred, and delusion that pervade the views and actions of those in power.

Buddhist practice reveals that compassion is the only rational response to the confusion and affliction that infuse the human realm. When we see that our every action can either cause or alleviate suffering, then the choices of nonviolence and non-greed are clear. The natural expression of the process of liberation is to act in ways that extinguish rather than fuel the fires that cause suffering.

This poses a personal and political dilemma. We know that samsara is a place of confusion, yet we also know that it is possible to understand this confusion and find personal freedom within this very realm. We know that we must respond with love and compassion to the suffering caused by those who have no understanding of these universal truths. We must then consider the implications of our empowering political leaders who are ignorant as to the nature of reality and the consequences of their actions.

We may never have the opportunity to empower an enlightened or even *wise* being in the modern American political arena. We may always be stuck with choosing the less deluded of two deluded beings. It may be that all we can do is make wise choices as to who we think will bring about less suffering and confusion to the world. From the perspective of non-harming we can see that no choice is the right one, but to make no choice at all is perhaps even worse.

So this is where our Buddhist practice becomes an engaged form of inner and outer rebellion—freeing ourselves from greed, hatred, and delusion and doing all we can to lessen the suffering in the world caused by fear, ignorance, and oppression.

FOUR NOBLE POLITICAL TRUTHS
by Ken Jones

WHEN we look at the state of the political and social world, we can see Four Noble Political Truths that, like the basic Buddhist principles they reflect, take us from suffering and bondage to liberation.

First is the truth that individual suffering and delusion are socially supercharged. Collectively, we commit immense follies that, if committed individually, would be pathological.

Second is the truth that the forces that drive history and politics are ultimately the same as those that characteristically drive the individual person. The latter experiences a profound sense of lack arising from the impermanence and insubstantiality of this flimsy self. Part of the social response to this has been to bond with other individuals to create a *belongingness* identity. It may be our race, our nation, our religion, our social class, or anything else.

This collective identity is reinforced by emphasizing the difference of other comparable groupings, and, better still, our superiority, and, even better still, the threat that they pose to us. Ideologies add a gutsy righteousness to this black and white picture. Hates condoned by our community enable us ethically to project all our rancor and frustration onto other communities. Hence the savage warfare, heartless economic exploitation, and ravaged environment that occupy such a large part of human history. Hence the ease with which former neighbors and schoolmates have slaughtered one another in countless killing fields.

The above process I call "antithetical bonding"—the heart of social delusion, and according to Buddhism the building block of history and society. The concept embodied in these two long words is easy to understand.

Ken Jones is secretary of the UK Network of Engaged Buddhists and author of The New Social Face of Buddhism.

Every citizen disgusted with conventional politics knows what they mean.

Third, there is a way out of social suffering. Reformers, radicals, and revolutionaries have been telling us this for centuries. The results have at best been mixed and at worst disastrous. In principle, we now have all the material resources to provide every citizen of our planet with a decent basic standard of living. Yet we are unable to do this. The latest ideology—free-market free-for-all capitalism—is actually making the majority of the world's people *poorer*. It provides a rationale for the greedy consumerism of a minority that is wrecking the planet. But there must be something else, something indispensable, that will enable us to find our way out of social suffering.

Fourth is the truth that we must cut the roots of our social problem, the roots of aggressiveness, acquisitiveness, and ignorance as to what we are really up to and why. We need to expose and wither those roots by creating a radical culture of awakening. This would be a culture in which the work of contemplative inquiry—alone and with others—is no less important than earning a living, raising a family, and keeping physically healthy. This would not heal our divisions overnight, but it would begin to dissolve the underlying bloody-mindedness that makes them so intractable. It would nurture wisdom and compassion, and a host of skillful means. Without these resources we cannot build the socially just and ecologically sustainable global commonwealth that is the collective expression of enlightenment. And which, in turn, would provide, for all, a positive environment for spiritual growth.

A BUDDHIST BRAWL
by Richard Reoch

ONCE a brawl broke out in a Buddhist shrine room. A close friend of mine was involved. The retreat leader was injured and needed treatment. It all happened in a very lovely retreat center near where I live. They were

---

Richard Reoch is the president of Shambhala and chair of the International Working Group on Sri Lanka, which is working to end the Buddhist world's longest-running war.

having a weekend devoted to nonviolence, and had invited a guest facil-
itator to lead the retreat. He wasn't a Buddhist, but knew about group
dynamics.

On the second day, the guest facilatator leading the retreat proposed
a role play. Two of the participants would be "kidnapped" by a terrorist
group. The rest would have to negotiate for their freedom. The retreat
leader was to play the terrorist with whom they would negotiate. He
opened a pack of cigarettes, took out a match, and lit up.

"Excuse me," said one of the participants, "there's no smoking in the
shrine room."

The leader paid no attention. He smoked on in silence.

"Please put out the cigarette. We don't smoke in the shrine room."

"I don't give a damn about your smoking rules," said the terrorist
coldly. "Do you want to talk about smoking, or do you want your friends
back?"

"We won't negotiate with you until you respect our shrine room," said
someone who was emerging as a leader for their side.

"Okay," said the terrorist, "I'll stop." He stood up slowly, sauntered over
to the shrine, took a last puff, and stubbed out his cigarette in the lap of
the Buddha.

Gasps filled the room. This was no longer play-acting. People rushed
up to see if the Buddha statue had been damaged.

"What do you think you're doing?" someone shouted. "That's a buddha!"

"I don't give a damn. It's not my buddha. This is not my shrine room.
I've stopped smoking. Do you want to talk about your friends or shall I
leave?"

People were irate! Events were overtaking them. No one wanted to talk
about the hostages; they were obsessed with the assault on the Buddha.
One person went up to the retreat leader and talked to him straight from
the heart. "We invited you here to lead this weekend. We know this isn't
your community or your tradition. But this is our sacred space. All we ask
is that you honor that."

"Would you like to see how much I respect your space?" he replied. He
walked over to the corner and pissed on the floor.

The whole room lunged forward. The first person to reach him knocked him to the ground. The rest joined in, shouting and kicking him as he curled up on the floor to protect himself from the blows. Eventually he managed to drag himself out of the shrine room, told the two "hostages" to rejoin their fellow practitioners, and abandoned the weekend.

Friends, this is the way these events were told to me. In these dark and turbulent times, I often find it helpful to remember this tale.

NOWHERE TO SPIT

by Alan Senauke

THE LONG political season is like one of those California seasons that has no clear beginning or end. Primaries, conventions, elections—and then it starts all over again the next year. In this process the question of "enlightened politics" naturally arises for people of all religious traditions. In our strange and violent world, what kind of Crazy Glue could make a compound of two notions headed toward very different horizons— enlightenment and politics?

The notion of *enlightened politics* points to two facts of life. First, all beings yearn for freedom and happiness. Second, we live in communities, nations, cultures, and global environments that bind our well-being to the well-being of others. This is what Thich Nhat Hanh calls "interbeing." It means that not only must we "think globally and act locally," but we must also think locally and act globally. The notion of enlightened politics brings to mind an old Zen saying: "There is no place in the world to spit." There is no place we can ignore, defile, or bomb, because we ourselves are everywhere.

Our current political leaders seem to have a lot of trouble understanding this.

Hozan Alan Senauke is senior advisor to the Buddhist Peace Fellowship, where he was executive director for eleven years.

The notion of enlightened politics implies policies rooted in the virtues of generosity, compassion, and wisdom, rather than the poisons of greed, hatred, and delusion. And then we need an "enlightenment platform" expressing these virtues. We could begin with what the ancients call "the four requisites": food, clothing, shelter, and medicine. I would humbly add a fifth requisite: self-determination.

This platform means that no one goes hungry, thirsty, or unclothed; that people have homes to protect them from the elements; that doctors and medicine are available to all, with an emphasis on hygiene and preventive care. Finally, it means that people have the economic and political power to determine the course of their lives. With these requisites in place, women, men, and children have an opportunity to develop a true spiritual life of sufficiency, contentment, and gratitude.

"Enlightened view" means, as Suzuki Roshi puts it, seeing "things-as-it-is." So we turn back to the real world where political realities—in fact, all realities—are impermanent and incomplete. This means compromise— working for and voting for candidates who will do the least harm: Who intends to end the downward spiral of war in the Middle East? Who intends to redirect our economy from military spending to education and health care? Who will admit that America's way in the world has been a path of arrogance and power, and intends to go another way? In faith that the dharma will flourish, that candidate will have my vote.

IT'S TIME

by Charles G. Lief

OUR American democracy is, for the most part, partisan in expression, hierarchical, and frequently inaccessible to those without wealth or personal connections. In the U.S., of course, there are models of grassroots democracy: I am writing this from Vermont, where there are literally dozens of town meetings at which any resident may show up and find a

---

Charles G. Lief is a cofounder of the Hartland Group, a community and economic development company in Burlington, Vermont.

way to be heard. There is, however, limited power in any of our voices at those democratic displays, beyond the occasional contrarian rejection of a school budget or the like. Even in Vermont, this home of a "purer democracy," the power is concentrated and guarded.

In order to bring systemic transformation to bear we need to find ways to engage within the system. Unfortunately, though, Americans generally become aware of the political world only every four years. And that experience is as "unenlightened" as one can get: We encounter the relentless begging for money, observe increasingly arrogant and nasty discourse, and hear the unending mantra that the ends justify the means (as if a pure lotus will arise from the mudslinging). Then, in November, following our solemn, secular ritual, we wake up hungover, and remember that maybe the means are important after all.

In 1968, I arrived at the Democratic national convention in Chicago a full-time volunteer for the reformist Eugene McCarthy presidential campaign, sleeping at the Hilton Hotel with the in-group, ready to change the system from within. I was steeped in the optimism of a seventeen-year-old, feeling that our country, wounded by war, racial injustice, and assassination, was ready for real transformation. By the end of the week, though, I discovered cynicism and tear gas. By the next year or so, I met a teacher and mixed that experience with the dharma. Thirty-eight years of fermentation is about enough, and it is time to get back to work.

SECTION TWO: PRACTICE

Phenomena are preceded by the heart,
    ruled by the heart,
    made of the heart.
If you speak or act
with a corrupted heart,
then suffering follows you—
as the wheel of the cart,
    the track of the ox
    that pulls it.

Phenomena are preceded by the heart,
    ruled by the heart,
    made of the heart.
If you speak or act
with a calm, bright heart,
then happiness follows you,
like a shadow
    that never leaves.

'He insulted me,
    hit me,
    beat me,
    robbed me'—
for those who brood on this,
    hostility isn't stilled.

'He   insulted me,
         hit me,
         beat me,
         robbed me'—
for those who don't brood on this,
         hostility is stilled.

Hostilities aren't stilled
         through hostility,
         regardless.
Hostilities are stilled
through non-hostility:
         this, an unending truth.

—Buddha, from *The Dhammapada*, "The Pairs"

"The great discovery of the meditative journey," says Joseph Goldstein, "is that all the forces for good and for harm playing out in the world are also right here in our own minds." The mindfulness, compassion, and wisdom developed through spiritual practice help us to understand ourselves. Can they also help us to understand and change the world?

★ ★ ★

THREE MEANS TO PEACE

by Joseph Goldstein

A CENTRAL QUESTION confronting spiritual life today is how we can best respond to the tremendous conflicts and uncertainties of these times. The "war on terror," the seemingly intractable violence of the Middle East, poverty and disease, racism, the degradation of the environment, and the problems in our own personal lives, all call us to ask: What is the source of this great mass of suffering? What are the forces in the world that drive intolerance, violence, and injustice? Are there forces that hold the promise of peace? Do we know how to cultivate love and kindness, energy and wisdom?

The great discovery of the meditative journey is that all the forces for good and for harm playing out in the world are also right here in our own minds. If we want to understand the world, we need to understand ourselves.

I believe something helpful has emerged from the interaction of various Buddhist traditions in the West over the last thirty years. Its defining characteristic is the very Western quality of pragmatism. It is allegiance to a simple question: *What works?* What works to free the mind from suffering? What works to engender the heart of compassion? What works to help us awaken from ignorance?

Rather than take religious views and teachings to be statements of absolute truth, they might be better understood as skillful means to liberate the mind. Instead of pitting one view against another, we might let go of rigid attachment to any view, and ask ourselves a very pragmatic question: "Is this teaching leading my heart and mind to greater wisdom and peace, to greater kindness and compassion? Or does it lead to more divisiveness, to more selfishness, to more violence?"

This approach to religion is of vital importance now, as we explore methods for understanding the various forces at work in the world. Whatever particular spiritual path we follow, we can draw on the harmonizing methods of mindfulness, the motivation of compassion, and the liberating wisdom of nonclinging. These three qualities—mindfulness, compassion, and wisdom—do not belong to any religion but are qualities in our own minds and hearts.

Mindfulness is the key to the present moment. Without it we simply stay lost in the wanderings of our minds. Tulku Urgyen, the great Dzogchen master of the last century, said, "There is one thing we always need and that is the watchman named mindfulness—the guard who is always on the lookout for when we get carried away by mindlessness."

Mindfulness is the quality and power of mind that is aware of what's happening—without judgment and without interference. It is like a mirror that simply reflects whatever comes before it. It serves us in the humblest ways, keeping us connected to brushing our teeth or having a cup of tea. It keeps us connected to the people around us, so that we're not simply rushing by them in the busyness of our lives.

The Buddha also spoke of mindfulness as being the path to enlightenment: "This is the direct path for the purification of beings, for the overcoming of sorrow and lamentation, for the disappearing of pain and grief, for the attainment of the Way, for the realization of nirvana."

We can start the practice of mindfulness meditation with the simple observation and feeling of each breath. Breathing in, we know we're breathing in; breathing out, we know we're breathing out. It's very simple—although not easy.

After just a few breaths, we hop on trains of association, getting lost in plans, memories, judgments, and fantasies. This habit of wandering mind is very strong, even though our reveries are often not pleasant and sometimes not even true. As Mark Twain so aptly put it, "Some of the worst things in my life never happened." So we need to train our minds, coming back again and again to the breath, simply beginning again.

Slowly, though, our mind steadies and we begin to experience some space of inner calm and peace. This environment of inner stillness makes possible a deeper investigation of our thoughts and emotions. What is a thought—that strange, ephemeral phenomenon that can so dominate our lives? When we look directly at a thought, we see that it is little more than nothing. Yet when it is unnoticed, it wields tremendous power. Notice the difference between being lost in a thought and being mindful that we're thinking. Becoming aware of the thought is like waking up from a dream or coming out of a movie theater after being absorbed in the story. Through mindfulness, we gradually awaken from the movies of our minds.

What, too, is the nature of emotions—those powerful energies that sweep over our bodies and minds like great breaking waves? In a surprising way, mindfulness and the investigation of emotions begin to deepen our understanding of selflessness: we see that the emotions arise out of conditions and pass away as the conditions change, like clouds forming and dissolving in the clear, open sky. As the Buddha said to his son, Rahula, "You should consider all phenomena with proper wisdom: This is not mine, this is not I, this is not myself.'"

On the subtlest level, we learn not to identify with consciousness itself, cutting through any sense of this knowing faculty as being "I" or "mine." As a way of cultivating this radical transformation of understanding, I have found it useful to reframe meditation experience in the passive voice; for example, the breath being known, sensations being known, thoughts being known. This language construction takes the "I" out of the picture and opens us to the question, "Known by what?" And rather than jumping in with a conceptual response, the question can lead us to experience directly the unfolding mystery of awareness, moment after moment.

The wisdom of understanding selflessness finds expression in compassion. We might say that compassion is the activity of emptiness. Compassion arises both on the personal level of our individual relationships and on the global level of great cultures and civilizations interacting with one another. The integration of the understanding of our own minds with what is happening in the world today has enormous implications.

Six weeks after 9/11, I was teaching loving-kindness (*metta*) meditation at a retreat for lawyers. In this practice, we start by sending loving wishes to ourselves, and then send those loving wishes to various categories of beings, including benefactors, friends, neutral persons, enemies, and, finally, all beings. At the retreat, I suggested the possibility of including in our metta even those involved in acts of violence and aggression. One of the participants from New York commented that he couldn't possibly send loving-kindness to al-Qaeda, nor would he ever want to.

For me, that simple and honest statement raised a lot of interesting questions. What is our response to violence and injustice? How do we understand the practices of loving-kindness and compassion? What are our bedrock aspirations for the world and ourselves?

In doing the meditation on loving-kindness, we repeat certain phrases; for example, "May you be happy, may you be free of mental and physical suffering, may you live with ease." However, when we get to people who have done us harm, either individually or collectively, often we don't want to include them in our loving wishes. We don't want to wish them happiness. In fact, we may well want to see them suffer for the great harm they have done. These are not unusual feelings to have.

But right there, in that situation, is the critical juncture of contemplative practice and our life of action in the world. If we want to enhance the possibilities for more compassion and peace in the world—and in ourselves—we need to look beneath our usual and, perhaps, instinctive emotional responses. In situations of suffering, whether small interpersonal conflicts or huge disasters of violence and destruction, there is one question that holds the key to compassionate response: in this situation of suffering, whatever it may be, what is our most fundamental wish?

In the current Middle East situation, with so much violence on both sides, I find my metta practice including all in the wish, "May you be free of hatred, may you be free of enmity." If our aspiration is peace in the world, is there anyone we would exclude from this wish, whether they are terrorists, suicide bombers, soldiers lost in violence, or government policy-makers? "May everyone be free of hatred, free of enmity." These are the mind states that drive harmful acts. If our own response is enmity or hatred or ill will, whether we acknowledge it or not, we are part of the problem.

This message is not new, but the challenging question remains of what to do with these feelings when they do arise, because for almost all of us, in different situations, they will. How do we find compassion in the middle of storms of anger, hatred, ill will, or fear?

Most importantly, we need to acknowledge that these feelings are arising. In this regard, it is mindfulness that can bring the gift of compassion, both for ourselves and others. Mindfulness sees the whole parade of feelings, however intense, without getting lost or drowning in them, and without judging ourselves for feeling them.

One of the transforming moments of my meditation practice happened when I was lost for several days in recurring feelings of intense fear. I tried being aware of these feelings as they arose, noting "fear, fear," but I still felt caught in the intensity of the emotion. Then, at a certain point, something shifted in my mind and I said to myself, "If this fear is here for the rest of my life, it's okay." That was the first moment of genuine acceptance, and it entirely changed my relationship to fear. Although it would still arise, I was no longer locking it in with my resistance. Genuine mindful acceptance allowed the fear to just wash through.

Through mindfulness, our hearts become spacious enough to hold the painful emotions, to feel the suffering of them, and to let them go. But it takes practice—and perhaps several different practices—to open to the difficult emotions that we're aware of and to illuminate those that are hidden.

There are some particular difficulties and challenges in being with difficult emotions. We often live in denial. It's not always easy to open to our shadow side. And even when we are aware, we can get caught in justifying these feelings to ourselves: "I should hate these people—just look at what they did!" From justifying these feelings of hatred and enmity (which is quite different from being mindful of them), there can come a strong feeling of self-righteousness. We forget that the feelings and emotions we have are all conditioned responses, arising out of the particular conditions of our lives. Other people in the same situation might feel very different things. Although at times it may be hard to believe, our feelings are not necessarily the reflection of some ultimate truth. As Bankei, the great seventeenth-century Zen master, reminded us: "Don't side with yourself."

Self-righteousness about our feelings and view is the shadow side of commitment. We sometimes confuse this self-justification with the feeling of passionate dedication. But great exemplars of compassion and social justice, people like Aung San Suu Kyi and others, illuminate the difference.

It is not a question of whether unwholesome mind states will arise in us—or in the world around us. Feelings of hatred, enmity, fear, self-righteousness, greed, envy, and jealousy all do arise at different times. Our challenge is to see them all with mindfulness, understanding that these states themselves are the cause of suffering and that no action we take based on them will lead to our desired result—peace in ourselves and peace in the world.

The method is mindfulness, the expression is compassion, and the essence is wisdom. Wisdom sees the impermanent, ephemeral nature of experience and the basic unreliability of these changing phenomena. Wisdom opens our minds to the experience of selflessness, the great liberating jewel of the Buddha's enlightenment. This understanding, in turn, engenders a compassionate engagement with the world. Dilgo Khyentse Rinpoche, a great Tibetan master, taught: "When you recognize the empty nature, the energy to bring about the good of others dawns, uncontrived and effortless." And wisdom reveals that non-clinging is the essential unifying experience of freedom. We see that non-clinging is both a practice to cultivate and the nature of the awakened mind itself.

T.S. Eliot expressed this well in a few lines from "The Four Quartets":

> *A condition of complete simplicity*
> *(Costing not less than everything)*
> *And all shall be well and*
> *All manner of thing shall be well.*

In this meditation instruction, Thich Nhat Hanh shows members of the U.S. Congress how they can transform the way they govern. Mindfulness, deep listening, and loving speech, he says, can restore communication and remove the wrong perceptions that are the foundation of all violence and hatred.

★ ★ ★

WE HAVE THE COMPASSION AND UNDERSTANDING NECESSARY TO HEAL THE WORLD

by Thich Nhat Hanh

DISTINGUISHED MEMBERS OF CONGRESS, ladies and gentlemen, dear friends, it is my pleasure to have this opportunity to talk with you about how to share our insight, compassion, and understanding to better serve those we want to serve and help heal the wounds that have divided our nation and the world.

When you sit in your car on your way to work, you might like to use that time to come home to yourself and touch the wonders of life. Instead of allowing yourself to think of the future, you might like to practice mindful breathing in order to come home to the present moment and be fully present. We breathe in and out all day, but we are not aware that we are breathing in and breathing out. The practice of bringing our attention to our breath is called *mindful breathing*.

"Breathing in, I know I am alive. Breathing out, I smile to life." This is a very simple practice. If we go home to our in-breath and out-breath and breathe mindfully, we become fully alive in the here and now. In our daily lives, our bodies are present, but our mind might be elsewhere, caught in our projects, our worries, and our anxieties. But life is only available in the present moment. The past is already gone; the future is not yet here. We have an appointment with life that takes place in the present moment. When we establish ourselves in the present moment, we are able to live our moments deeply and to get in touch with the healing, refreshing, and nourishing elements that are always within us and around us.

With this energy of mindfulness, we can very well recognize our pain and embrace it tenderly, like a mother whose baby is crying. When a baby cries, the mother stops everything she is doing and holds the baby tenderly in her arms. The energy of the mother will penetrate into the baby and the baby will feel relief. The same thing happens when we recognize and embrace the pain and sorrow within ourselves. If we can hold our anger, our sorrow, and our fear with the energy of mindfulness, we will be able to recognize the roots of our suffering and we will be able to recognize the suffering in the people we love as well.

Mindfulness helps us not to be angry at our loved ones, because they are suffering as well. Instead, we will want to do something to help them transform their suffering. The person you love has a lot of suffering and has not had a chance to be listened to. It is very important to take the time to sit down and listen with compassion. We call this practice "deep listening," and you can use it, with the practice of loving speech, to help restore communication with the people you care about. To listen like this is to give the other person a chance to empty his or her heart. If you can keep your compassion alive during that time, even if what the other person says is full of accusations and bitterness, it will not touch off irritation and anger in you. Listen in order to help the other person to suffer less.

When you communicate with compassion, you are using language that does not have the elements of anger and irritation in it. In this way, we can help each other remove wrong perceptions. All the energies of anger, hatred, fear, and violence come from wrong perceptions. Wrong perceptions result in a lot of anger, mistrust, suspicion, hate, and terrorism. You cannot remove wrong perceptions through punishment. You have to do it with the tools of deep and compassionate listening and loving speech. With deep, compassionate listening and loving speech, we can bring harmony to our families and our communities can become communities of understanding, peace, and happiness.

When I was in India a number of years ago I spoke to Mr. R.K. Narayan, a member of the Indian parliament, about the practice of deep listening and compassionate dialogue in the National Assembly. When you represent the people, you are expected to offer the people the best of your understanding and compassion. I said that such legislative assemblies could become communities with a lot of mutual understanding and compassion. They could have strong collective insight to support the decision-making process and the people of the nation. Before a session of Congress, for example, one person could read a short meditation:

> Dear colleagues, we are elected by our people and our people expect us to listen to each other deeply and to use the kind of language that can convey our wisdom and insight. Let us bring together our individual experiences and wisdom so that we can offer our collective insight and make the best decisions for the country and the people.

When a member of Congress is speaking from her insight with this kind of language, she is offering the best in her. If we only act and speak in the line of our party, then we are not offering the best compassion and understanding we have. Each of us, if we have enough mindfulness and concentration, is able to understand the suffering and the difficulties of our people.

Congress-members are very concerned about the levels of violence in our families, in our schools, and in our society. Each concerned person may have his or her own ideas and insight about how to bring down that level of violence. If we can combine all our insight and experiences, we will have the collective insight that will help to decrease the amount of violence in our society. If we are not able to listen to our colleagues with a free heart, if we think only that he or she is in the other party and we only consider and support ideas from our own party as worthwhile, then we are harming the foundation of our democracy.

That is why we need to transform our community, in this case the Congress, into a compassionate community. Everyone would be considered to be a brother or sister to everyone else. Congress would be a place where we learn to listen to everyone with equal interest and concern. The practice of deep and compassionate listening and loving speech can help to build brotherhood, can remove discrimination, and can bring about the kind of insight that will be liberating to our country and to our people.

Two days after the event of September 11, I spoke to four thousand people in Berkeley. I said that our emotions are very strong right now. We should be able to calm ourselves down because with lucidity and calm we will know what to do, and especially what *not* to do in order not to make the situation worse. I have suggested a number of things that could be done to decrease the level of violence and hate.

The terrorists who attacked the Twin Towers must have been very angry. They must have hated America a lot. They must have thought of America as having tried to destroy them as people, as a religion, as a nation, and as a culture. We have to find out why they have done such a thing to America.

America's political leaders can ask the question, calmly and with clarity, "Dear people over there, we don't know why you have done such a thing to us. Have we done anything that has made you suffer so much? We want to know about your suffering and why you have hated us that much. We may have said something or done something that has given you the impression that we wanted to destroy you. But in fact that is not the case. We are confused. That is why we want you to help us understand why you have done such a thing to us."

We call this kind of speech loving or gentle speech. If we are honest and sincere they will tell us and we will recognize the wrong perceptions they have about themselves and about us. We can try to help them to remove their wrong perceptions. All these acts of terrorism and violence come from wrong perceptions. Wrong perceptions are the ground for anger, violence, and hate. You cannot remove wrong perceptions with a gun.

When we listen deeply to another person, we not only recognize their wrong perceptions but we can also identify our own wrong perceptions about ourselves and about the other person. That is why mindful dialogue and mindful communication is very crucial to removing anger and violence. It is my deepest hope that our political leaders can make use of such instruments to bring peace to us and to the world. I believe that using force and violence can only make the situation worse. Since September 11th, America has not been able to decrease the level of hate and violence on the part of the terrorists. In fact, the level of hate and violence has increased. It is time for us to go back to the situation, to look deeply, and to find another, less costly way to bring peace to us and to them. Violence cannot remove violence; everyone knows that. Only with the practice of deep listening and gentle communication can we help remove wrong perceptions that are at the foundation of violence.

America has a lot of difficulty in Iraq. I think that America is caught in Iraq in the same way that America was caught in Vietnam. We have the idea that we have to go and search and destroy the enemy where we believe they are. That idea will never give us a chance to do the right thing to end violence.

During the Vietnam War, America thought that it had to go to North Vietnam to bomb. The more America bombed, the more Communists they created. I am afraid that the same thing is happening in Iraq. I think that it is very difficult for America to withdraw now from Iraq. Even if you wanted to leave, it would be very difficult. The only way for America to free itself from this situation is to help build the United Nations into a real body of peace so that the United Nations will take over the problem of Iraq and of the Middle East. America is powerful enough to make this happen. America should allow other nations to contribute positively to building the United Nations into a true organization for peace with enough authority to do her job. To me, that is the only way out of our current situation.

I think we have to wake up to the fact that everything is connected to everything else. Our safety and well-being cannot be individual matters anymore. If they are not safe there is no way that we can be safe. Taking care of other people's safety is, at the same time, taking care of our own safety. To take care of their well-being is to take care of our own well-being.

It is the mind of discrimination and separation that is at the foundation of all violence and hate. My right hand has written all the poems that I have composed. My left hand has not written a single poem. But my right hand does not think, "You, left hand, you are good for nothing!" My right hand does not have the complex of superiority at all. That is why it is very happy. My left hand does not have any complex at all, including the complex of inferiority. In my two hands there is the kind of wisdom called the wisdom of nondiscrimination. One day I was hammering a nail and my right hand was not very accurate and instead of pounding on the nail it pounded on my finger. It put the hammer down and it took care of the left hand in a very tender way, as if it were taking care of itself. It did not say, "You, left hand, you have to remember that I, the right hand, have taken good care of you and you have to pay me back in the future." There was no such thinking. And my left hand does not say, "You, right hand, have done me a lot of harm. Give me that hammer, I want justice." The two hands know that they are members of one body; they are in each other.

I think that if Israelis and Palestinians knew that they were brothers, that they are like my two hands, then they would not try to punish each other any more. The world community has not helped them to see that. Muslims and Hindus also, if they know that discrimination is at the base of our suffering, would know how to touch the seed of non-discrimination in them. That kind of awakening, that kind of deep understanding, will bring about reconciliation and well-being.

I think it is very important for individuals to have enough time to look deeply and to see that violence cannot remove violence. Only kind, deep listening and loving speech can help restore communication and remove the wrong perceptions that are the foundation of all violence, hatred, and terrorism. I believe that in America there are many people who are awakened to the fact that violence cannot remove violence. They realize that there is no way to peace; peace itself is the way. These people have to come together and voice their concern strongly and offer their collective wisdom to the nation so that the nation can get out of this current situation. Every one of us has the duty to bring together that collective insight. With that insight, compassion will make us strong and courageous enough to bring about a solution for us and the world.

Every time we breathe in and go home to ourselves and bring the element of harmony and peace into ourselves, that is an act of peace. Every time we know how to look at another living being and recognize the suffering in him that has made him speak or act like that, we are able to see that he is the victim of his own suffering that he cannot handle. When that understanding is in us, we can look at this other person with the eyes of understanding and compassion. When we can look with the eyes of compassion, we don't suffer and we don't make the other person suffer. These are the actions of peace that can be shared with other people.

In Plum Village, we have had the opportunity to practice together as a community. We are several hundreds of people living together like a family in a very simple way. We are able to build up brotherhood and sisterhood. Although we live simply, we have a lot of joy because of the amount of understanding and compassion that we can generate. We are able to go to many countries to offer retreats of mindfulness so that people may have a chance to heal, transform, and reconcile. Healing, transformation, and reconciliation is what always happens in our retreats. That can be very nourishing to you.

We have invited Israelis and Palestinians to our place to practice with us. When they come they bring anger, suspicion, fear, and hate. But after a week or two of the practice of mindful walking, mindful breathing, mindful eating, and mindful sitting, they are able to recognize their pain, embrace it, and find relief. When you are initiated to the practice of deep listening, you are able to listen to others and realize that people from other groups suffer as you do. When you know that they suffer also from violence, from hate, from fear and despair, you begin to look at them with the eyes of compassion. At that moment you suffer less and you make them suffer less. Communication becomes possible with the use of loving speech and deep listening.

Israelis and Palestinians always come together as a group at the end of their stay in Plum Village and they report to us the success of their practice. They always go back to the Middle East with the intention to continue the practice and to invite others to join them.

We believe that if this practice could be done on the national level, it would bring about the same kind of effect. Unfortunately, our political leaders have not been trained in these practices of mindful breathing, mindful walking, and embracing pain and sorrow to transform their suffering. They have been trained only in political science. It is very important that our friends here try to bring a spiritual dimension into our life, not vaguely, but in concrete practices. Talking like this will not help very much. But if you go to a retreat, the practice of breathing mindfully, eating mindfully, walking mindfully, and going home to yourself to take care of the pain inside you becomes a daily practice. You are supported by hundreds of people practicing around you, and after only a few days, you will find transformation and healing. When you are in a retreat like that you are in touch with people who are experienced in the practice, and they can offer you their collective energy of mindfulness, which can help you to recognize and embrace the pain in you for your transformation and healing. That is why in a retreat we always bring enough experienced practitioners to offer the collective energy of mindfulness and concentration for healing. A teacher, no matter how talented she or he is, cannot do that. You need a community of practice where everyone knows how to be peace, how to speak peace, how to think peace, so that practitioners who are beginners are able to profit from the collective insight.

I think that we should bring a spiritual dimension into our daily life. We should be awakened to the fact that happiness cannot be found in the direction of power, of fame, of wealth or sex. If we look deeply around us we see many people with plenty of these things, but they suffer very deeply. But when you have understanding and compassion in you, you don't suffer. You can relate well to other people around you and to other living beings also. That is why a collective awakening about that reality is very crucial.

One of the concrete things that the Congress could do is to look deeply into the matter of consumption. We think that happiness is possible when we have the power to consume. But by consuming we bring into us a lot of toxins and poisons. The way we eat, the way we watch television, and the way we entertain ourselves brings us and our children a lot of destruction. Because we consume so much, the environment suffers. Learning to consume less, learning to consume only the things that can bring peace and health into our body and into our consciousness, is a very important practice. Mindful consumption is the practice that can bring us out of much of our unhappiness. We also need to practice mindful production of items that can bring only health and joy into our body and consciousness.

By consuming unmindfully, we continue to bring the element of craving, fear, and violence into ourselves. There is so much suffering in people. They consume in order to forget because they do not know how to handle the suffering. Something should be done to help people in the context of families, schools, and communities to go home to themselves and take care of the suffering inside. The spiritual dimension is very important. When we are able to touch joy by living with compassion and understanding, we don't need to over-consume and we don't need to destroy our environment anymore. Consuming in this new way, we can preserve the compassion and understanding in us.

The Buddha said that if we consume without compassion it is like we are eating the flesh of our own son and daughter. In fact we destroy our environment and we destroy ourselves just because of unmindful consumption. Congress could find ways to encourage people to consume mindfully and encourage people to produce mindfully, instead of creating products that can bring toxins and craving into the hearts and bodies of people.

In the name of freedom, people have done a lot of damage to this nation and its people. I think there should be some kind of law that prohibits people from producing items that bring toxins into our body and our mind. To produce with responsibility is our practice.

We have the Statue of Liberty on the East Coast. I think we have to make a Statue of Responsibility on the West Coast to counterbalance liberty. Liberty without responsibility is not true liberty.

In films, movies, and entertainment, we are producing food for the soul. If we know how to forbid the kind of food that can bring toxins into our bodies, we have to also forbid the kind of food that can bring toxins into our collective consciousness. I think these things have to be looked at deeply by people in Congress. We hope that people in Congress can see where our suffering and their own suffering comes from. Unmindful consumption and unmindful production of items of consumption are part of the root of our problem. We are creating violence and craving by consuming and producing these.

My strongest desire is that the members of Congress will have time to look into this matter and look deeply into the roots of their own suffering, the suffering of this nation, and the suffering around the world. This suffering does not have to continue. We already have the compassion and understanding necessary to heal the world.

What makes things really turn bad—in our own lives and in political situations? Generally it's when people get swept away by hot, strong emotion. The antidote to anger, fear, hurt, and other powerful emotions, says the renowned American Buddhist nun Pema Chödrön, is patience. This kind of patience is not passive or weak. It's the courage to wait and simply experience the intensity of emotion, without suppressing it or acting it out. Thus the chain of escalation is broken.

★ ★ ★

THE POWER OF PATIENCE: ANTIDOTE TO ESCALATION

by Pema Chödrön

THE BUDDHIST TEACHINGS tell us that patience is the antidote to aggression. When we feel aggression in all its many forms—resentment, bitterness, being very critical, complaining, and so forth—we can try to apply different practices we've been given and all the good advice we've heard and given to other people. But those often don't seem to help us. That's why the teaching on patience caught my interest a few years ago, because it's so hard to know what to do when one feels aggression.

It's said that patience is a way to de-escalate aggression. I'm thinking here of aggression as synonymous with pain. When we're feeling aggressive—and in some sense this would apply to any strong feeling—there's an enormous pregnant quality that pulls us in the direction of wanting to get some resolution. It hurts so much to feel the aggression that we want it to be resolved.

So what do we usually do? We do exactly what is going to escalate the aggression and the suffering. We strike out; we hit back. Something hurts our feelings, and initially there is some softness there—if you're fast, you can catch it. But usually you don't even realize there is any softness. You find yourself in the middle of a hot, noisy, pulsating, wanting-to-just-get-even-with-someone state of mind: it has a very hard quality to it. With your words or your actions, in order to escape the pain of aggression, you create more aggression and pain.

At that point, patience means getting smart: you stop and wait. You also have to shut up, because if you say anything it's going to come out aggressive, even if you say, "I love you."

Once, when I was very angry at a colleague of mine, I called him on the telephone. I can't even remember now what I was angry about, but at the time I couldn't sleep because I was so furious. I tried meditating with my anger and working with it and doing practices with it, but nothing helped. So I just got up in the middle of the night and called him. When he answered the phone, all I said was, "Hi." But he immediately asked, "Did I do something wrong?" I thought I would very sweetly cover over what I was really feeling and say something pleasant about all the bad things he had done, whatever they were. But just by the tone of my greeting to him, he knew. That's what it's like with aggression: you can't speak because everyone will feel the vibes. No matter what is coming out of your mouth, it's like you're sitting on top of a keg of dynamite.

Patience has a lot to do with getting smart at that point and just waiting: not speaking or doing anything. On the other hand, it also means being completely and totally honest with yourself about the fact that you're furious. You're not suppressing anything—patience has nothing to do with suppression. In fact, it has everything to do with a gentle, honest relationship with yourself. If you wait and don't feed your discursive thought, you can be honest about the fact that you're angry. But at the same time, you can continue to let go of the internal dialogue. In that dialogue you are blaming and criticizing, and then probably feeling guilty and beating yourself up for doing that. It's torturous, because you feel bad about being so angry at the same time that you really are extremely angry, and you can't drop it. It's painful to experience such awful confusion. Still, you just wait and remain patient with your confusion and the pain that comes with it.

Patience has a quality of enormous honesty in it, but it also has a quality of not escalating things, allowing a lot of space for the other person to speak, for the other person to express himself or herself, while you don't react, even though inside you are reacting. You let the words go and just be there.

This suggests the fearlessness that goes with patience. If you practice the kind of patience that leads to the de-escalation of aggression and the cessation of suffering, you will be cultivating enormous courage. You will really get to know anger and how it breeds violent words and actions. You will see the whole thing without acting it out. When you practice patience, you're not repressing anger; you're just sitting there with it—going cold turkey with the aggression. As a result, you really get to know the energy of anger and you also get to know where it leads, even without going there. You've expressed your anger so many times, you know where it will lead. But you realize that such actions don't get rid of the aggression; they escalate it. So instead you're patient, patient with yourself.

Developing patience and fearlessness means learning to sit still with the edginess of the energy. It's like sitting on a wild horse, or on a wild tiger that could eat you up. There's a limerick to that effect:

> *There was a young lady of Niger,*
> *who smiled as she rode on a tiger.*
> *They came back from the ride*
> *with the lady inside,*
> *and the smile on the face of the tiger.*

Sitting with your discomfort feels like riding on that tiger, because it's so frightening.

When we examine this process we learn something very interesting: there is no resolution. The resolution that human beings seek comes from a tremendous misunderstanding. We think we can resolve everything! When we human beings feel powerful energy, we tend to be extremely uncomfortable until things are resolved in some kind of secure and comforting way, either on the side of *yes* or the side of *no*. Or the side of right or the side of wrong. Or the side of anything at all that we can hold on to.

But the practice we're doing gives us nothing to hold on to. Actually, the teachings themselves give us nothing to hold on to. In working with patience and fearlessness, we learn to be patient with the fact that we're human beings, that everyone who is born and dies from the beginning of time until the end of time is naturally going to want some kind of

resolution to this edgy, moody energy. But there isn't any. The only resolution is temporary and just causes more suffering. We discover that as
a matter of fact joy and happiness, peace, harmony, and being at home
with yourself and your world come from sitting still with the moodiness
of the energy until it rises, dwells, and passes away. The energy never
resolves itself into something solid.

So all the while, we stay in the middle of the energy. The path of touching in on the inherent softness of the genuine heart is to sit still and be
patient with that kind of energy. We don't have to criticize ourselves when
we fail, even for a moment, because we're just completely typical human
beings; the only thing that's unique about us is that we're brave enough
to go into these things more deeply and explore beneath the surface reaction of trying to get solid ground under our feet.

Patience is an enormously wonderful and supportive and even magical
practice. It's a way of completely changing the fundamental human habit
of trying to resolve things by going either to the right or the left, calling
things right or calling things wrong. It's the way to develop courage, the
way to find out what life is really about.

But patience is not ignoring. In fact, patience and curiosity go together.
You wonder, *Who am I? Who am I at the level of my neurotic patterns? Who am I at
the level beyond birth and death?* If you wish to look into the nature of your own
being, you need to be inquisitive. The path is a journey of investigation,
beginning to look more deeply at what's going on. The teachings give us
a lot of suggestions about what we can look for, and the practices give us
a lot of suggestions on how to look. Patience is one extremely helpful
suggestion. Aggression, on the other hand, prevents us from looking: it
puts a tight lid on our curiosity. Aggression is an energy that is determined to resolve the situation into a hard, solid, fixed pattern in which
somebody wins and somebody loses.

When you begin to investigate, you notice, for one thing, that whenever there is pain of any kind—the pain of aggression, grieving, loss, irritation, resentment, jealousy, indigestion, physical pain—behind the pain
there is always something we are attached to. There is always something
we're holding on to.

As soon as you discover that behind your pain is something you're holding on to, you are at a place that you will frequently experience on the spiritual path. After a while it seems like almost every moment of your life you're there, at a point where you realize you actually have a choice. You have a choice whether to open or close, whether to hold on or let go, whether to harden or soften.

That choice is presented to you again and again and again. For instance, you're feeling pain, you look deeply into it, and you notice that there's something very hard you're holding on to. And then you have a choice: you can let go of it, which basically means you connect with the softness behind all that hardness. Perhaps each one of us has made the discovery that behind all the hardness of resistance, stress, aggression, and jealousy, there is enormous softness that we're trying to cover over. So we can either let go and connect with that softness or we can continue to hold on, which means that the suffering will continue.

You don't have to let go of the big things you're holding on to, because usually you can't. That's too threatening. It may even be too harsh to let go right then and there, on the spot. But even with small things, you may—perhaps just intellectually—begin to see that letting go can bring a sense of enormous relief, relaxation, and connection with the softness and tenderness of the genuine heart. True joy comes from that.

Holding on increases the pain, but that doesn't mean you're going to be able to let go, because there's a lot at stake. What's at stake is your whole sense of who you are, your whole identity. You're beginning to move into the territory of egolessness, the insubstantial nature of oneself—and of everything, for that matter. Theoretical, philosophical, distant-sounding teachings can get pretty real when you're beginning to have an inkling of what they're actually talking about.

I've come to find that patience has a lot of humor and playfulness in it. It's a misunderstanding to think of it as endurance, as in, "Just grin and bear it." Endurance involves some kind of repression or trying to live up to somebody else's standards of perfection. Instead, you find you have to be pretty patient with what you see as your own imperfections. Patience is a kind of synonym for loving-kindness, because the speed of loving-kindness can be extremely slow. You are developing patience and loving-kindness for your own imperfections, for your own limitations, for not living up to your own high ideals. There's a slogan someone once came up with that I like: "Lower your standards and relax as it is." That's patience.

There's a slogan that says, "One at the beginning and one at the end." That means that when you wake up in the morning you make your resolve, and at the end of the day you review, with a caring and gentle attitude, how you have done. The path of developing loving-kindness and compassion is to be patient with the fact that you're human and that you make mistakes. That's more important than getting it right. And, interestingly enough, that adds up to something: it adds up to loving-kindness for yourself and for others. You look out your eyes and you see yourself wherever you go. You see all these people who are losing it, just like you do. Then, you see all these people who catch themselves and give you the gift of fearlessness. You say, "Oh wow, what brave ones—they caught themselves." You begin to appreciate even the slightest gesture of bravery on the part of others because you know it's not easy, and that inspires you tremendously. That's how we can really help each other.

We all have the seeds of compassion within us, for the human heart is basically good. But how do we develop our compassion and extend it beyond our immediate circle to all people? The Tibetan Buddhist teacher Gehlek Rinpoche teaches us "taking and sending," a meditation practice to develop such universal compassion. We can make no greater contribution to transforming the world than learning this.

★ ★ ★

GIVING AND TAKING: A PRACTICE TO DEVELOP COMPASSION

by Gehlek Rinpoche

OUR WORLD TODAY is very unstable, irritable, and impulsive. We have perfected our ability to harm each other to an unprecedented degree, and the need to protect our own interests is used to justify terrible violence nearly every day. In the name of "self-protection," people are confused into doing all kinds of horrible things to each other.

Deep inside, all beings want happiness. We all want to be free from suffering. But we act in ways that bring about its exact opposite. *Me* and *mine* are always given as justification for our negative actions, no matter how destructive they might be.

Many of us who are interested in spiritual development have come to see it as a means of challenging these destructive tendencies. At the very least, we would like to be good spiritual practitioners in order to find peace of mind in the face of suffering. Spiritual development, however, carries certain responsibilities. His Holiness the Dalai Lama refers to this as "universal responsibility." In his book *Ethics of the New Millennium*, he describes this as the "foundation of human happiness regardless of religious belief."

Universal responsibility develops when we begin to see the deep similarities among us all. Out of this arises a feeling of respect for ourselves and others as being fundamentally equal. This kind of respect can be a powerful instrument for social change. Respect for oneself and others allowed Mahatma Gandhi to peacefully challenge the might of the British Empire. People may remember that at one time it was said that the sun never set on the British Empire. But Gandhi, a simple man wearing a dhoti made from homespun cloth, was able to change the course of that empire not through violence, but by refraining from it.

The same sense of universal responsibility allowed Nelson Mandela to endure long years in jail without wavering in his non-violent challenge to the unjust system of South Africa. Whatever freedom South Africans are able to enjoy today is due to his respect for the equality of individuals.

This same view has allowed His Holiness the Dalai Lama to deal peacefully and consistently with the Chinese Communists. He has held to the principle of non-violence even after fifty years of Chinese occupation of Tibet.

When you think about this, universal responsibility seems like a big statement; most of us don't have this expansive view of our everyday activities. When we consider the actions of people like Gandhi, we may think, "Oh, these are important people and I am not." That is not true. Our individual actions make a big difference to society. A nation is nothing more than the collection of its citizens. A nation does not belong to a single individual nor is it a single individual's responsibility. "Of the people, by the people, for the people," as Lincoln said at Gettysburg. If you consider that every human act has a universal dimension, it takes you beyond that narrow view.

Compassion alone can bring about the kind of change that truly benefits society. The change has to come from within. Love, caring, compassion, respect, universal responsibility—these are the keys. Forcing people to change through fear and violence never works in the long run. You can twist their arms and put a gun to their heads and force them to *say* they agree. But this has never really brought change and will never work. It only creates more fear and anger among the people. Hatred will grow in their hearts until it emerges as revenge. Violence will never change people's minds. It will never put an end to the hatred that gives rise to more violence.

When I was still living in Tibet, there was great admiration for America. One thing we really admired was America's example of freedom, liberty, and individual rights. These are so important. Without these liberties, we are in danger of suffering under terrible dictatorships and fascism and communism. We cannot afford to lose our individual rights and our freedom. It is our responsibility to look after them.

Spiritual people have even greater responsibilities in that regard than politicians. Spirituality really means caring for and loving people, including ourselves, our children, and all those around us. If we don't protect them, who else will? The protection of our rights is not just a matter that the politicians sort out and we don't need to care. If we do this we will lose.

Compassion benefits us all. Every great religion recognizes compassion as the key. The Dalai Lama has said, "We can reject everything else— religion, ideology, all received wisdom—but we cannot escape the necessity of love and compassion."

How can we expand our view in order to recognize and begin to practice universal responsibility? When we develop compassion in ourselves, this compassion will lead to positive changes. Every human being has the capacity to develop this compassion. We all have the seed within us.

We need to develop our minds to the level where every action we take is influenced by compassion. If we only practice on the mind level, we run a great risk of our compassion being just talk. To develop true compassion, we have to put our money where our mouth is. We need not only to feel compassion, but to act on it.

Western traditions have tremendous examples of compassion in action. We build hospitals and schools. We contribute to feeding the hungry and providing shelter for refugees. There are groups that address human rights. Others work tirelessly to protect the environment. When these efforts are made with kindness and compassion, they are great examples of compassion in action.

In our society, however, it is often considered enough to reach for our checkbook and help that way. That is fine, but we can't leave it there. The real help comes from the difficult work of changing our own minds. Positive change in society comes from having compassion for others. Positive change in ourselves comes from having compassion for ourselves. Without it, our compassion for others will lack a solid foundation.

Right now, the ego is our biggest obstacle, not only to helping others but, most importantly, to helping ourselves. We may understand intellectually that we cannot really help anyone until we have learned how to help ourselves. But the ego prevents us from helping ourselves by presenting a false notion of what it means to help ourselves.

This ego continuously makes demands. It wants only the best, to be the most important one, to have more than anyone, more fame, power, and wealth. It is the opposite of universal responsibility.

If you're a business-person, you want to be the most successful one and, if it comes at the expense of others, you may justify it as healthy competition. Your ego always demands superiority, although you call it may call it performance, excellence, or some other business term. Motivational speakers go from company to company explaining how to achieve success. But they also want to be the most famous motivational speaker, with the highest fees and the biggest book sales. Even if you are a spiritual practitioner, the ego will want to be the best meditator, the holiest holy person, someone everyone will recognize and bow down to with respect. There is no telling what ego wants, because its desire has no limit; therefore, its demands continually increase.

As spiritual practitioners, we try to train our mind to destroy our ego— the ego that ignores all others, the one that thinks we are the most important one. Once we have been able to destroy our selfish, egoistic thoughts, we begin to act as our true selves, with a real ability to benefit ourselves and others.

To develop real compassion for ourselves that will enable us to practice compassion for others as well, we need to turn the tables on ego's demands. So, whatever the ego wants, you should turn around and do the opposite. That is the premise of the practice called *tonglen,* or "give and take."

Tonglen practice is united with the flow of the breath. As I said earlier, we need to develop our minds to the level where every action we take is influenced by compassion. With tonglen, we try to associate love and compassion with the action of each breath.

If you are a reasonable person, what you want to do is to make your nearest and dearest ones happy. We normally try to make our dear ones happy by removing their pain. What makes them unhappy? Their mental, physical, and emotional suffering. In the practice of tonglen, we utilize our normal desire to free our near ones from pain and suffering. The tool that we use is our breath. We employ visualization where we use the power of our inhalation to remove their sufferings. Then we use the power of exhalation to give them our joy and happiness.

To do the practice, you breathe in through the left nostril, holding the right nostril closed with your finger. While breathing in, you take in their sufferings. You take them completely, without any fear, without any hesitation, and you don't leave anything out. Then, breathing out from the right nostril, you give all your happiness and the causes of your happiness, without any attachment, without any hesitation, without any stinginess at all. It reaches them and we visualize that they become happy and full of joy.

At first, we may not have that much difficulty with imagining this. But when we begin to think about it more seriously, we may become afraid. We may grow hesitant, both of taking their suffering and giving away all our joy. That's the ego-controlled part of our human nature exerting its self-cherishing fears. Remember, though, that the enlightened ones work solely for the benefit of others, giving whatever is needed without the slightest hesitation. Can any one of us say for an instant that we came out as losers because of our generosity and compassion?

If you are afraid of taking somebody else's pain, it is recommended to start with taking your own *future* suffering. In the morning, you can take the sufferings that you are going to experience in the evening. Today, you may take the suffering you are going to experience tomorrow, or next week, or next month, or next year, or next life. It's much easier at first to take your own problems than to take someone else's.

Before we take in any suffering, either our own future suffering or the suffering of others, the question arises, "What do I do with this suffering? Where am I going to put it?" We have to be prepared for that. We need an appropriate place to dump it. We have an enemy inside. Its name is ego. That is our target. Let that one take it. This method is actually known as "special give and take."

Collect your own negativities, which are the deeds of your ego. Collect your negative emotions, which are the reactions of your ego. Collect all of this negativity and visualize it in the form of whatever you dislike—a big spider or a heap of darkness at the heart level at the center of your body. This is your ego.

As you breathe in, take in your future suffering or the suffering others. Take in not only the suffering but also the causes of suffering, such as attachment, hatred, and ignorance. All of these things come in through the breath. Breathe it in and let it strike the ego at your heart level like a bolt of lightening, completely destroying it. Not even a trace is left. Nothing! Instead, it is replaced by what can be of benefit to others: our body, wealth, and virtue. We exhale this in the form of brilliant white light and liquid as a source of joy and happiness.

As you visualize the suffering of others, or your own future suffering, you need to develop a feeling that puts you in touch with what you're doing and why you want to do it. Visualize the person you care about right in front of you. Think of that person's suffering, the mental, physical, and emotional pain that the person is going through. When you really see your friend suffering with unbearable pain, tears will come. That is true caring. It may not be universal, unlimited compassion, but it is a true feeling of compassion. Try to feel it in your heart.

If you don't feel anything when visualizing the person you love the most, then you have to change focus and try to recollect your own sufferings that you have gone through. Think about when you experienced similar difficulties, or other difficulties: how unhappy your were, how much pain you went through, how much anxiety you had, and how many times you woke up in the middle of the night with a heavy heart. Think of that, and then try to understand that this person you care for is going through the same kind of pain. Everybody can say, "Poor little thing!" but if we have no strong feelings in our heart, we will remain out of touch. Being out of touch with compassion doesn't work. We have to have the feeling. We can only understand and develop that feeling if we think about when we went through that. If we think that way, we get a better understanding of what the other person is going through.

This particular feeling is not necessarily just for tonglen. It is important to develop it in relationships within your family: the relationship between husband and wife, the relationship between children and parents, and the relationships between all members of the family. If you don't understand the other person's problems, you have to sit down, calm your mind, and think about when you had that pain and how you felt. If you can remember that, then your attitude toward your family members will be different. You will no longer be that short-tempered, snappy person. It will give you a better understanding of what other peoples' pain is all about. Otherwise there is a danger for us of falling into saying, "Oh, the poor little things, how they are all suffering!" That kind of pity is definitely not compassion.

Once you have the feeling, once you can really appreciate and understand what the other person is going through, you are giving rise to real caring. You would like to destroy his or her pain right at this moment. You feel, "If I can do something about it, let me do it right now to make that pain go away." That desire and eagerness are what we need. We have to train our minds to that level so that we see others suffering and we can't bear not doing something about it. Without hesitation we say, "Let me take the pain. Is there any way I can take it to free them from suffering?"

When we have that kind desire to relieve suffering from ourselves and others, we visualize the suffering as an undesirable color such as a dark, sooty cloud or dirty laundry water, and breathe it in. Breathe in whatever that suffering might be. Breathe in the suffering itself and the cause of suffering. In your visualization, literally bring it in. And like a powerful bolt of lightning, it hits that mountain of ego, that heap of darkness you have at your heart level, and destroys it.

Then you give. You give love, affection, and virtue without any hesitation. You give your own positive karma, your own body. Whatever the desire or need of the person may be, you give it to him or her. You are giving three things: your body, your wealth, your virtue. That's the best that you have to offer, so you give that. And whatever the need of the individual might be, it manifests in that form. That individual becomes free of pain and instead is filled with happiness, just as you wanted.

The moment you have any hesitation in your giving, the moment you attach a condition, it is not good. People appreciate generosity, but when it is attached to a condition, it becomes difficult to accept it.

I remember living in India, which is such a poor country. In the '70s and '80s, America gave a lot of aid but it came with strings attached. India didn't appreciate it. The Indians kept on saying, "We'd rather have trade than aid." They even forced the U.S. aid office to close. If aid comes with strings attached, the recipient becomes a puppet who has to dance according to the pull of the puppeteer. Even India could say no to that. They were very proud of it, and justifiably.

True generosity does not look for anything in return. Whatever is given is given without attachment or hope of gaining something in return. With true generosity, we are not looking for gratitude. We are certainly not looking for control, influence or power. So when you give, give without any hesitation, without any reservation. Just give.

With practice, we can expand our wish to help beyond just our nearest and dearest, until we leave no one out. In Buddhism, we have six realms of beings: the human realm, hungry ghosts, animals, demigods, samsaric gods, and beings in the hell realm. In our tonglen practice, we try to relieve the suffering and fill the needs of beings in all these realms.

You may ask if we are really helping others with this tonglen practice, giving and taking on the breath. How does meditating and breathing develop a sense of universal responsibility and help us put compassion into action? It works because tonglen practice helps us reduce the force of our ego. It is this demanding, grasping ego that stands in the way of our ability to help ourselves and others.

With practices such as tonglen, our minds begin to be more and more influenced by compassion, so that our actions in the world take on this compassionate influence as well. As long as we understand that meditation is not a goal but a means, we will lessen the risk of becoming one of those all-talk-and-no-action people. This way, even something as basic as our breathing is no longer simply hot air.

Traditionally, the Buddhist precepts address our individual behavior toward others—not to kill, lie, cheat, steal, etc. It is modern Buddhism's contribution to recognize that we also do harm in more subtle ways—as citizens and consumers, through our denial and rigid views, and in the ways we seek entertainment and pleasure. The Order of Interbeing proposes these fourteen mindfulnesses of the ways we create suffering in the modern world and vows not to continue them.

★ ★ ★

THE POLITICAL PRECEPTS
The Fourteen Mindfulnesses of the
Order of Interbeing

1

Aware of the suffering created by fanaticism and intolerance, we are determined not to be idolatrous about or bound to any doctrine, theory, or ideology, even Buddhist ones. Buddhist teachings are guiding means to help us learn to look deeply and to develop our understanding and compassion. They are not doctrines to fight, kill, or die for.

2

Aware of the suffering created by attachment to views and wrong perceptions, we are determined to avoid being narrow-minded and bound to present views. We shall learn and practice nonattachment from views in order to be open to others' insights and experiences. We are aware that the knowledge we presently possess is not changeless, absolute truth. Truth is found in life, and we will observe life within and around us in every moment, ready to learn throughout our lives.

3

Aware of the suffering brought about when we impose our views on others, we are committed not to force others, even our children, by any means whatsoever—such as authority, threat, money, propaganda, or indoctrination—to adopt our views. We will respect the right of others to be different and to choose what to believe and how to decide. We will, however, help others renounce fanaticism and narrowness through practicing deeply and engaging in compassionate dialogue.

4

Aware that looking deeply at the nature of suffering can help us develop compassion and find ways out of suffering, we are determined not to avoid or close our eyes before suffering. We are committed to finding ways, including personal contact, images, and sounds, to be with those who suffer, so we can understand their situation deeply and help them transform their suffering into compassion, peace, and joy.

5

Aware that true happiness is rooted in peace, solidity [groundedness], freedom, and compassion, and not in wealth or fame, we are determined not to take as the aim of our life fame, profit, wealth, or sensual pleasure, nor to accumulate wealth while millions are hungry and dying. We are committed to living simply and sharing our time, energy, and material resources with those in need. We will practice mindful consuming, not using alcohol, drugs, or any other products that bring toxins into our own and the collective body and consciousness.

6

Aware that anger blocks communication and creates suffering, we are determined to take care of the energy of anger when it arises and to recognize and transform the seeds of anger that lie deep in our consciousness. When anger comes up, we are determined not to do or say anything, but to practice mindful breathing or mindful walking and acknowledge, embrace, and look deeply into our anger. We will learn to look with the eyes of compassion at ourselves and at those we think are the cause of our anger.

7

Aware that life is available only in the present moment and that it is possible to live happily in the here and now, we are committed to training ourselves to live deeply each moment of daily life. We will try not to lose ourselves in dispersion or be carried away by regrets about the past, worries about the future, or craving, anger, or jealousy in the present. We will practice mindful breathing to come back to what is happening in the present moment. We are determined to learn the art of mindful living by touching the wondrous, refreshing, and healing elements that are inside and around us, and by nourishing seeds of joy, peace, love, and understanding in ourselves, thus facilitating the work of transformation and healing in our consciousness.

8

Aware that lack of communication always brings separation and suffering, we are committed to training ourselves in the practice of compassionate listening and loving speech. We will learn to listen deeply without judging or reacting and refrain from uttering words that can create discord or cause the community to break. We will make every effort to keep communications open and to reconcile and resolve all conflicts, however small.

9

Aware that words can create suffering or happiness, we are committed to learning to speak truthfully and constructively, using only words that inspire hope and confidence. We are determined not to say untruthful things for the sake of personal interest or to impress people, nor to utter words that might cause division or hatred. We will not spread news that we do not know to be certain nor criticize or condemn things of which we are not sure. We will do our best to speak out about situations of injustice, even when doing so may threaten our safety.

10

Aware that the essence and aim of a sangha is the practice of understanding and compassion, we are determined not to use the Buddhist community for personal gain or profit or transform our community into a political instrument. A spiritual community should, however, take a clear stand against oppression and injustice and should strive to change the situation without engaging in partisan conflicts.

11

Aware that great violence and injustice have been done to our environment and society, we are committed not to live with a vocation that is harmful to humans and nature. We will do our best to select a livelihood that helps realize our ideal of understanding and compassion. Aware of global economic, political, and social realities, we will behave responsibly as consumers and as citizens, not supporting companies that deprive others of their chance to live.

12

Aware that much suffering is caused by war and conflict, we are determined to cultivate nonviolence, understanding, and compassion in our daily lives, to promote peace education, mindful mediation, and reconciliation within families, communities, nations, and in the world. We are determined not to kill and not to let others kill. We will diligently practice deep looking with our sangha to discover better ways to protect life and prevent war.

13

Aware of the suffering caused by exploitation, social injustice, stealing, and oppression, we are committed to cultivating loving-kindness and learning ways to work for the well-being of people, animals, plants, and minerals. We will practice generosity by sharing our time, energy, and material resources with those who are in need. We are determined not to steal and not to possess anything that should belong to others. We will respect the property of others, but will try to prevent others from profiting from human suffering or the suffering of other beings.

14

Aware that sexual relations motivated by craving cannot dissipate the feeling of loneliness but will create more suffering, frustration, and isolation, we are determined not to engage in sexual relations without mutual understanding, love, and a long-term commitment. In sexual relations, we must be aware of future suffering that may be caused. We know that to preserve the happiness of ourselves and others, we must respect the rights and commitments of ourselves and others. We will do everything in our power to protect children from sexual abuse and to protect couples and families from being broken by sexual misconduct. We will treat our bodies with respect and preserve our vital energies (sexual, breath, spirit) for the realization of our bodhisattva ideal. We will be fully aware of the responsibility of bringing new lives into the world, and will meditate on the world into which we are bringing new beings.

The political journey is often one of emotional transformation, of healing divisions and wounds. This is especially so in places of seemingly intractable conflict, where politics is a matter of life and death. When people hate each other, when they want to kill each other, and often do, peace comes only through a long and difficult journey, which is ultimately spiritual. The following three essays take us along this path of emotional healing, beginning with a discussion on dissolving enmity by the well-known British writer on Engaged Buddhism, Ken Jones.

★ ★ ★

BEYOND US AND THEM

by Ken Jones

ENMITY ENCOMPASSES ill will, rancor, hostility, envy, bitterness, resentment, animosity, and much other mind-disturbing, guilt-inducing stuff. We may feel it in ourselves, or may be on the receiving end of it, or both. We may feel it toward a parent, child, or spouse; toward a co-worker or toward a public figure.

Enmity can give Buddhists a lot of trouble. In many instances our enmity may make us feel doubt, regret, guilt, or even pain, especially when someone close to us is involved. At work it may add a disagreeable complication to the everyday demands of the job. And a sense of outrage about the public figures we love to hate does little for our sense of well-being and peace of mind. It is also likely to get in the way of a more objective understanding of what they are up to and hence of doing something effective about it.

The difficulty with enmity is that in many cases there may appear to be very evident grounds for it, whether it be felt or received. We may be trapped in strong feelings of the injustice done to us, of the unreasonableness of another person. Surely we have some *right* to feel enmity toward them? Why not give them what they deserve, in a bloody good row, a thorough humiliation, a well-merited sacking, or even a bloody good revolution? And sometimes the sheer force of righteous outrage does appear to flatten the other party and resolve the problem.

However, badly hurting a person or a social class or a movement, nation, or natural environment, commonly has a price. It is a paid over the years, poisoning perpetrator and victim alike. There is more than pious homily in the warning in the Dhammapada that "Hate is not conquered by hate; hate is conquered by love. This is the eternal law." The twentieth century has given us the appalling example of so-called 1914–1945 "war." The Treaty of Versailles that concluded the First World War so humiliated and punished the Germans as to lead directly to Hitler's rise and the even more destructive Second World War. Usually, whether on the public or personal level, enmity leads not to an outright victory, but only to a deepening polarization, as in the long running enmities of Northern Ireland. And on the personal level, the unforgiving rancor of divorcing parents can blight several childhoods late into life.

DISSOLVING ENMITY THROUGH EMOTIONAL AWARENESS

Another response to enmity is that we try to deny our feelings, or feel guilty about them. We may even develop a corrosive enmity against our ourselves, because we don't feel as a good self *should* feel. This is the path of spiritual lobotomy, of the saint as zombie.

But there is a third response to enmity, beyond either denial or letting it rip. For Buddhists the golden rule is always to look within first, to be scrupulously self-aware. For the present, forget the other. The feelings we experience are *our* feelings, not theirs. It is *our* problem (whoever else's it also is), something that *we* are carrying around with us and which is disturbing *us*. Just getting to this point of turning the question round may itself bring some relief.

We do not usually respond to others as if we were dispassionate, reflecting mirrors. We respond as precarious, needy beings, struggling in the world to affirm some reassuring sense of self-identity. It is this that characteristically drives our feelings, perceptions, and behaviors, and, largely unbeknown, distorts our mirror view of others.

In this connection the Buddha likened our discomfit to being struck by two arrows, when we believe we have been struck by only one. The first arrow is the objective ground for our enmity—the incident, the alleged injury, or whatever. The second is how we *react* to the blow—what it feels like for us. To be aware of this distinction is a vital step in the development of the practice of emotional awareness.

Sometimes enmity may arise on the merest pretext. Probably most of us carry around with us in one pocket or another at least a bit of enmity ready for use. After all, surely someone or something must be responsible for the mess! Some books do have a quarrelsome smell about them. Over issues like veganism even Buddhists have been known to grow somewhat shrill.

The most difficult and important stage in dissolving the experience of enmity lies in cultivating a level of awareness in which we are able to open ourselves clearly, intimately, and profoundly to the bare acceptance of that experience. Such emotional honesty can appear hurtful and threatening to our self-esteem, to our very sense of self. We therefore need to be no less aware of our characteristic evasions—fixating on the injury done to us, projecting our indignation on the perpetrator, trying to rationalize our emotional discomfort away (or just denying it altogether), beating ourselves up with guilt, and so on.

FREED FROM OUR SUBJECTIVE CONTAMINATION OF REALITY

As we learn to become intimate and accepting of our own feelings of enmity they begin to release their grip on us. We begin to view the objects of our enmity in their own light, as it were, rather than in ours. George Orwell warned that "one cannot get away from one's subjective feelings, but at least one can get to know what they are and make allowances for them."

Accepting our feelings just as they are, we not only start to accept others (with *their* enmity) just as they are also, but also start to see more clearly the overall situation in which the mutual enmity occurs. The problem may then appear more as a situation to be resolved than another person or group to be corrected or punished or defeated. This revelation is commonly accompanied by a release of tension. Once we get the knack of this practice a new lightness of being is possible.

Whether at the public or personal levels, none of the foregoing implies any endorsement or acceptance of wrongdoing or injustice. Instead it is about a shift in perception that empowers us to respond to the situation

with a new clarity. Freed of what Orwell called "subjective contamina-
tion" we are in a much better position to achieve a satisfactory resolution.
Mahatma Gandhi, in his use of creative non-violence, was very clear
about this. He was always adamant that there should be no compromise
on fundamental, reasonable, and minimum demands for redress. To the
extent that the adversary refused to meet such demands the struggle
should resolutely be sustained. But it should no less be a struggle to
deepen the adversary's awareness of the suffering and injustice that is
being perpetuated, and to do so through mutual respect, genuine communication, and some recognition of common interest.

A willingness to enter into authentic dialogue and a tireless search
for an optimal resolution of the problem is the mark of the dissolution
of enmity, in at least one party. Where there is a raging enmity the
prospect of constructive dialogue is unwelcome, as a threat to the seamless righteousness with which one or both sides identify. Through such
dialogue a constructive and mutually beneficial reconciliation is possible, as in the historic achievement of Nelson Mandela and F. W. de Klerk
in South Africa, underpinned by the subsequent Truth and Reconciliation confessionals.

I believe the two most important breakthroughs are when we can distinguish the arrow of affliction from the arrow of reacting to that affliction,
and when we can take full responsibility ourselves for the way in which we
react to enmity, regardless of the alleged culpability of whoever we may
hold responsible. This is nicely illustrated by a parable of the Taoist sage
Chuang-Tzu. Rowing across a river our passage may be impeded by empty
boats that have got adrift. These we push aside without concern. However, if there are people in the boats, although the problem is the same, we
get angry and shout at them for willfully obstructing us.

Through awareness and acceptance, enmity can be dissolved and reconciliation achieved. Beaming loving-kindness (*metta*) to the next
crooked politician we see posturing on television may take longer. However, reconciliation does provide favorable conditions for the arising of
loving-kindness and compassion, though best at first to people we can
get to know well. And when our awareness practice makes us familiar

and accepting of our own frailties, and we come to love ourselves, our hearts are opened more readily to accepting in fellow-feeling the frailties of others.

Is there anything more powerful than forgiveness? Is there anything more difficult than truly to forgive? "An eye for an eye" drives so many of the world's conflicts, and in subtler form, it drives much of our personal conflict. Only forgiveness breaks the cycle. As Ezra Bayda tells us, forgiveness is a spiritual practice that benefits the forgiver even more than the one forgiven.

★ ★ ★

THE PATH TO FORGIVENESS

by Ezra Bayda

MANY OF OUR CONFLICTS, both personal and on the global level of politics, come from our inability to break free of underlying cycles of fear and resentment. The practice that deals with this most directly is forgiveness. Forgiveness is about practicing with resentment and healing it. To make this real, bring to mind a person or group toward whom you have the strongest resentment. In other words, who in your life don't you *want* to forgive? It could be anyone toward whom you feel anger or bitterness—anyone for whom there is active agitation in your heart. It could include political leaders, political parties, or even whole countries.

When I was in my teens I worked in a retail store, and I remember people feeling such strong resentment toward the Japanese people that they wouldn't buy anything made in Japan. Have we really evolved very much since then when we can't even watch or listen to someone from the opposite political party without feeling contempt or disgust?

If we examine the current world situation, we can see what happens when resentment solidifies and takes over whole countries. The Israeli-Palestine conflict is one obvious example. Without forgiveness, how can these opposing groups break the cycle of fear, resentment, and revenge that perpetuates the ongoing conflict? Closer to home, we have our own history, including the continuing battles over civil rights, woman's rights, gay rights, blue states versus red states—wherever we hold onto the arrogance of certainty and rightness.

Unfortunately, "forgiveness" is a word that is often fraught with subjective associations, particularly ideals of how we're supposed to be. Spiritual practitioners in particular might equate "forgiving" with some form of magnanimous acceptance of another "even though he did us wrong." Actually, in forgiveness practice we look deeply into *ourselves*—into our own emotional reactions. The path to forgiveness requires our open-hearted attention to the things that block our way to it.

This is a very interesting situation, because the part of us that wants to be awake wants nothing more than to be free of the attachment of resentment. But we have to be honest about this, because the part of us that feels a perverse satisfaction in holding onto feelings of resentment is often stronger than the part of us that wishes to awaken. Even though the resentment makes our life narrow, dark, and constricted, we still cling to it with a stubbornness that defies all reason. That is why the practice of forgiveness has to start with addressing the part of us that wants to stay closed.

In order to work with the resentment and inability to forgive, we have to be willing to look deeply and honestly into our own experience, instead of pointing the finger of blame outside of ourselves. This is why we need to pay attention to *whatever* arises when we bring to mind the ones toward whom we feel resentment. Holding onto resentment often has the feeling of an unsettled account—"So-and-so has hurt me and therefore, they somehow owe me." The human mind has so many strange twists that as we cling to the hard, bitter feeling that someone owes us, at the same time we also may feel the need to pay this person back. As resentment festers, the attitude of "I'll show them!" takes over and hardens us. We shore up our hardened heart with the sense of false power and righteousness that arises with resentment.

If someone were to ask a spiritual teacher, "What should I do with all this resentment I feel?," many teachers might respond, "It's not good to hold onto resentment. Why don't you just let it go?" But can we "just let it go"? Even when we know how much it hurts us, we often don't have that option. We wouldn't be stuck in the throes of resentment if we could "just let it go"; consequently, letting go is not a real practice. It's a fantasy practice based on an ideal of how we'd like things to be.

But why is forgiveness so hard to do? Why do we want to hold on to resentment? The answer, in part, may be rooted in our evolutionary

development. At one point, back when life was very dangerous and prim-
itive, perhaps there was a value in holding on to resentment, perhaps it
better prepared us for inevitable battle. The chemicals that are emitted
when we feel these emotions are very powerful, and on some level they
actually feel good. The problem is that this physiologically-based defen-
sive state is no longer appropriate, nor is it at all conducive to living from
the heart that seeks to awaken.

Genuine forgiveness has three stages. The first is simply acknowledging how *unwilling* we are to forgive. We let ourselves experience the degree
to which we prefer to hold onto our resentment, anger, and bitterness,
even when we see how it closes us to living a genuine life. By bringing a
nonjudgmental awareness to how we resist forgiveness, we can actually
experience resistance for what it is, a complex of unpleasant physical sensations and deeply believed feelings.

We have to experience *in the body* how our unwillingness to forgive
feels. Staying with the experience in the body is not that easy, because
often the sensations that we feel are not particularly pleasant. However,
the trick is to bring the mindset of curiosity—just wanting to know what
resistance actually feels like. One way to do this is to ask the koan question, *"What is this?"* This is not asking what the resistance is *about;* it's asking what it *is.* And the only real answer to this question is the actual
experience of the present moment itself. The only real answer is *just this.*

For example, as we ask the question, *"What is this?,"* we might first feel
the tightness in the mouth, the heaviness in the shoulders, the ache in
the heart, the rigidity of the muscles. Staying with the physical experience, we continue to ask, *"What is this?,"* striving to avoid getting hooked
into thoughts of self-justification and blame. We come back again and
again to the physical reality of the moment, including the feeling of the
air, the sounds, the environment.

In this way, a sense of spaciousness begins to gradually develop
around the resistance, within which the tight fist of our resentment can
be loosened. We can't move on to the second stage of forgiveness until
we've entered into and experienced the depth to which we're *unwilling*
to forgive.

The second stage is bringing awareness to the emotional reactivity toward the person whom we resent: to experience it without judgment, to see it with an open mind. As we visualize the person we resent, we notice what reacting emotions arise. Is it anger, resentment? Is it bitterness, fear, or grief? Again, we ask the koan question, *"What is this?"* With whatever arises, we just experience it within the body itself.

If we get lost in thoughts, memories, or justifications, we keep coming back to what we feel in the body. Where is the tightness, the contraction? What's the overall or gestalt texture of the feeling? We stay with the awareness of our physical-emotional reactions as long as it takes to reside in them. That means relaxing into them, as painful as they are, until at some point we no longer need to push them away.

The third stage of a forgiveness practice is to say words of forgiveness. It's important to realize that saying these words has nothing to do with condoning the actions of another. It's about forgiving the *person*, not the action. It means seeing that the person who harmed only acted from his or her own conditioning and pain. And the way we do this isn't by looking for the other's pain, but by attending to our own. Once we've attended to our own, we're more open to truly seeing the other's. At this point, saying words of forgiveness helps us open into the heart. Trying to open to the other's pain before passing through the first two stages of forgiveness practice—being willing to feel our resistance and then directly experiencing our anger—won't work; then we're just adding cosmetic mental constructs over our suppressed feelings.

Only after we've experienced how our own emotional reactivity stands in the way of real forgiveness can we truly understand that the other was just mechanically acting in the only way he or she could—out of beliefs and conditioning. To truly understand on this level *is* to forgive. When our self-imposed prison walls come down, all that remains is the connectedness that we are. We can then say words like these:

> *I forgive you.*
> *I forgive you for whatever you may have done*
> *from which I experienced pain.*

I forgive you because I know
that what you did came from your own pain.

Thich Nhat Hanh's famed poem "Please Call Me By My True Names" (reprinted in this volume) is a reminder that we must acknowledge *all* of our names, not just the ones we like or identify with. This is how we can access those closed-hearted parts of ourselves that we otherwise rarely encounter. In so doing, we can come closer to genuine compassion and forgiveness.

A few years ago I saw a documentary about the decision to drop the atomic bomb during World War II. My understanding had been that the decision was made to avoid losing over 100,000 men in a land invasion of Japan. Whether or not I agreed with this rationale, at least it had some merit. But the film pointed out that Japan had tried to surrender shortly before the bomb was dropped, approaching a third party (Russia) to broker peace with the Allies. President Truman and his advisors decided not to negotiate, refusing even to hear the terms of surrender before they dropped the bomb. Dropping the bomb wasn't just about ending the war and saving American lives, it was also about showing Russia who had the biggest stick. At that point in the program I had such a strong reaction that I had to turn the television off. I felt tremendous self-righteous indignation against the people I had once believed at least were acting from some positive moral position.

In practicing with the rage—experiencing my own anger without the blaming thoughts—I remembered Thich Nhat Hanh's poem and what he had said about it. I realized, *experientially,* that I was not so different from President Truman or his advisors. Nor was I different from the person who dropped the bomb, or from the millions of people who cheered when they heard the news that a bomb was dropped on Japan, killing countless people and causing suffering that is still with us. This was a sobering moment. Whether or not the documentary had the facts straight, my belief-based rage was solid as a rock. In looking at my anger and opening to what had appeared to be so abhorrent, I saw that the fear-based, protected stance that had resulted in the death of so many wasn't really foreign to me at all. In fact, that conditioned trait was equally present in me.

This realization came from experiencing and seeing through my own anger. This is an important point. It's easy to comprehend intellectually that others are acting from their own protectedness and pain, and that we share certain traits that we may not like. But such conceptual understanding doesn't really touch our lives. It can never lead to the compassionate and genuine forgiveness that's possible once we've practiced with our own closed-heartedness and seen through it.

In practicing forgiveness, it is possible to move from living in our own isolated pain—which usually manifests as anger and resentment—to experiencing the universal pain that we all share. We realize this experientially when we're able to see that we're not essentially different from those we've been quick to judge. As we experience this truth of our basic connectedness, we no longer view the world through the lenses of "us" versus "them." We no longer perceive the other as an enemy. We no longer seek revenge for what we regarded as wrongdoing. We no longer demand recompense.

To enter into the process of forgiveness at this level, where the illusion of separation between self and other begins to dissolve, is a profoundly transformative practice. It's also challenging, partly because we don't want to do it, and partly because entering into our own pain is never easy.

FORGIVENESS MEDITATION

When anger and resentment have calcified the heart, practicing forgiveness as a specific meditation can be very useful. The purpose of the following guided meditation is to help us see through the emotional reactions that stand in the way of real forgiveness. Essentially, it's an accelerated way of clarifying and healing our resentment.

The meditation has three parts.

In the first part we *see* how unwilling we are to forgive. We experience the degree to which we prefer holding onto our resentment.

In the second part we bring into awareness all of the emotional reactivity we feel. The point is to *experience* it without judgment, to see it with the open mind of curiosity. Only after we are no longer caught in resentment can we proceed to the third part.

In the third part we actually "forgive." But this is not the same as condoning their actions. It means that, through practicing with our own resentment, we come to *see* that the other was simply acting from his or her own conditioning and pain.

One of the most important aspects of this meditation is to bring awareness of the person or group toward whom we feel resentment into the area in the center of the chest. Doing this may feel foreign and uncomfortable at first, which is a natural consequence of habit and resistance. Bringing awareness into the heart area makes it less likely that we'll spin off into simply thinking about our feelings. Rather, it allows us to experience them in a way that is both genuine and transformative.

Here are the instructions.

> Sit or lie in a comfortable position, staying as still as possible. Take two or three deep breaths, then just breathe naturally.

> Bring into awareness the particular person or persons toward whom you feel resentment.

> Feel for a moment what arises with even the thought of forgiveness. How much longer do you wish to keep your heart closed to this person, and consequently to life as a whole?

> Now remember the latest situation that sparked your resentful feelings. Feel whatever arises. Don't try to do anything; just experience the feeling in your body. Experience the degree to which you do not *want* to forgive. Acknowledge your unwillingness and bring a nonjudgmental awareness to the sensations of resistance. How does it feel, in your body, to push them away?

Allowing the resistance to just be, bring to awareness sensory phenomena from outside the body: hear the sounds, feel the air temperature. Let the container of awareness widen around the resistance. Feel how the texture of the resistance changes as a sense of spaciousness surrounds it.

Begin breathing into the center of the chest. Feel the texture of the heart.

Now try to bring awareness of the person closer to your being. Breathing into the center of the chest, bring his or her presence, via the inbreath, into the heart. On the outbreath, just breathe out—not trying to do anything special. Without self-judgment, experience all of the arising emotions. Is there anger, resentment, bitterness? Is there fear or grief? With whatever arises, ask *"What is this?"* The answer to this question is to directly experience the emotion in the body. When you get lost in thoughts, memories, or justifications, come back via the breath into the center of the chest, to the physical feelings of the body. Where do you feel tight, contracted, stiff? Where is the pain, the rigidity, the nervous quivering? How does it actually feel?

Asking, *"What is this?"*—feel it. Stay with the gestalt awareness of your bodily-emotional reactions. Stay with them as long as is necessary to be able to reside in them, painful as they may be, without having to push them away. Stay here. Breathe into the center of the chest. Hear the sounds outside, hear the sounds in the room, feel the air around you. Breathe again into the heart. Reside here.

Return to your visualization of whomever you wish to forgive. Draw their presence, via the inbreath, even deeper into the center of the chest. Then say these words:

> *I forgive you.*
> *I forgive you for whatever you may have done,*
> *whether intentional or unintentional,*
> *from which I experienced pain.*
> *Whether it was from something you did*
> *or from something you said, I forgive you.*
> *I forgive you,*
> *because I know that what you did*
> *came from your own pain.*

Repeat these words until you feel the barrier between you and the other begin to dissolve.

If you still don't feel the sense of forgiveness, if some measure of hardness around the heart remains, just continue to breathe into the heart for a while, at least acknowledging the possibility of forgiveness at some future time. It is rare that the transformation of resentment could occur in just one or two sittings. If the resentment is deep, it could even take months. Timing is also an important element. Sometimes the pain is too raw; we have to wait until the feelings are less intense. However, as you practice this meditation regularly, the process of forgiveness will gradually loosen the tight grip of resentment, and will allow you to live increasingly from the lightness of the heart. If your wish to live more awake is sincere, this is one area of practice that can't be ignored.

The fruition of the peace process is reconciliation, a return to trust and friendship. The American Theravadan monk Thanissaro Bhikkhu tells us that this means more than just forgiveness: reconciliation requires the acknowledgment of past wrongs, honest inquiry into their roots, and the intention not to repeat them. The Buddha's instructions on healing divisions within his monastic community provide valuable advice on how to achieve this.

★ ★ ★

THE BUDDHA'S ADVICE ON HEALING THE COMMUNITY

by Thanissaro Bhikkhu

These two are fools. Which two? The one who doesn't see his/her transgression as a transgression, and the one who doesn't rightfully pardon another who has confessed his/her transgression. These two are fools.

These two are wise. Which two? The one who sees his/her transgression as a transgression, and the one who rightfully pardons another who has confessed his/her transgression. These two are wise.—The Buddha, Anguttara Nikaya

It's a cause of growth in the Dhamma and Vinaya of the noble ones when, seeing a transgression as such, one makes amends in accordance with the Dhamma and exercises restraint in the future.—The Buddha, Digha Nikaya

THE BUDDHA SUCCEEDED in establishing a religion that has been a genuine force for peace and harmony in the world. He succeeded not only because of the high value he placed on these qualities but also because of the precise instructions he gave on how to achieve them. Central to these instructions is his insight that forgiveness is one thing, and reconciliation is something else.

In Pali, the language of early Buddhism, the word for "forgiveness"—*khama*—also means "the earth." Thus having forgiveness means having a mind like the earth, nonreactive and unperturbed. When you forgive me for harming you, you decide not to retaliate, to seek no revenge. You don't have to *like* me. You simply unburden yourself of the weight of resentment and cut the cycle of retribution that would otherwise keep us ensnarled in an ugly samsaric wrestling match. This is a gift you give us both, totally on your own, without my having to know or understand what you've done.

Reconciliation means a return to amicability, and that requires more than forgiveness. It requires the reestablishing of trust. If I deny responsibility for my actions, or maintain that I did no wrong, there's no way we can be reconciled. Similarly, if I insist that your feelings don't matter, or that you have no right to hold me to your standards of right and wrong, you won't trust me not to hurt you again. To regain your trust, I have to show my respect for you and for our mutual standards of what is and is not acceptable behavior. I have to admit that I hurt you, that I was wrong to do so, and promise to exercise restraint in the future. At the same time, you have to inspire my trust, too, in the respectful way you conduct the process of reconciliation. Only then can our friendship regain a solid footing.

Thus there are right and wrong ways of attempting reconciliation: those that skillfully meet the requirements for reestablishing trust, and those that don't. To encourage right reconciliation among his followers, the Buddha formulated detailed methods for achieving it, along with a culture of values that encourages putting those methods to use.

These methods are contained in the Vinaya, the Buddha's code of monastic discipline. Long passages in the Vinaya are devoted to instructions for how monks should confess their offenses to one another, how they should seek reconciliation with lay people they have wronged, how they should settle protracted disputes, and how a full split in the sangha— the monastic community—should be healed. Although directed to monks, these instructions embody principles that apply to anyone seeking reconciliation of differences, whether personal or political.

The first step in every case is an acknowledgment of wrongdoing. When a monk confesses an offense, such as having insulted another monk, he first admits to having said the insult. Then he agrees that the insult really was an offense. Finally, he promises to restrain himself from repeating the offense in the future. A monk seeking reconciliation with a lay person follows a similar pattern, with another monk, on friendly terms with the lay person, acting as mediator.

If a dispute has broken the sangha into factions that have both behaved in unseemly ways, then when the factions seek reconciliation they are advised first to clear the air in a procedure called "covering over with grass." Both sides make a blanket confession of wrongdoing and a promise not to dig up each other's minor offenses. This frees them to focus on the major wrongdoings, if any, that caused or exacerbated the dispute.

To heal a full split in the community, the two sides are instructed first to inquire into the root intentions on both sides that led to the split, for if those intentions were irredeemably malicious or dishonest, reconciliation is impossible. If the group tries to patch things up without getting to the root of the split, nothing has really been healed. Only when the root intentions have been shown to be reconcilable and the differences resolved can the sangha perform the brief ceremony that reestablishes harmony.

Pervading these instructions is the realization that genuine reconciliation cannot be based simply on the desire for harmony. It requires a mutual understanding of what actions served to create the disharmony, and a promise to try to avoid those actions in the future. This in turn requires a clearly articulated agreement about—and commitment to—mutual standards of right and wrong. Even if the parties to a reconciliation agree to disagree, their agreement needs to distinguish between right and wrong ways of handling their differences.

This is one of the reasons why genuine reconciliation has been so hard to achieve in the modern world. The global village has made instant neighbors of people with deeply conflicting standards of right and wrong. In addition, many well-funded groups find it in their interest—narrowly defined—to emphasize the points of conflict that divide us, such as race, religion, social class, and education, and to heap ridicule on sincere efforts to establish a widely acceptable common ground.

Although the weapons and media campaigns of these groups may be sophisticated, the impulse is tribal: "Only those who look, think, and act like us have the right to live in peace; everyone else should be subjugated or destroyed." But though the global reach of modern hate- and fear-mongers is unprecedented, the existence of clashing value systems is nothing new. The Buddha faced a similar situation in his time, and the way he forged a method for reconciling conflicting views can be instructive for our time.

The beliefs he encountered in the India of his day fell into two extreme camps: absolutism—the belief that only one set of ideas about the world and its origin could be right—and relativism, the refusal to take a clear stand on issues of right and wrong. The Buddha noted that neither extreme was effective in putting an end to suffering. So he found a pragmatic Middle Way between them: right and wrong were determined by what actually did and didn't work in putting an end to suffering.

The public proof of this Middle Way was the sangha that the Buddha built around it, in which people agreed to follow his teachings and were able to demonstrate the results through the inner and outer peace, harmony, and happiness they found. In other words, instead of forcing other people to follow his way, the Buddha provided the opportunity for them to join voluntary communities of monks and nuns, together with their lay supporters, whose impact on society lay in the example they set.

The obvious implication for modern Buddhist communities is that if they want to help bring peace and reconciliation to the world, they'll have to do it through the example of their own communal life. This is one area, however, where modern Western Buddhist communities have often been remiss. In their enthusiasm to strip the Buddhist tradition of what they view as its monastic baggage, they have discarded many of the principles of monastic life that were a powerful part of the Buddha's original teachings. In particular, they have been extremely suspicious of the idea of right and wrong, largely because of the ways in which they have seen right and wrong abused by the absolutists in our own culture—as when one person tries to impose arbitrary standards or mean-spirited punishments on others, or hypocritically demands that others obey standards that he himself does not.

In an attempt to avoid the abuses so common in the absolutist approach, Western Buddhists have often run to the opposite extreme of total relativism, advocating a nondual vision that transcends attachment to right and wrong. This vision, however, is open to abuse as well. In communities where it is espoused, irresponsible members can use the rhetoric of non-duality and nonattachment to excuse genuinely harmful behavior; their victims are left adrift, with no commonly accepted standards on which to base their appeals for redress. Even the act of forgiveness is suspect in such a context, for what right do the victims have to judge actions as requiring forgiveness or not? All too often, the victims are the ones held at fault for imposing their standards on others and not being able to rise above dualistic views.

This means that right and wrong have not really been transcended in such a community. They've simply been realigned: If you can claim a non-dual perspective, you're in the right no matter what you've done. If you complain about another person's behavior, you're in the wrong. And because this realignment is not openly acknowledged as such, it creates an atmosphere of hypocrisy in which genuine reconciliation is impossible.

So if Buddhist communities want to set an example for the world, they have to realize that the solution lies not in abandoning right and wrong, but in learning how to use them wisely. This is why the Buddha backed up his methods for reconciliation with a culture of values, whereby right and wrong become aids rather than hindrances to reconciliation. Twice a month, he arranged for the members of the sangha to meet for a recitation of the rules they had all agreed to obey and the procedures to be followed in case disputes over the rules arose. In this way, the sense of community was frequently reinforced by clear, detailed reminders of what tied the group together and made it a good one in which to live.

The procedures for handling disputes were especially important. To prevent those in the right from abusing their position, the Buddha counseled that they reflect on themselves before they accuse another of wrongdoing. The checklist of questions he recommended boils down to this: "Am I free from unreconciled offenses of my own? Am I motivated by kindness, rather than vengeance? Am I really clear on our mutual standards?" Only if they can answer "Yes" to these questions should they bring up the issue. Furthermore, the Buddha recommended that they determine to speak only words that are true, timely, gentle, to the point, and prompted by kindness. Their motivation should be compassion, solicitude for the

welfare of all parties involved, and desire to see the wrong-doer rehabil-
itated, together with an overriding desire to hold to fair principles of right
and wrong.

To encourage a wrongdoer to see reconciliation as a winning rather than
a losing proposition, the Buddha praised the honest acceptance of blame
as an honorable rather than a shameful act: not just *a* means, but *the* means
for progress in spiritual practice. As he told his son, Rahula, the ability to
recognize one's mistakes and admit them to others is the essential factor
in achieving purity in thought, word, and deed. Or, as he said in the
Dhammapada, people who recognize their own mistakes and change their
ways "illumine the world like the moon when freed from a cloud."

In addition to providing these incentives for honestly admitting mis-
behavior, the Buddha blocked the paths to denial. Modern sociologists
have identified five basic strategies that people use to avoid accepting
blame when they've caused harm, and it's noteworthy that the early
Buddhist teaching on moral responsibility serves to undercut all five. The
strategies for avoidance are: to deny responsibility, to deny that harm was
actually done, to deny the worth of the victim, to attack the accuser, and
to claim that they were acting in the service of a higher cause. The
Buddhist responses to these five strategies are:

(1) We are always responsible for our conscious choices.

(2) We should always put ourselves in the other person's place.

(3) All beings are worthy of respect.

(4) We should regard those who point out our faults as if they were
     pointing out treasure.

And

(5) There are no—repeat, no—higher purposes that excuse breaking
     the basic precepts of ethical behavior.

In setting out these standards, the Buddha created a context of values
that encourages both parties entering into a reconciliation to employ

right speech and to engage in the honest, responsible self-reflection basic to all Buddhist practice. In this way, standards of right and wrong behavior, instead of being oppressive or petty, engender deep and long-lasting trust. In addition to creating the external harmony conducive to practice, the process of reconciliation thus also becomes an opportunity for inner growth.

Although the Buddha designed this culture of reconciliation for his monastic community, its influence did not end there. Lay supporters of the sangha adopted it for their own use—parliamentary procedure in Thailand, for instance, still uses terminology from the Vinaya—and supporters of other religions who had contact with Buddhism adopted many features of this culture as well.

The Buddha never placed a patent on his teachings. He offered them freely for all who found them useful in any way. But regardless of whether anyone else followed his example, he stuck to his principles in all his actions, secure in the knowledge that true change has to begin by taking solid root within. Even if its impact isn't immediate, a solid inner change is sure to have long-term results.

If Buddhist groups are to bring reconciliation to modern society, they have to master the hard work of reconciliation among themselves. Only then will their example be an inspiration to others. And even if their impact is not enough to prevent a general descent into the madness of fascism, terror, and war, they will be planting seeds of civilization that can sprout when the madness—like a fire across a prairie—has passed.

The Buddha admitted that not all disputes can be reconciled. There are times when one or both parties are unwilling to exercise the honesty and restraint that true reconciliation requires. Even then, though, forgiveness is still an option. This is why the distinction between reconciliation and forgiveness is so important. It encourages us not to settle for mere forgiveness when the genuine healing of right reconciliation is possible, and it allows us to be generous with our forgiveness even when it is not.

As we master the skills of both forgiveness and reconciliation, we can hold to our sense of right and wrong without using it to set the world ablaze.

There is an old Buddhist metaphor: For those whose hearts are closed, the world's suffering is like sticking a hair in their finger: it is hardly noticed. But for those whose hearts are open, it's like a hair stuck in their eyeball: it is acutely painful. We can become discouraged when we feel deeply the world's suffering, particularly when we know how little is being done to stop it. The organizational therorist Margaret Wheatley, best-known for her book *Leadership and the New Science*, has worked with community development in southern Africa and has observed South Africa's Truth and Reconciliation process. She offers four ways we can remain sane and effective activists in a world of unsolved problems.

★ ★ ★

FOUR FREEDOMS: NOT LOSING HEART IN A HEARTLESS WORLD

by Margaret Wheatley

I HAVE NEVER QUESTIONED, as a Buddhist, how active I should be in the world. I suppose because I came at this from the other direction: I was already active in a world that was breaking my heart. I became Buddhist so that I could stay in this world and allow my heart to *keep* breaking.

I work in many different places where people are suffering. These people live in third world countries, confronting a future that is no future. Or they live in modern organizations, confronting the loss of self and meaning. I used to differentiate, believing that those who suffer from poverty and disease deserve more support than those whining in comfortable offices. But Pema Chödrön dissolves this distinction when she explaines, "Suffering is suffering."

This is true.

Today as I write this, Robert Kennedy Jr. is speaking just down the road before several hundred people, all of whom care about this world. He will talk to them about environmental issues. About vaccinations containing mercury that have led to a huge increase in childhood autism, clear cause and effect denied by authorities. In his gestures and demeanor, he will remind them of his father, that passionate, strident voice striving to awaken our anger about poverty and the forgotten. People will leave incensed, inspired, frustrated. I have been to many of these events and given speeches myself that activate these emotions. The anger rises and stirs us awake; we speak out, we protest, we rage and rally. And then, when nothing changes, we deflate, feeling weak, powerless, and sickened by our own anger.

Later this day in October, CNN broadcasts former president Clinton's Global Initiative Summit—dozens of powerful leaders from around the world gathered by him to create change in the world. So many brilliant, passionate people speaking from the depth of their clarity. I can't listen to another summit. Or panel. Or speech. We don't need one more session where we sit, adamant in our positions, blaming the other. Because we already know what to do. The solutions we need are already here. Why can't we use what we know works? Where is the courage to stop doing what is destroying so many? As the show continues (CNN gives them an hour), I am back in a familiar place—pulsating with anger and frustration.

I became Buddhist so I could see this insanity and not go insane.

Many years ago, I learned to bear witness, to stand with those enduring great harm. To do nothing but be there, listening. I was in South Africa a number of times as people learned how to live together as a free nation. When there, I would hear experiences of such horror, and of such forgiveness, that some nights I couldn't sleep, tossed and turned by these stories, forced to reconsider human nature. I didn't want to hear one more horror. But I reasoned with myself to become a good listener. If they had experienced it, I told myself, the least I could do was listen.

How do I bear witness to the unbearable?
Why are people so deliberately cruel?
How do I not bring more rage into the world?

This is why I became Buddhist. To be free from these and many other cries.

FOUR FREEDOMS

Buddhists relish enumerated concepts. Everything has a number in front of it, collections of concepts from two to 84,000. Here is my own addition. I could call these "Four Freedoms," because practicing these I feel free to walk into difficult places, even free to remain sane. But truly, I think of them more gratefully as, "thank-god-I-know-these." The four I have learned from my Buddhist practice are to be hopeless, groundless, empty, and fearless.

1. Free from Hope

I was listening to the most eloquent speaker I'd ever heard, a man who has worked in the United Nations for years, first on issues of children, now on issues of HIV/AIDS. With images that took us to heartbreak, he described the fate of children in this world. He described the legions of child soldiers, the children enslaved in industry, the millions orphaned by AIDS, nine-year-olds struggling as heads-of-household to keep their siblings together. Everywhere children learning only to be silent, craven, or brutal.

This is what he confronts each day. At the very end, he stated quietly: "This is a world that does not care about its children."

Someone in the audience asked him how he sustained himself, as day-to-day he looked such horror in the face. He replied: "It's increasingly difficult to keep my anger under control. It's eating away at me. I don't know how much longer I can continue this work."

I practice to avoid descending with him into anger, fear, sorrow, and illness. My new faith frees me from the awful question, "Why would a loving God allow this to happen?" No longer seeking explanation, I can stay in this world of escalating inhumanity.

After all, what other species is so stupid as to stop caring for its children?

"Beyond hope and fear" is a frequent teaching in Buddhism. Dante admonished Christians condemned to hell, "Abandon all hope, ye who enter here." But we all need to abandon hope. Hope plays hell with us, the siren call of accomplishment, the seduction of success. We can change the world. We can make a difference. If only we work hard enough. If only we get more resources. If only...If we...If we...

Thomas Merton, a Christian mystic, counseled a friend: "Do not depend on the hope of results...you may have to face the fact that your work will be apparently worthless and even achieve no result at all, if not perhaps results opposite to what you expect. As you get used to this idea, you start more and more to concentrate not on the results, but on the value, the rightness, the truth of the work itself.... you gradually struggle less and less for an idea and more and more for specific people.... In the end, it is the reality of personal relationship that saves everything."

I often read Merton's letter to groups. Nobody wants to hear it. It's not the usual career advice: Your work will be worthless, achieve no results, or even create results contrary to what you want. Oh my God.

People are terrified of hopelessness. They ask: What will motivate me if there's no hope? Why would I try to do anything if it won't work? Deprived of hope they anticipate only endless hours of depression. For a worthless life.

Their questions introduce a key problem with hope. It never enters a room without fear at its side. If you hope to accomplish something, you also are afraid that you will fail. What if our actions don't work? What if we can't save the world? What if we truly are powerless?

I gave up saving the world about three years ago. It was more difficult than letting go of a love relationship. I felt I was condemning the world to its bitter end. Some of my colleagues were critical, even frightened by my decision. How could I be so irresponsible? If we give up on the world, what will happen? They still refuse to resign as savior (especially the younger ones). I watch them force their failing spirits and tired bodies back into action one more time, wanting vehemence to give them vigor.

I didn't give up saving the world to protect my health. I gave it up to discover what I'm supposed to be doing—how best to help. Beyond hope and fear, freed from success or failure, I'm learning what right action feels like. Its clarity, its energy. I still get angry, enraged, and frustrated. But now I know to retreat, to not be driven to action by these emotions. I don't do anything until I have relocated myself beyond hope and fear. Then I can act, rightly. I hope.

And Merton spoke truthfully. Outcomes don't matter. People do. Can we be kind, loving, generous, even as everything caves in?

Beyond hope and fear, this question I can answer. My answer is yes.

2. Free from Safety

The flags are flying at half-mast. Again.
This one drapes across the highway as I drive toward it.
It's oversized, the type of flag that became popular
  when patriotism needed to be more visible.
It suffocates the road, limp, lifeless.
   Wind attempts to lift its spirit but
the flag refuses so
  laden with sorrow.

This flag is for Katrina.
I remember another massive flag that
 flared out defiantly in the fierce wind after 9/11.

The world I see will soon be lost in lifeless flags.
We are only at the beginning.

  Last night I threw out a salt container that still had some salt in it.
  I wanted to clear space in my crowded cabinet.
  As I tossed it in the garbage, it came to me. There will
  come such scarcity that even those few grains will be treasure.
  I still threw it out, but vowed to remember this night.

Now, how do I live whole-heartedly?

Every time a flag gets lowered, I tell myself:
  This is what it feels like as a culture dies.
  This is what it feels like in the age of destruction.
  This is what groundless feels like.
  Don't grasp for ground.
  Don't grasp.

Groundlessness has to be learned.
I am teaching myself with these terrifying mantras.

3. Free from Self

Nothing remains the same.
   Nothing has solid lasting form.
      Nothing is as it appears.
         Nothing means what I think it means.
            Nothing that grabs my attention will remain.
                           If I let it.

     Nothing exists by itself.
     Nothing has independent identity.
   Nothing I am means what I think I mean.
  Nothing I cling to is real.
Nothing to protect, defend, prefer.

Whew.

4. Free from Fear

Fearless

      Trickster   sage   prankster   magician

Fearless

    Acting   out
     crazy   wisdom

Fearless

    The lion's roar
        the dragon's soar

       Lift off.

Beyond hope and fear

no ground

no base

soaring, roaring

Wings flared wide

free

no hope

no self

no safety

Fearless

Up here the world looks lovely

Spacious, welcoming, open

grateful for gifts that only appear as

risk, bravery, foolishness
on the ground.

Fearless

Speak out

act out

make love

do nothing

there's nothing else to do.

Soar sweet dragon   beyond   beyond

Fearless

True love.

Coda

The course of true love never runs smooth.
True love never runs.

Yet here I am, again restrained from flight by the terrible gravity of events. It doesn't matter what day it is. Natural catastrophes, manmade disasters, greed, violence—the senselessness doesn't cease. Every day we undo the future. (A Chilean poet created this new verb, *to undo-the-future.* We need new terms, she said, to describe what we're really doing.) Another new descriptor appears on the evening news: "disastered out." The commentator asks whether we are so overwhelmed with the world that we can't take it anymore, we can't give anymore.

Confronted by so much turmoil and tragedy, how can we help but grasp for ground anywhere we can find it? How, with so much horror, could we ever give up hope?

I have a colleague, famous in my circles, who has decided his legacy is to make life better for billions of people. He plans to create leadership programs for eliminating poverty, creating health, literacy, and prosperous communities. He repeatedly stresses that it is only billions served that will satisfy him. He knows, as I do, that the solutions we need are already here. He is investing his money and his last passion in making sure that we learn these solutions and apply them everywhere. He will save the world.

I sit there exposed, naked in hopelessness. The longer his energy and optimism fill the room, the more I doubt myself. Have I done right to stop dreaming, to surrender my visions? Have I done right to treat this world as illusion? Is it true that nothing I see means what I think it means?

Am I bringing any good to the world selfless, hopeless, groundless? Or is he right? Can we still save the world? Oh my God.

I want to flee in self-defense from these questions. But they only hold me to this troubled earth. Really, there is only one question.

> *Where do I find the winds of fearlessness?*
> > *For this, I know the answer.*
> *Retreat. Relocate. Beyond hope and fear. True love.*

SECTION THREE:
ACTION

How do we act in the world? With a boundless mind of friendliness toward others,
    like a mother protecting her only child. This is the Buddha's platform for joining
    dharma and political action.

Whatever living beings there are, whether they be weak or strong—omitting none—
Whether long, large, average, short, big or small,
Seen or unseen, dwelling near or far,
Born or to be born—may all beings be happy.

Let no one deceive another or despise anyone anywhere.
Let none out of anger or hostility wish suffering upon another.

Just as a mother would protect with her life her own child, her only child,
So should one cultivate a boundless mind toward all beings and friendliness toward
    the entire world.

One should cultivate a boundless mind—above, below, and across,
Without obstruction, hatred, or enmity.

Standing, walking, sitting, or lying down, throughout all one's waking hours,
One should practice this mindfulness; this, they say, is the supreme state....

—Buddha, from the *Metta Sutta*

Nowhere is the Buddhist principle of interdependence more important—and more violated—than in our relationship with the environment. Our presumed dominion over the Earth—our belief that its plants, animals, and resources exist for human consumption—is the foundation of all our economic systems. This attitude is not only destructive of other beings; it is self-destructive, because the quality of human life, if not our actual survival, depends on the health and balance of the Earth's complex systems. Because Buddhism has long understood this principle, says Stephanie Kaza, a teacher of environmental ethics and ecophilosophy, it can offer some important guidelines for environmental activism.

★ ★ ★

AGENT IN INDRA'S NET

by Stephanie Kaza

THESE DAYS it can be overwhelming to think about the state of the environment. Ravaging consumption, exploding population growth, and high-impact technologies now circle the globe; the problems seem intractable. Methods of resource extraction have become rapacious in their efficiency, and ecosystem health is plummeting on every continent. In the midst of such a challenge to planetary stability, what really can one person do? This is the question my students ask every semester, and it is crucial to have some answers or we cannot move forward toward any hope of sustainability.

Often people ask me, "Where should I begin?" I usually ask in reply, "What do you care about the most?"—because most environmental work is incremental and cumulative, strong motivation is essential to hang in there for the long haul. And since the problems are endless, no one can possibly address all of them effectively. So it is important to choose a specific area to do some work, to be grounded in the physical, political, and economic realities of a specific situation. I won't tell you where you should put your energy, but I would like offer several Buddhist approaches that can be applied to any environmental work.

BEING WITH THE SUFFERING

If you look at the state of the world today, the suffering is enormous. Global agriculture, urban sprawl, and industrial development have caused wide-scale loss of habitat, species extinction, land and water degradation, and unstable climate. In the last century, the rate of loss has accelerated significantly, to the point of threatening ecosystem health and the continuity of life.

One of the earliest Buddhist teachings, the Four Noble Truths, begins with the suffering of impermanence. Birth, sickness, old age, and death—every stage of life for every form of existence is conditioned by the inevitability of change and loss. Facing this suffering and the delusions it generates is the place where all Buddhist practice begins. In his precepts of the Order of Interbeing, Thich Nhat Hanh urges, "Do not avoid contact with suffering or close your eyes before suffering." He directs students to be present with suffering to understand the nature of existence. This requires patience and equanimity in the face of upsetting realities, whether it is a clear-cut forest reduced to stumps, a once-fertile wetland deadened by chemical waste, or a coral reef blasted by fishing dynamite. It is not easy to gaze clear-eyed at these troubling manifestations of human activity.

Most of the time we would rather not consider the consequences of such activities. Yet from a Buddhist perspective, this is the best place to start, for it is grounded in reality, undistorted by visionary ideals. Mindful awareness supports what Zen teachers call *direct knowing*, or direct experience of the actual state of things. Such authentic perception is freeing and motivating at the same time. Practices that quiet and focus the mind provide a stable mental base from which to observe the full range of human impact.

To be with environmental suffering means being aware of the suffering produced by our own cultural conditioning toward other beings. Those of us in the West have been raised with views which emphasize objectivity: seeing plants and animals, forests and rivers as autonomous objects and potential resources. This human-centered bias, so central to Western politics and economics, is one of the greatest deterrents to being fully present with other living beings. If we see the environment as primarily for human use—whether for food, shelter, recreation, or spiritual development—it is hard to see the intrinsic nature of another being and how it suffers under the thumb of human dominance.

Part of being with the suffering is learning what is actually going on in any given environmental conflict. The Four Noble Truths can be applied as a framework for diagnosis through four questions, each corresponding to one of the truths:

First, what is the problem or suffering? Second, what are the causes of the suffering? Third, what would put an end to the suffering? And fourth, what is the path to realize this goal? This analysis is deceptively simple, yet it is radical in including all forms of suffering—people, animals, trees, species, habitats, ecosystems.

This method of questioning provides straightforward guidelines for how to become more informed and therefore more able to bear witness to the suffering involved. It also provides some analytical balance to the inevitable emotions that arise when you glimpse the nature of another being's suffering.

CULTIVATING SYSTEMS MIND

Analyzing environmental problems almost always requires some under-standing of ecological principles, or what I call *systems thinking*. Buddhist philosophy provides an excellent foundation for systems thinking in the law of dependent co-arising, or interdependent origination. According to this perspective, all events and beings are interdependent, interre-lated, and mutually co-creating. The universe is dynamic in all dimen-sions and scales of activity, with every action affecting and generating others in turn.

A Chinese Buddhist metaphor for this view is the Jewel Net of Indra. Imagine a net extending infinitely across horizontal and vertical dimen-sions of space. Then add more nets criss-crossing on the diagonals. And then imagine an infinite number of these nets criss-crossing every plane of space. At each node in every net, there is a multifaceted jewel which reflects every other jewel in the net. There is nothing outside the Net and nothing which does not reverberate its presence throughout this Net of infinite capacity. The jewels and the infinite links across space are all changing constantly, and always reflecting each other in that process.

From an ecological perspective, this metaphor makes obvious sense: ecological systems are exactly such complex sets of relations shaping and being shaped over time by all the members in the system. You do not have to study formal ecological science to understand this; it is a matter of observing cause and effect in whatever system you engage closely— your family, the workplace, your backyard.

Systems thinking develops through looking at patterns in time and space, such as seasonal cycles or animal paths. For an ecologist these are essential tools. For a mindful citizen, these tools enable you to ask very useful questions in addressing environmental concerns. Rather than focusing too narrowly on only one or two actors in the drama, you can ask about the origin and history of the conflict, the patterns in policy decisions that have determined decisions, the economic and social needs of the parties involved, and the specific ecological relations at stake. A systems thinker looks across several scales of time and space, always piecing together the puzzles of relationship, of the many causes and the many effects.

Astute observers of systems can decipher the patterns of feedback that reflect the dominant shaping forces. Too much heat, the cat seeks shade. Too much cold, the cat finds a warm car-hood to sleep on. Systems are created by self-regulating patterns, such as those that keep you at a constant body temperature, and by self-organizing patterns that allow the system to adapt and respond when new opportunities arise.

Self-regulation (which maintains the stability of the system) and self-organization (which allows the system to evolve or "learn") are both happening all the time at all levels of activity in every system. You can practice observing this in your own body/mind to see how such feedback works. How do you respond to rainy days? To the short days of the year? To being hungry? To getting enough and not enough sleep? You can practice observing yourself in nature to see which places nourish you, and why and in what season. This is all very useful for developing a systems mind to address complex environmental situations.

So far this is fairly straightforward biogeophysical reality. From a Buddhist perspective, however, the law of interdependence, or systems thinking, as I'm calling it, also includes the role of human thought and conditioning. Intention and mental attitudes count; they are a significant force in the universe. So Buddhists see human thought as a very critical part of any environmental dialogue. What people think about the environment will have a major determining effect on what they choose to do. The serious Buddhist systems thinker taking up a perplexing environmental controversy would want to know as much about the human actors and their attitudes as about the affected trees and wildlife.

This leads to a key aspect of systems thinking, *agency*: who is actually doing what? It can be intoxicating to taste the grand interdepending awe of the whole universe, that "oneness" experience where everything makes sense. But this is only a first step of insight. It is crucial to keep going— to study closely what is actually going on and who is causing what to happen. With environmental issues, this means determining who is responsible for the decisions or actions that impact the earth and human community. It means tracing the chain of cause and effect back to those who have generated the environmental damage and who are in a position to reverse their course of action.

The vast web of relations in the dynamic unfolding is not made up of equal partners. Some agents definitely carry more weight than others, and identifying key actors and policy decisions can be very helpful in choosing appropriate strategies to re-orient the system to healthy goals.

Liberty Hyde Bailey, an American naturalist at the turn of the twentieth century, said "the happiest life has the greatest number of points of contact with the world, and it has the deepest feeling and sympathy with everything that is." I believe he is describing the experience of a systems thinker, who brings awareness to all his or her relationships with specific human and non-human beings. A Buddhist might call it a penetrating experience of interdependence. The point is that such awareness is available to everyone and is foundational to doing effective environmental work. If you learn the topography of local rivers and mountains, if you hike their latitudes in all seasons, if you converse with those who use and protect the local rivers and mountains, this becomes the basis for seeing yourself as one who is shaped by—as well as shaping—the relations of Indra's Web.

TAKING UP THE PATH OF NONHARMING

All religions and cultures have established ethical guidelines and moral frameworks to guide human actions. Both historically and recently, a number of these have been interpreted to support environmental protection.

In Buddhist ethics, there is one central principle to all ethical teachings: the practice of nonharming, or *ahimsa*. This is the first precept of the monastic vows, and it informs all other ethical commitments. Understanding how deeply life is conditioned by suffering at many levels, the Buddhist student aims not to add to the suffering, and to reduce suffering where possible; in other words, to cause minimal harm. In its deepest sense, *ahimsa* means the absence of even the urge to kill or harm. Such a compassionate response arises naturally out of a broadly-felt connection to other beings.

Nonharming is not meant as an unreachable ideal, but rather a pragmatic basis for making choices. It can serve as a guiding principle for environmental decisions. The U.S. National Environmental Protection Act (NEPA) was written with this intention: environmental impact statements were mandated as a way to measure how much suffering would be caused by a federal project and to suggest mitigation measures to reduce the impact. That can mean changing harvest methods, for example, from clear cutting to selective cutting. It can mean providing protection for endangered species that are close to extinction. It can mean forming a watershed council so that all voices are included in decisions about watershed basin planning.

The practice of nonharming has been codified in the Mahayana model of the *bodhisattva*, the enlightened being who returns lifetime after lifetime to help all suffering beings. The bodhisattva's vow is all-encompassing, requiring endless compassion. Green Buddhists have coined the term *ecosattva* to conjure an archetypal bodhisattva who has vowed to end environmental suffering. Ecosattvas take their work into any field of environmental concern. Agriculture, water pollution, climate stabilization, wilderness protection—the opportunities are endless—and their work carries the strength of the bodhisattva vow to help all who are suffering.

Having such a vow as a reference point relieves some of the anxiety about getting quick results. Many environmental problems are quite intractable and will take lifetimes to turn around. A steady intention can provide a grounding point for what may be a very long battle for environmental stability.

Two places where I hear a lot of discussion these days about reducing harm are in relation to food and energy. The suffering of modern meat production for both animals and workers has been well documented (see *Fast Food Nation*, by Eric Schlosser, for example). Likewise, industrial agriculture has been exposed for its chemical assaults on soil and human health. Many people are choosing ethical principles for eating that reduce harm to animals, plants, soils, and the human body. For some, this means eating food produced organically, and if possible, grown by local farmers, which reduces the energy use of long-distance transportation. For others, this means choosing fair trade products that reduce the suffering of field-laborers and producers caught in a global economic system. Some people are committed to reducing the anonymity of food shopping by participating in community-supported agriculture food shares.

College students are especially concerned about alternative energy choices. They know that oil production will peak in their lifetime and that other sources of energy must be developed. Biodiesel fuel is quite popular, since it offers a way to recycle used vegetable oil. Wind and solar energy are both seen as causing relatively little harm to the environment, while other potential energy sources, such as hydrogen fuel cells, are questioned because of their high costs of production. Many students would love to have a hybrid electric vehicle, because with better gas mileage they would be less dependent on the petroleum economy. While "nonharming" may not be a key word in the conversation, the direction seems clear to these students: why cause any more harm to the environment? Hasn't there been enough already, enough Chernobyls and Love Canals and Exxon Valdez oil spills? Getting "off-grid" is seen as a moral ideal, a way to reduce your ecological footprint and be a better neighbor to the rest of the world.

GETTING TO PEACE

William Ury, and internationally-recognized conflict negotiator, has laid out a number of principles for "getting to peace," meaning solutions that stabilize political conflicts at many levels. His work applies well to environmental issues, which often involve conflict between different parties and different points of view. Some have said that we are now fighting World War Three—the ongoing war not against terrorism, but against the environment. Pesticides, nuclear waste, toxic chemicals, clear-cutting—all these and more are direct assaults on life forms of many kinds. Getting to peace would mean finding a less harmful way of living with the environment, a way that supports peaceful loving relations with other beings.

In his recent book (also called *Getting to Peace*), Ury lays out a role for what he calls "the third side," a party outside the immediate conflict but with a vested interest in a peaceful outcome. This seems to me to be a useful role for people concerned about the environment. The third-side party can clarify differences, provide protection to threatened parties, and educate where knowledge is needed. Someone with Buddhist sensibilities in these roles can draw on the three approaches outlined above: being with the suffering, cultivating systems mind, and practicing nonharming. Holding to such an intention in itself can help to stabilize an ongoing conflict. Ury sees the third-side role as an active one—it engages the conflict but doesn't take sides. For most of us groomed in polarizing thinking, which is so caustic and destructive in modern politics, such a third side can be hard to imagine. But over and over again in a wide variety of conflict situations, Ury has observed the third-side role as crucial in finding a way forward.

Ury describes ten roles for the third side that address reasons why conflict escalates. These he categorizes as preventing, resolving, or containing conflict. All of them might apply to environmental situations, but I'd like to focus on three roles that seem particularly well-suited for a Buddhist approach.

Among the roles that prevent conflict from escalating or getting started in the first place, the bridge-builder role seems appropriate for Buddhist sensibilities. The bridge-builder works to strengthen weak relationships between human parties, or between human and nonhuman parties. An example is efforts to protect the Everglades built on conversations among cotton-growers, wildlife biologists, and tourism operators. Very often environmental problems arise from overuse of a resource or an area; with shared discussions among the users, it is possible to achieve some restraint and coordination of activities. This is essential in recreation conflicts between, for example, jet-skiers and canoers, or hunters and hikers. A third-party role would support creative problem-solving through bringing the parties together to discuss the situation.

To resolve existing conflicts or environmental problems, Ury suggests roles that settle disputed rights and power imbalances. Of the four prevention-oriented roles, I imagine the role of healer, one who cares for injured relationships, would be well supported by Buddhist practice. With relational thinking at the heart of systems mind and compassionate action, a Buddhist practitioner is both skilled and sensitized to the health of relationships. Where relations have been injured, the Buddhist third party would work to heal brokenness and damage. This would take diplomacy, courage, and patience, depending on the degree of injury.

A third-side party with clear intention to heal and to serve with compassion would be a valuable asset in moving a situation out of the stuck place of conflict. One could bring this healer role to cases of bad neighbor relations, where injury has been caused through felling a beloved tree or spraying a lawn with pesticides. One could be proactive in healing relations with the soil through local community gardens or by supporting organic agriculture.

In cases where environmental conflict has become entrenched and resolution is not obvious, the third-side role requires more courage. I think of the massive gold-mining operations in Indonesia, for example, where the mining company pays the military to support its ravaging of the land in search of gold. Such a deeply-ingrained history of assault, which has engaged local political, economic, and military systems to sustain it, will not be easy to resolve. Here a good role for the Buddhist would be as witness—to offer active attention, to make public what is happening, and to articulate the impacts on plants and animals and impaired ecosystems.

The third-side witness documents and records what is going on. This can be the role of a journalist or a tour guide or a scientist. Within government agencies, third-side witnesses are often whistleblowers who reveal illegal or improper activity. This role, as the others, is not without risk and difficulty. When what is being exposed is very threatening to an agency or business, they may decide to eliminate the messenger. Whistleblowers have lost their jobs; journalists have been killed. A Buddhist approach is not necessarily more effective than other approaches, but it may be less prone to adding antagonism to the situation. The Buddhist can take a systems view and act compassionately toward all parties involved, bearing witness without accusation, reporting facts without condemnation.

To carry out such challenging environmental work, it is essential to regard yourself as an active and effective agent in Indra's Net. This is part of the peacekeeping effort. Thich Nhat Hanh refers to this as planting seeds of joy and peace internally, actively choosing to do environmental work with clear intention and a joyful heart. Such joy may come from sensory contact with the natural world or quiet meditative practices which renew the heart. By cultivating an internal reference point of joy, independent of changing circumstances, a spiritually committed environmentalist is prepared to work for the long haul. In the ancient tradition of *gathas*, or meditation poems, Zen teacher Robert Aitken offers such a long haul vow:

> *Hearing the crickets at night*
> *I vow with all beings*
> *to find my place in the harmony*
> *crickets enjoy with the stars.*

Reciting such a mantra or vow of intention can be a force of renewal in the universe, opening up your creativity in peace negotiations. When you actively cultivate an attitude of loving-kindness it encourages others to plant seeds of joy, and this joy can spread to catalyze the desperately needed transition to ecological sustainability.

The Dalai Lama advocates a policy of kindness no matter how troubling the situation. This is practicing buddhism-with a-small-*b*, taking up the everyday challenge of getting along peacefully with the environment. A policy of kindness toward trees, rivers, sky, and mountains means paying caring attention to all the relations that make up Indra's Net. Engaging environmental problems is not easy work; it is not for the faint-hearted. But working with these Buddhist principles—being with the suffering, cultivating systems thinking, and getting to peace—the task seems more possible.

So I haven't told you whether to get involved with climate protection or waste reduction. I haven't said whether population or consumption are causing more damage to the earth. There are many, many fine resources in print and online that take up just these questions. What I hope is that anyone working at any level, as a citizen or professional, as a parent or student, can take up these Buddhist approaches and put them to good use. The Buddha felt the true test of his teachings was whether they were helpful in everyday life. Those I've offered here are core to my environmental work; may they be of good use to you, dear reader, in whatever small piece of the puzzle you take on.

Most nations measure economic progress by a simple material measure—how much more stuff they are producing and consuming. Clearly that does not reflect the full range of human needs and aspirations. Bhutan, a Buddhist country, is trying to develop a more holistic standard for economic policy, which they call Gross National Happiness. Here, Jigmi Thinley, Minister of Home and Cultural Affairs in Bhutan, outlines a development philosophy that's attracting interest around the world.

However, it is important to note that while many Western Buddhists romanticize Bhutan, the Bhutanese government has been criticized internationally for its repression of non-Buddhist Bhutanese of Nepali origin (and the discussion here of cultural preservation could be read as a defense of that policy). King Jigme Singye Wangchuck has announced his intention to create a constitutional monarchy in Bhutan. When that happens, perhaps the country will become a shining and unblemished model for these principles, and the whole world benefit from its example.

★ ★ ★

GROSS NATIONAL HAPPINESS

by Jigmi Thinley

GROSS NATIONAL HAPPINESS is the guiding philosophy of Bhutan's development process, pronounced by King Jigme Singye Wangchuck soon after his enthronement in 1972. Our King was clear that happiness is the ultimate end desired—but not necessarily pursued—by every Bhutanese and indeed, every human being. All else for which we labor are but means to fulfilling this wish. Yet it is ironic that human society is pervasively susceptible to confusion between this simple end and the complexity of means. This explains why conventional development or economic-growth paradigms are seriously flawed and delusional.

It is heartening to observe that toward the end of the last century and at the beginning of this millennium, the reflective and the analytical across all sections of society are seeing the need to search for a clearer purpose and a more rational approach to development. There is a growing level of dissatisfaction with the way in which human society is being propelled, without a clear and meaningful direction, by the force of its own actions. It is also noteworthy that there is a general consensus that the conventional development process and the contemporary way of life are not sustainable.

The gross national happiness (GNH) offers a more rational and human approach to development.

First, GNH stands for the holistic needs of the human individual, both physical and mental well-being. It reasons that while material development measures contribute, undeniably, to enhancing physical well-being, the state of mind, which is perhaps more important than the body, is not conditioned by material circumstances alone.

Second, which is a corollary to the first point, gross national happiness seeks to promote a conscious, inner search for happiness and the requisite skills to harmonize that search with the beneficial management and development of outer circumstances.

Third, GNH recognizes that happiness should not be approached or viewed as yet another competitive good to be realized by the individual. It supports the notion that happiness pursued and realized within the context of the greater good of society offers the best possibility for the sustained happiness of the individual.

Further, while acknowledging that happiness may not be a directly deliverable good or service, it insists that it is far too important to be left as a purely individual responsibility, without the state having a direct role. It may be emphasized that the society as a whole cannot obtain happiness if individuals compete irresponsibly for it—at all cost, in a zero-sum game.

It is King Jigme Singye Wangchuck's belief that the legitimacy of a government must be established on the basis of its commitment to creating and facilitating the development of those conditions that will assist citizens in the pursuit of their single most important goal and purpose in life. To this end, GNH stresses collective happiness, to be addressed directly through public policies in which happiness becomes an explicit criterion in development projects and programs.

Fourth, as happiness is the most common yearning of the electorate, both individually and collectively, and as it transcends ideological or contentious values, public policies based on GNH will be far less arbitrary than those based on standard economic tools.

This helps explain why the world should move toward a more holistic approach to development which recognizes happiness as the primary, and perhaps only, purpose of development.

THE WORLD'S NEED FOR GROSS NATIONAL HAPPINESS

In general, models for both developed as well as developing countries do not explicitly include happiness as a goal, and contemporary measures of progress do not usually address happiness, which is assumed to be the collateral result of social and economic policies. This is not to suggest that we should reject altogether current approaches and their indices. In fact, the purposes of human development, sustainable development, and millennium development goals are noble and supported by fairly well-developed indicators.

What GNH calls for is a holistic, comprehensive approach to development. It is a matter of some satisfaction to note that the media, academia, development experts and social engineers alike have shown growing interest in the subject of happiness in recent years. The desirability and feasibility of happiness as an essential goal and purpose of society have been bolstered by empirical findings of and an upsurge in research. The Genuine Progress Index pioneered in Nova Scotia, Canada, is a noteworthy measure of true human advancement. Equally, there are other institutions and individuals, both in North America and Europe, who are doing similar work.

Surely, this work is a reflection of the rising popular concerns and interests of society—that society is not content with our unsustainable, unfulfilling, and unhappy way of life, amid ominous signs of our collective future. This should help engender further understanding, knowledge, and wisdom. I am certain that public interest and concern in the subject is not a passing trend, and that public acceptance of the powerful and compelling reasons for GNH will serve to impel deeper research and policy intervention.

The first reason, as corroborated by unquestionable data, is that the manifold rise in real income in several highly industrialized countries over the last fifty years has not led to similar increases in happiness. It is evident that triumphs in the rat race to earn more, have more, and consume more do not bring true and lasting happiness. The rich, the powerful, and the glamorous, it appears, are often the ones who are more impoverished spiritually and socially and thereby are less happy. While there is certainly considerable room for improvement to what and how we measure both wealth and happiness, the lack of any correlation between the two, after meeting basic needs, clearly indicates that happiness cannot be found on the unending, rudderless journey powered by man's insatiable greed.

This brings me to the second reason: the illusion of market-led happiness. The market demands ever greater efficiency and higher productivity. It demands ruthless competition and maximization of profit and employs enticement as the means. But these are the very causes that serve to dehumanize society and undermine the factors that create happiness. As has been well documented, the demanding and grinding work life that is necessary for efficiency and productivity is difficult to balance with the leisure and social life that give us satisfaction. Moreover, the mobility and job changes imposed by the market are inconsistent with the vital need for sustained community life, just as emotional security is diminished by market economics. And it bears repeating that, edging out the weak, making profit the main motive for industry, and capitalizing on the baser instincts of envy and greed, are not the ingredients for a harmonious society.

Related to mobility and locational changes as dictated by our professional lives is our attempt, at the same time, to stay connected through better communication. Yet this third concern springs from the reality that people are living ever more apart, despite being ever more connected. We only have to remind ourselves of the near complete disintegration of the extended family structure in urban and industrialized societies, the higher rates of divorce and single parenting, the erosion of trust and loss of genuine friendship that are known to be factors in unhappiness. If upbringing by single parents is an increasing aspect of modern life, aging alone is also a rising prospect. It is ironic that longer life spans afforded by science and medicine should serve to prolong the pains of loneliness and desolation.

The fourth reason is to be found in the rise in mental illness, alcoholism, and related crime across all categories of age. Then there is suicide, which is a clear sign of the absence of emotional and psychological anchors in society. It is symptomatic of the failure to see any purpose in life and the loss of hope for happiness. Depression rates seem to be substantial in many societies and the latest American statistics in this regard are alarming.

This list is, of course, not exhaustive. These simply represent some of the more popular concerns that academia and media have brought into sharper focus. Given the socio-cultural impulses from within and evidences from without, it was with no little consideration or conviction that we in Bhutan opted for a development process that some say offers a new paradigm.

FOUR PILLARS OF GNH POLICY

GNH is a broader concept, and more profound in its implications, than is conveyed by the current set of four policy priorities in Bhutan. Within Bhutan, the four pillars of GNH are perceived as a normatively defined means toward promoting GNH. Their objective is to create the conditions that would enable every citizen to pursue happiness with a reasonable chance of success.

What is clear to us is that in a state bearing responsibility for collective happiness, GNH must be a serious arbitrator of public policies. If promotion of happiness is the primary purpose of a GNH state, then it is essential that the institutional arrangements of the society reflect this value. Yet it is very challenging to even contemplate what a GNH state should be like. The nature and theoretical foundations of a modern developing or liberal democratic state are well-known. But the structures and processes of a GNH state are yet to be defined clearly. Should it be distinct from either the ascendant liberal state or the declining socialist state. What will be the nature of GNH political economy? What will be appropriate social welfare, legal, and constitutional foundations for GNH? What will be its educational and health policies? How would the polity have to change? And so forth.

There are many questions that require examination, beginning with the basic principles. I would not suggest that at this moment Bhutan is a GNH state, although it aspires to be so. At this stage in Bhutan, the creation of an enabling environment for GNH is being undertaken through a set of four key strategies, popularly known as the four pillars. These are:

(1) sustainable and equitable socio-economic development,
(2) conservation of the environment,

(3) preservation and promotion of culture, and

(4) promotion of good governance.

These thematic areas may very well be an incomplete catalogue of policy areas for good development, but they do encompass the important areas of concentration to serve the intended purpose. In building and strengthening the four pillars, we must be mindful of their interdependence to ensure holistic development. Only with such a holistic perspective can the externalities which are eliminated as costs in one sector not reappear in another.

Sustainable and Equitable Socioeconomic Development

The necessity for materialistic development is obvious from the scale of economic suffering faced by the majority of global population. Ignorance, ill health, deprivation, and poverty in their most abject forms are still serious challenges faced by much of the developing world. Economic growth is of absolute necessity to eradicate poverty. It is, therefore, true to say that for many countries and for vast sections of our global community, where physical survival is an everyday challenge, economic policies are what matters most. Securing jobs and livelihood are prerequisites of happiness.

In general, there appear to be three considerations that must guide GNH-driven economic development.

First, in a GNH economy, the means and nature of economic activities chosen are as important as their result in terms of economic growth. As research by Genuine Progress Index has shown, a GNH economy must make qualitative distinctions among mixes of economic activities that would deliver the same level of growth.

Second, the measurement system for a gross national happiness economy must necessarily be different from conventional measurement of gross domestic product. It must value the social and economic contributions of households and families, as well as free time and leisure, given the roles of these factors in happiness. The indicators must not be biased toward consumption. They must take into account conservation of social, environmental, and human capitals.

Third, a GNH economy must concentrate on the redistribution of happiness through income redistribution. This is not only an ethical proposition; we cannot escape from the reality of living in a world of distorted perceptions, where people derive satisfaction from relative, and not absolute, wealth or consumption. The self-defeating, vicious spiral of catching up with or bettering the Jones's amid unconscionable inequality is a hindrance to collective happiness. Orientation of our perceptions toward actual and absolute needs, and the ability to find satisfaction upon having fulfilled such needs, is a difficult but inevitable challenge for a GNH economy.

Conservation of the Environment

It would seem from happiness research that environment and biodiversity are not strong correlates of happiness. Nevertheless, it is difficult to argue against the value of the environment to our happiness, given that our health and aesthetic experiences depend on the quality of physical environment around us. This is particularly true for the Bhutanese, who live in an extremely fragile environment. The majority of Bhutanese live in farming communities, where livelihood depends directly on richness of their immediate natural environment, which bestows on them free, wholesome foods, medicines, pleasure, and a host of essential materials. Thus, I would argue that there is a demonstrable relationship between happiness and natural environment.

Given our intuition about environment and happiness, and our fear of the immediate consequences of tampering with the wrathful nature of the Himalayan ecology, Bhutan launched vigorous greening and biodiversity preservation policies, the implementation of which have not been without costs in terms of foregone industrial and commercial opportunities. But our country is greener than it has been in living memory, with 26% of it dedicated as wildlife sanctuaries and 72% forest coverage.

But it is not enough that we take local or national actions. There are so many external factors that do and can directly affect our survival. Global warming has already led to very visible and alarming rates of the withdrawal of glaciers, which are the sources and natural regulators of our river systems. Predictions about the definite possibility of the disappearance of all the glaciers in the third Polar region, namely the Himalayas, within the next thirty to fifty years are terrifying to say the least.

The latest report of Bhutan's department of geology and mines, which has been studying glacial behavior since 1967, is not encouraging at all. For not only could Bhutan eventually become a barren desert, but the process leading to it could be devastatingly painful and prolonged. Much of our fertile valleys could be swept away by the glacial lake outburst floods that are no longer a rare phenomenon in the mountain regions of the world. The impact of all this on the two and a half billion people living on either side of the Himalayas and on the security of the whole world is unthinkable especially given that water scarcity is already a major concern. It would not only be the Maldives and other low-lying islands and coastal real estates that are at risk unless greenhouse gas emissions are controlled and reduced. Likewise, Bhutan's susceptibility to the harmful rays of the sun on account of the depletion of the Ozone layer could be significantly more than those in the lower elevations.

The world needs to desperately recognize the Earth as a mortal organism that must be nourished and protected. It desperately needs to accept the mountains of evidence which prove that our finite natural resources are running out while nature's magic of regenerating and replenishing are fading away. Someone called Bhutan an acupuncture point in the leviathan body of our ailing planet!

Preservation and Promotion of Culture

Culture received rare global attention last year through the UNDP's human development report entitled "Cultural Diversity in Today's World," which stated that cultural liberty is central to human rights and human development. Throughout, the report resonated with the message that an individual must have the right to choose, change, and revise various elements of his multiple cultural identities.

But while there should be all the space for choice, we should distinguish between situations where individuals change their identities voluntarily and situations where powerless individuals are changed by profoundly pervasive forces, such as open-sky and free trade regimes that spawn cultural hybridization and displacement of vernacular economies.

This is particularly true in highly asymmetric situations such as Bhutan, where massive external cultural influences could literally overwhelm local cultural values when the borders open wide under the onslaught of globalization. Hence the need for a vigorous promotion of indigenous cultures as a context for making available true choice to individuals. We believe that a state which does not preserve its cultural richness is one where the choices and well-being of its citizens are diminished and greatly constrained.

It is, however, true that there is also a difficulty in reconciling human rights with cultural rights, which are group-based rights. As it has been pointed out, group-based rights do not sit easily with the concept of individuals as autonomous choosers. What we can say in favor of group-based traits implied by culture is that choice is instrumental for pursuit of well-being and happiness. But as is well known, well-being and happiness are largely a shared pursuit. Happiness exists and grows with sharing. I find it rather difficult to accept that human development should be seen only from the point of view of individual liberty and choices without relating to any larger societal good.

The matter about human rights and cultural liberty seems to be more complex in reality. We need to be attentive to human beings not only as bearers of the same set of universal rights, but also as far more complex individuals with cultural and social particularities that define them. We need to adhere to human rights and liberty as basic universal minimum standards to mediate individuals' claims against each other or between individuals and the state. But we could explore further the view that completely meaningful interdependence can arise only when and if we do not see ourselves as just independent and separate bearers of rights, but as relational beings. As one scholar put it, suffering and unhappiness in the end arise not so much from factual conditions of loss or misfortune, but when the flow of meaningful relationships is blocked or interrupted.

GOOD GOVERNANCE

In one sense, securing any public good, such as collective happiness, depends on realizing governance oriented to it. Logically, if a government should reflect the ultimate democratic desire or opinion of the people, which is happiness, then the nature of governance should also be attuned to it. But I must admit that both theoretically and practically, we are far from grounding GNH in any contemporary system of government and political structures, of which the most well-established is the liberal democratic system.

However, in keeping with the times, we in Bhutan are about to formally take up parliamentary democracy. King Wangchuck has recently circulated the Draft Constitution of the Kingdom of Bhutan, which opts for liberal democratic institutions. We have taken such a system as the best institutional arrangement for securing any public good and good governance. But we should not betray ourselves with the belief that a liberal democratic system is the climactic manifestation in a linear and convergent evolution of political institutions, as some scholars have supposed.

Even in the best of the great democratic societies, the signal values like freedom and equality that humanity has struggled to attain seem set at one moment but unsteady at another. We are well aware of the tension between freedom and equality and the shifting boundary between them. Likewise, we are reminded time and again of the vacillating lines between the private and public domains, and between secularism and politics.

All human institutions are systems of relationships between and among actors; in themselves they have no inherent nature. We can always attempt to move in a direction of improving our shared situations or "relationalities," which are where happiness arises and dissolves in dependence on the quality of relationships. In so doing, we can improve any institutional arrangement and human conditions. For example, even alleviating poverty—a primary objective of most governments and international agencies—is only partly a matter of alleviating objective material circumstances. Poverty also results from the failure of personal, social, and cultural relationships, which can be revived or strengthened by better values and intentions in the heart of institutions.

What seems to demand attention even among democratic states is the motivational values that drive the institutions holding power, not just their forms alone. We need to ask whether the values and intentions that guide them and the processes employed for governance, both at the national and international levels, are aligned with the search for happiness, where every person's happiness matters to an equal degree. The fact that national governance and international relations are intertwined as never before also presents opportunities. It provides scope and reason to question and rethink the aims, content, and nature of international relations and global institutions: We must ask whether focusing on happiness can lead us to a more peaceful, harmonious, and equitable world and truly sustainable and civilized human society.

To sum up, gross national happiness is a balanced and holistic approach to development. It is based on the conviction that man is bound by nature to search for happiness, and that happiness it is the single greatest desire of every citizen.

The only difference between Bhutan and others is that we do not dismiss this as a utopian quest.

Obvious injustices such a gender inequality can bring up anger and dualistic thinking, and that causes many spiritually-oriented people to shy away from political activism. The key, says feminist and Buddhist scholar Rita M. Gross, is to see the wisdom and insight inherent in the strong emotions that arise when we fight injustice. That way, politics becomes spiritual practice, and as a bonus, we become more effective activists.

★ ★ ★

THE WISDOM IN THE ANGER

by Rita M. Gross

WHEN DUALISTIC WORLDVIEWS prevail, Buddhist political think-ing and acting become very difficult, if not impossible. Fundamentally, Buddhism discourages us-and-them analyses as much as it discourages evaluating complex situations as black-and-white dichotomies. Buddhism claims that all beings are equal in the sense that they share the same basic nature, whether they are friends or enemies, and sharing the same basic nature is more important than their status as friend or enemy, which is impermanent in any case. Though the difference between friends and enemies, between those who are right and those who are wrong, can feel very real, Buddhist analytical meditation always shows that such feelings, though temporarily real, are ultimately illusory. Acting upon them leads to grief, regret, and suffering.

By contrast, politics, at least as frequently practiced, easily divides the world, the country, the neighborhood, or the dharma center into those who are right and those who are wrong. Common political prac-tice also encourages passionate belief that one's own cause is just and good, and that following the views of the other side would bring disas-ter. Decisive choice is required, we are told. Therefore, many involved in politics who try to befriend those on both sides of a conflict experi-ence the same fate as Thich Nhat Hahn experienced in Vietnam: becoming regarded by both sides as a disloyal enemy. "If you are not for us, then you are against us," a common current political slogan, is the epitome of dualistic thinking. Such dualism is antithetical to Buddhist ways of viewing reality.

As a result, many Western Buddhists are deeply suspicious of "causes," of being involved too much in politics, or of having seemingly political issues, such as justice and peace, be discussed at dharma centers. (The engaged Buddhist movement is a notable exception, but its overall impact on Western Buddhism is somewhat limited.) Asian and historical forms of Buddhism are often perceived as deeply apolitical and without significant social involvement by many Westerners, both scholars and practitioners. (This perception may not be accurate, but that question cannot be discussed in this context.)

The widespread Buddhist suspicion of "causes" has always been a difficult issue for me. I was a feminist before I became a Buddhist and have never been convinced that Buddhists' reluctance to take its feminist critics seriously is appropriate. While I have learned much about the perils and pitfalls of involvement in a cause such as feminism through my Buddhist practice, I also have learned that continuing involvement in a cause can teach one much about the dharma. What I have learned and how I learned it is the subject of this essay.

POLITICS AND BUDDHIST ETHICS

Early in my life as a Buddhist practitioner, I was repeatedly told that concern with feminism and gender issues was not in accord with Buddhist dharma. I was told that involvement in a political cause inevitably involves attachment, while Buddhism and enlightenment are about "detachment." I wasn't the only practitioner to receive this advice, and it is a long-held position in dharma debates. On many occasions, I have heard newer meditation students express their feelings of frustration and anger concerning environmental destruction, social injustice, racism, sexism, or impending war. Often their concerns were dismissed with the slogan, "Just sit more," implying that if their practice were better, they would not care about such things. Sometimes they were told that because enlightenment is the only ultimate solution to peoples' woes, formal practice was the only useful response to political issues and social problems, which is one traditional Buddhist position.

But Buddhism, despite its deep loyalty to nonduality, also emphasizes ethics as the basis of the spiritual path and a prerequisite for the
successful pursuit of meditation and wisdom. And do not ethics, by
their very nature, involve the duality of discriminating right from
wrong, the duality of knowing what to cultivate and what to avoid?
Does not politics involve a similar duality? Political issues at a minimum call for discriminating between better and worse alternatives and
occasionally require discriminating right from wrong in a more absolute
sense. Because both politics and ethics involve discriminating between
better and worse, it would be difficult not to see a connection between
ethics and politics. So how can Buddhists hide behind ultimate metaphysical nonduality as a justification for avoiding the ethical issues
brought up by politics?

Some Buddhists might argue that Buddhist ethics are directed toward
individual choices and behaviors, whereas politics involves struggles for
power and material wealth between groups of people. As a result, ethical
uprightness is much more difficult in politics. Furthermore, clashes for
power and wealth easily intensify the polarization and demonizing of
others that so often characterizes politics.

Other Buddhists concerned to bring individual and group ethics
together would respond that those political struggles often have a great
deal to do with individual well-being, including having enough time and
money to practice spiritual disciplines. Especially given the Buddhist
claim that all things are interdependent, it is not so easy to separate individual choices from group decisions. Indeed, one of the most cogent modern criticisms of traditional Buddhist thought is that, though Buddhism is
adamant in asserting non-harming as its most basic ethic, it lacks an
understanding of structural violence. Buddhist thought has not usually
noted the harm wrought by a social system that automatically favors
some, such as men, over others, such as women. It should be noted in
passing that traditional Buddhism cannot be faulted too much for this
lack of awareness. Many religions traditionally regarded political and
social systems as inevitable fiats rather than the results of choices made
by many human beings over many years.

Nevertheless, some Western Buddhists justify their opposition to political involvement by arguing that political action is only an attempt to "fix samsara," to rid it of its pain, which is impossible. Changing group fates through politics, they tell us, is only an attempt to subvert karma, which controls peoples' positions in samsara.

But in Buddhist thought, karma is not predestination. If it were, there would be no point to practicing Buddhist spiritual disciplines, because the development of awareness, insight, and compassion would have no effect on predestined outcomes. If karma were predestination, one might as well sleep and engage in frivolous activities as practice, because the predetermined outcomes would be the same in any case. But Buddhists have never rejected the possibility that individuals can change their future karma through present choices. Why should it be different for groups, which are only collections of individuals seeking to change their karma?

It is true that Buddhist thought can seem ambiguous, sometimes claiming that the best course of action is to avoid taking sides because no real differences can be found between one thing and another, while at other times clearly urging that choices be made between what to cultivate and what to avoid. This line, so difficult to discuss, runs between absolute and relative truths, however, not between ethics and politics. Balancing absolute and relative truths and properly honoring their inseparability is one of the most difficult issues in Buddhism, both to discuss and to accomplish. That balance cannot be achieved by cultivating individual ethics, which is a necessary discipline in Buddhism, while abjuring causes devoted to peace and justice, such as feminism, because they too easily degenerate into name-calling and polarization.

POLITICS AS PRACTICE

Two difficult tests of individual attainment confront the Buddhist concerned about the politics of peace and justice. Accomplishing them could be considered the *siddhis* or "powers" of Buddhist social action. One must be able to retain equanimity and awareness while caring about a "cause"

and in the midst of conflict. Finally, one must be able to maintain contentment and cheerfulness in the midst of failure and the seemingly unending obstacles to any real attainment of justice, peace, and gender equity.
Advice about and practices leading to this delicate but essential state of
mind are the most important contributions Buddhists can make to political discussions, including discussions of feminism.

For a Buddhist another fact deserves attention. In my long experience of
being involved with gender, a peace and justice issue that many Buddhists
prefer to ignore, I have found that the most interesting dimension of politics for a Buddhist is the way in which caring about a "cause" provides constant fuel for working through the three poisons of aversion, attachment,
and ignoring. Given that these three are at the very hub of the wheel of
cyclic existence (samsara), it is no wonder that they are the constant pitfalls
besetting Buddhists concerned about political causes. However, against
those who decry Buddhist political involvement, one must realize that the
three poisons cannot be avoided merely by avoiding politics.

Practitioners of Vajrayana Buddhism understand that, like any unenlightened energy, each of the three poisons includes the potential for its
transmuted form. Aversion contains muted clarity; attachment contains
unrealized compassion; and ignoring contains complete, all-inclusive
spaciousness.

Because one can learn so much about the most profound dimensions of
Buddhist realization by contemplating carefully one's actions and reactions to political and social concerns, I simply cannot agree that serious
Buddhists should avoid politics as a diversion from serious practice. Rigid
dualities are always conceptual mistakes in Buddhist practice, and perhaps the most inappropriate duality of all is that between "real practice"
and politics.

I do agree with more conservative Buddhists who claim that Buddhist
attainment is primarily about individual transformation rather than social
change. I also agree with those Buddhists who claim that until one has
enough attainment to sustain equanimity and awareness through distractions, one should perhaps limit one's involvement in causes. One may well
do more harm than good if the three poisons immediately take over when

conflict or frustration occurs. Having heeded such warnings, I will explore what one can learn about the dense interweaving of aversion, attachment, and ignoring, as well as the possibility of their transmutation, through devotion to a cause such as feminism.

THE THREE POISONS AND THEIR ENLIGHTENED ASPECT

At least in Western contexts, aversion takes the lead among the three poisons that beset those who work on political causes such as feminism, but its enlightened counterpart, clarity is not far behind. I claim that aversion takes the lead for at least three reasons. First, one is devoted to a cause only because of aversion to some well-established practice, such as the straitjacket of traditional gender roles. Second, no matter how well or poorly one voices feminism, one will be on the receiving end of aversion from those who despise this cause. Third is the extreme aversion, expressing itself as aggression toward "the other side," so frequently found among those who espouse a cause. While examining each of these forms of aversion, we will see that one of the three poisons usually brings the others in tow, as well how each transforms into its enlightened aspect through greater awareness and equanimity.

The whole thing began, at least for me, with intense aversion to the male-dominant gender practices of my society and my chosen profession (academia). My aversion was intense and unremitting. I tried to control expressing my anger because for women, such expression was disapproved completely. But I felt completely justified in my rage and did express my aggression whenever such expression seemed "safe," that is to say when the social consequences would not be too high. I also experienced some seeming satisfaction, some relief from my intense emotion, whenever I could express my anger, and even experienced some satisfaction simply from mentally skewering my tormentors.

Then I began to practice meditation, never expecting that such practice could change my relationship with feminism. After all, I was very sure of the correctness of my analyses. After several years, I could no longer dredge up the same feelings of release and emotional satisfaction by aggressive expressions of my frustrations and rage. I also began to see that little was being accomplished by these expressions, and that, if anything, I was only causing mutual entrenchment.

Over the long term, what changed was not my analyses, but the emotionalism and attachment with which I expressed those analyses. That change has had mixed results. While I have been much more successful in convincing people that sexism of any stripe is simply inappropriate and not in accord with Buddhist dharma than would ever have been possible if my intensely angry expressions had continued, nevertheless, many people remain hostile to these analyses and prefer to ignore them. Unpacking this short story reveals the many dense links between the three poisons and their enlightened counterparts.

The utter accuracy of regarding clarity as the enlightened, transmuted form of aversion has been intensely vivid to me since my early days as a practitioner. According to Vajrayana Buddhist psychology, every negative emotion contains some enlightened energy which can be unleashed through practice. Anger transmutes into clarity, or, more accurately, when angry expressions subside, underlying clarity can shine through. Water is the element associated with anger; murky water veils what is in its depths while clear water both allows those depths to be seen and reflects perfectly what is on its surface. That is how political analyses are. Even the seemingly most misguided contain some intelligence and accuracy; even the most angry are right, in least in part.

For example, male-dominant institutional forms simply cannot be made to square with Buddhist dharma, no matter what arguments may be enlisted by male dominant traditions. The most frustrated, unskillful, out-of-control feminist has that much straight. Aggression, anger, and aversion mask clarity, but the clarity is there nevertheless. Friends mistakenly assured me that as practice matured, my caring about feminism would vanish, but what vanished was my rage, leaving the clarity of what I had already seen much sharper and more vivid.

In people lacking deep spiritual discipline, anger usually overwhelms clarity, making the clarity indiscernible to others and often only a minor part of one's own awareness. Instead, one experiences pain and grief

about the perversions of peace and justice one sees so clearly. Directing
verbal (or physical) attacks at others seems to bring satisfaction; it is so
tempting to lash out with sarcasm and angry humor when one sees clearly
but is powerless to do anything to bring real change. At least one can yell
and make cutting remarks, but these reactions only temporarily mask the
pain one feels, soon making another outburst necessary. Meanwhile, others can be excused if aggression is more evident to them than the clarity
contained in these outbursts.

The interplay between anger and clarity has never been more ade-
quately demonstrated than by an interchange I witnessed some years ago
between the Venerable Khandro Rinpoche, a leading female Tibetan
Buddhist teacher, and a student. The student asked what one should do
about things that made one angry. Khandro Rinpoche replied quite
sharply, "Anger is always a waste of time." The student, looking shocked,
blurted out, "But what about things you should be angry about, like
abuse?" Without losing a second, Khandro Rinpoche replied, "I didn't tell
you to give up your *critical intelligence*. I told you anger is a waste of time."
(Notice that she did not tell the student just to "sit more"!) So the trick is
to tame anger while not losing critical intelligence. To tame anger by dis-
connecting one's critical intelligence would be to fall into apathy and
ignoring, not to attain realization.

"But what about the things about which one *should* be angry" was this
student's expression of critical intelligence, phrased in perhaps poorly
chosen words. *Should* is a word more connected with attachment and passion than with aversion. Though one's devotion to feminism may be triggered by aversion to existing practices, it also contains a strong element
of passion and desire: "I hate the way things are and I desire them to be
different." Outsiders to Buddhism are often mystified by the way in which
Buddhists see hope and fear as two sides of the same coin, not radically
opposed emotions, and the same analysis applies to aversion and attachment. They are not as opposed to each other as we often think.

Devotion to feminism involves great passion as well as great aversion.
One is passionately devoted to an alternative vision of how things could
be. Like every other expression still involved in dualism, political passion

is double edged. In Vajrayana Buddhist psychology, the enlightened expression of attachment *is* compassion—concern for the entire matrix not based on the distinction between self and others. I have always regarded my activities as a Buddhist feminist as an attempt to fulfill my bodhisattva vows, not as a worldly diversion from those vows.

Without the gentling effects of deep spiritual discipline, attachment prevails and expresses itself as ideological fixation—an expression deeply tinged with aggression. Nothing is so repellant as a good idea grasped without flexibility, gentleness, and humor. What makes involvement in political causes and organizations nearly impossible for many Buddhists is the self-righteousness of so many people who have good ideas. Their good ideas are expressed in an entirely dualistic manner, with no aware-ness of the basic goodness of those on the other side. I find it difficult now to be involved with many of my feminist colleagues because of their ideological rigidity and prefer the company of colleagues who are less self-consciously feminist in their outlook, but whose compassion does include concern for gender justice.

Some might ask, "But if you *really* care about something, will you not have strong and fixed opinions on that issue?" With careful attention, it becomes evident that cogent analysis and clarity of expression are not the same as aversion or attachment. Telling the difference between them is not so easy. Usually the actual words used are not so critical; rather, tone of voice and body language communicate whether fixation or clar-ity is driving the expression. It is possible both to care about something and be non-ideological and non-fixated in that caring. If it were not pos-sible, the Buddhist ideal of nondual compassion would be an illusion.

Gradually, one's speech and expressions are tamed and one can talk about difficult issues without reeking of aversion and attachment. When that happens, communication is possible and one may succeed in getting one's message across. There is a middle path between fighting with oth-ers and simply turning numb and passive, deaf and dumb to clearly evi-dent injustice and violence.

BEING CORRECT IS NOT ENOUGH: THE NEED FOR SKILLFUL MEANS

Avoiding the pitfalls of aversion and attachment, both in oneself and others, is only the beginning. One may practice not speaking out on an issue if the murky emotionalism of aversion or attachment still clouds one's mind, and such a practice is essential. Even with this practice well in place, however, one will still be widely ignored and will often be the recipient of aggression and aversion from others. Clear analysis does not always penetrate, and even when it does, many people prefer to ignore the analysis or may even become hostile because clarity makes them uncomfortable.

The intermingling of willful ignoring and hostility that greet clear analysis presented without aversion or attachment is evident in a conversation the following example: I had just presented a talk in which I discussed the fact that many Buddhist liturgies do not include any references to women or any feminine imagery, even though we women are supposed to feel that the liturgies include us. With some amazement, the woman with whom I was speaking said that she enjoyed Buddhist liturgies a great deal and had never noticed that they really did not include her. "You spoiled it for me!" she said somewhat angrily. Apparently she preferred inaccurate, though pleasant, ignoring to deeper insight and greater clarity.

Such a reaction is not at all uncommon. It is the usual reaction to Buddhism's most profound teachings, such as teachings about egolessness. Ignoring is always the deepest and most intractable of the poisons, the root out of which the others grow. Amazingly, even in many Buddhist contexts, the response to unfamiliar but cogent feminist analyses, is some variant of "I don't like the message, so let's kill the messenger." Ignoring quickly is displaced by aversion to the message and attachment to what is familiar. I could recount countless examples of being blamed for the information about gender inequity in Buddhism that I brought to people. People often say, not in so many words, that if only I didn't bring them information about traditional male dominance in Buddhism, the problem would not exist. And, in a certain sense, those of us who carry feminist messages do make information exist for those who were formerly ignorant. The only

difference is that after the message has been delivered, unconscious ignoring is replaced by willful ignoring, a far more violent and aggressive act.

Thus we see the utter cogency of regarding clarity and aversion as the
enlightened and deluded forms of the same energy. A message containing unwelcome clarity *feels* aggressive to those who prefer ignorance. As
we know from elementary Buddhist psychology, the conventional
response to feeling attacked is to attack the source of those feelings,
which we conventionally believe lies with someone else outside ourselves.
Thus, someone who works on issues of social and political awareness must
also learn to develop equanimity and accommodation regarding the indifference and rejection with which one's work is greeted. One could probably be more accepted and honored in one's community if one did not
draw attention to things the community prefers to ignore. This dimension
of being able to greet distasteful situations with equanimity rather than
aversion is especially important and difficult.

When a Buddhist cares about feminism or other social justice causes
long enough, one begins to see, as I put it in one of my more recent slo-
gans, that "being correct is not enough." In fact, being correct is the easy
part. How does one express righteousness nondualistically?

It is easy to be clear that male dominance is unjust and harmful. How
does one express that conviction and caring skillfully, without alienating
people? How can one really accommodate disagreement concerning issues
about which one cares deeply and has great conviction? Do I really think
that people who would argue that male dominance is necessary and is good
for everyone, including women, might have a case? I don't think so. That
clarity is the easy part. Going further with such an insight is the hard part.

Contemplations about political involvement help us understand certain
deep insights of the Buddhist tradition. When a Buddhist works long
enough on a political issue, one begins to understand why skillful means
(*upaya*) is the seventh perfection (*paramita*) and discriminating wisdom
(*prajna*) is the sixth paramita. One also begins to understand why clarity
is useless without an ability to express clarity skillfully, why in Vajrayana
Buddhist symbolism and practice, clarity is never invoked alone but only
in partnership with skillful means.

WHAT BUDDHISM CAN CONTRIBUTE TO FEMINISM

Buddhism has two things to contribute to those involved in feminism. One is the immediate need for the skillful means of developing and maintaining equanimity and peacefulness in the face of opposition, oppression, and conflict. And what of the long term? After people have expressed their outrage long and forcefully enough, they often burn out. Exhaustion replace aversion as the chief outcome of caring about a cause. How does one keep going, year after year, when things do not get better, and even seem to be getting worse, as is the case with many of issues about which feminists have cared for years?

The second great gift of Buddhism to political causes such as feminism is its ability to develop staying power in those who practice its spiritual disciplines. To stay concerned about social issues, one has to develop the ability to keep on working cheerfully year after year without hope of success and fear of failure. In my own case, I cannot imagine still caring about and working on feminist issues after forty years if I had not discovered Buddhist practices. Or if I were still concerned, I would probably also be filled with the pain of bitterness and frustration, which I am happy to report is not at all the case. This discovery too is in deep accord with fundamental Buddhist teachings, especially Mahayana Buddhist teachings on the third paramita, patience.

Buddhist realization is about seeing deeply into the fundamental nonduality of experience, but politics seems riven with duality. I have argued that part of one's practice as Buddhist might be to practice the inseparability of spiritual disciplines and politics. As we know, practicing nonduality is practicing the inseparability of absolute and relative truths. It could be tempting to think when we practice spiritual disciplines, we are practicing on the absolute level, and when we practice politics, we are practicing on the relative level. But that would be much too dualistic an assumption. With true inseparability, we learn much about deep Buddhist insights through involvement with causes, and our immersion in Buddhist practices teaches us how to remain involved in politics—skillfully.

In our families, businesses, and nations, whether we are ordinary or powerful people, conflict is an inescapable part of our lives. The challenge is to work with conflict in a way that minimizes damage and helps everyone achieve their goals. The *Sun Tzu*, the ancient Chinese text known in the West as *The Art of War*, calls this "taking whole." James Gimian, general editor of the Denma Translation group's translation of *The Art of War*, says we can practice this strategy by approaching conflict with the open and supple mind of contemplative practice.

★ ★ ★

TAKING WHOLE: THE ART OF LESS WAR

by James Gimian

IT'S A MYSTERY how some conflicts in the world seem to get resolved without a lot more bloodshed, or at least without a lot more yelling and screaming. The celebratory fall of the Berlin Wall—fabulous! The peaceful transition from an authoritarian apartheid regime to a racially egalitarian democracy in South Africa—amazing! My daughter picking the expensive clothes I bought her off the floor of her room and hanging them up neatly—I never saw that coming. A situation that seems stuck, tense, and impossible one day now seems workable, even creative. How did that happen? It didn't seem connected to any particular action or effort.

Are these sudden, almost mysterious, shifts in direction brought about by accident, serendipity, or unseen intervention? No, according to the wisdom text now commonly known as *The Art of War*, it's a kind of ordinary magic, which comes from being connected to and working with reality at a deeper, more intuitive level. Attributed to a Chinese general named Sun Tzu who lived 2,500 years ago, the text tells us that this kind of ordinary magic arises when we respond to conflict in a more profound and subtle manner, resisting heavy-handed attempts to wrestle the world into submission. Beyond being simply a hit-or-miss occurrence, it can be cultivated as a way of being and acting in the world. The Chinese text calls it *shih* (pronounced "shir," almost with no vowel sound).

In order to understand shih, we must first understand the way the *Sun Tzu* text views the world, for it is from the depths of this view that skillful action arises. The *Sun Tzu* sees the world as a whole—interdependent,

interconnected, constantly in flux. The world is less about specific locations and solid things than it is about potentialities, processes, and relationships. There are "things" and causal chains that appear to us as linear,
but each is part of a whole system, and each whole system is interrelated
and interactive. As the *Sun Tzu* sees it, we are part of a web of interconnectedness, fluid and rapidly changing. The frame of reference we take for
granted today may well evaporate by next week, and one little thing way
over there can affect one little thing way over here.

Sound familiar? That's probably because this view of the world from
500 B.C.E. China is not unlike the view of our world emerging today,
whether on the frontiers of theoretical physics or in the way we lead our
everyday lives. From Google searches and personal networks to quantum
mechanics and chaos theory, viewing the world as an interconnected
whole is becoming commonplace. Think synchronicity, the tipping point,
and the flat world. Or how cellphone photos of a disaster halfway across
the globe quicken our heartbeats as they bring the experience of human
suffering to us seconds after it occurs.

In this interconnected and ever-changing world, the challenging experience we call conflict arises as a matter of course. Conflict is not regarded
as an aberration that occurs because people have acted badly. It arises as
an inevitable outgrowth of the differing conditions, views, and aspirations of people who find themselves nevertheless connected to each
other. To the extent that there is any duality whatsoever—and the relative world is nothing but a web of dualities—one thing will rub against
another.

Having taken conflict as a naturally occurring feature of life, the text
offers a way to work with it directly and skillfully. The *Sun Tzu* text came
into being to address the conflict that generals faced during the Warring
States period in China (475–221 B.C.E.), when they battled to take control of critical territory in order to ward off threats to their state's existence. While most of us are not vying for control of cities and farms, we
may have a keen interest in the *Sun Tzu* because, as "generals" trying to
maintain command of our own worlds, we routinely attempt to carry out
objectives, from simple inspirations to grand plans. And in so doing, we

are met with indifference, resistance, or open hostility. Conflict is a tough part of life, and we long for ways of working with it that are more creative and profound than our habitual extremes of avoidance or aggression.

The *Sun Tzu* text's view of how to work with conflict conveys its most profound teaching. The core wisdom of the text is that it is possible to accomplish your objective without resorting to aggression, or as the text famously states, "to subdue the other's military without battle." The text calls this *taking whole*. Once you see the world as whole, then "taking whole" becomes the consummate skill in working with the phenomenal world. Taking whole means keeping things intact, as much as possible, rather than destroying them, and it applies to the aspirations of the "enemy" as much as to their physical well-being. Incorporating and including the enemy leaves something to build upon. The Chinese general realized that the farmers who were his enemies today could be producing food for his people tomorrow, and so destroying them in the battle for more territory was only depriving himself of resources for his future, larger kingdom.

But how does the general take whole in the midst of the chaos and confusion of the battlefield? How do we take whole, in the midst of our tough battles at corporate headquarters, in our social action project, or at our children's school? Here the *Sun Tzu* is again resoundingly clear: skillful action begins with knowledge. In the battlefield this obviously means knowing all the details that affect critical decisions: the weather, what our soldiers have had to eat, how far enemy troops marched last night. But the text expands from this to a more profound understanding of knowledge:

> *Know the other and know oneself,*
> *Then victory is not in danger.*
> *Know earth and know heaven,*
> *Then victory can be complete.*

While knowledge includes the accumulation of information, it goes beyond that to become a more active openness, a knowing, an unbiased perception of all the elements of a situation and the patterns they form. When the general acts with a fixed view, each new bit of information is interpreted in relation to that view, and emerging possibilities are missed. "Knowing" in the *Sun Tzu* is relating directly to the way things are—connecting to the interrelated, changing world rather than clinging to one's smaller, fixed view. It lays the ground for taking whole and makes it possible to attain a larger-scale victory, one that goes beyond applying old solutions to new, emerging circumstances. Thus the text tells us: "Victory can be known; it cannot be made."

This active openness can be fostered by a contemplative approach to working with the world and to studying the *Sun Tzu*. A contemplative approach here refers to the simple human faculty of holding open a space to see things clearly. It is a state of mind that occurs naturally to human beings and that can be developed with effort and discipline.

One of the most powerful ways of developing this basic human faculty of clear seeing is through the practice of sitting meditation, or mindfulness-awareness practice, from the Buddhist contemplative tradition. Mindfulness-awareness meditation is the simple practice of letting things be. It loosens the grip of the internal narrative—ego's relentless story-line that perpetuates the separation between "self" and "other" and shields us from seeing what is. Buddhist meditation nurtures the experience of a gap in this story-line, and this experience fosters a direct perception of the world as interconnected, interdependent, and constantly in flux.

The *Sun Tzu* text and Buddhist contemplative practice are two very different traditions, yet both are known for presenting profoundly effective ways of working with conflict and chaos. Their common ground is insight into the fundamental misstep of solidifying one's existence. Whether at the level of ego-building or fortification of the nation-state, solidification of "this" perpetuates a false separation from "that." In addition, this solidification takes a tremendous amount of effort and story-line to maintain, which creates obstacles to clear seeing and effective action.

From the shared ground of this insight, each tradition proceeds in its unique way to offer an antidote to the cycle of conflict and aggression that follows from dualistic separation. The *Sun Tzu* presents taking whole, and so the Chinese general in 300 B.C.E. saw that it was shortsighted to destroy the enemy soldier who was also the farmer growing wheat for his army. The Buddhist teachings lead to kindness and compassion, and so the practitioner of mindfulness-awareness begins to exhaust the habitual pattern of projecting external causes for his or her own suffering.

The connection between Buddhist contemplative practice and the *Sun Tzu* text has been made in recent times by Buddhist meditation master Chögyam Trungpa Rinpoche. In general, he presented meditation in a number of contexts as a way of developing this contemplative approach to knowing and seeing. (See his teachings on Dharma Art, for example.) In particular, Trungpa Rinpoche wove study of *The Art of War* into one of the unique forms he devised to extend the practice of meditation into the world of daily life, training students to respond skillfully to chaos and conflict. The use of the *Sun Tzu* in this way encourages us to go beyond the practice of formal meditation and explore its implications for the conduct of war, politics, and society.

This exploration begins with the insight that the experiences and lessons of meditation practice are not separate from what happens in the world. Rather, learning about the patterns of ego's aggression toward oneself and others in the practice of meditation can be applied directly to the realm of politics and war. The analysis that war is a more extreme manifestation of ego's individual aggression mirrors modern definitions of war, for example, the German military theorist Carl von Clausewitz's dictum that war is the extension of politics by other means. This analysis creates a common ground for discussion among those in business, government, and the military who understand the importance of knowing and who experience shih as an observable, familiar, and highly-valued skill.

The sage commander of the Warring States period in China faced the same challenge we do today: How do we successfully work with the chaos and conflict that arises as we seek to attain our objective, to bring about victory in our particular battleground? The *Sun Tzu* tells us that skillful mastery of shih is the primary way of working with the phenomenal world.

In general, shih refers to action that rearranges the environment to our advantage, but in a different way than we're used to. Though the world is a whole system, it is possible to carve off discrete areas and take action. Within the constant change, there are tendencies or norms that the text calls *tao*. These can be simple things, such as the fact that water seeks the low ground, soldiers get tired at the end of the day, and round rocks roll downhill. These conditions combine to make up clusters of events, patterns that we can recognize and work with. In the interconnected web, the convergence of small movements changes the relationships between all the elements. Imagine the crossing wave patterns made by two motorboats on a small mountain lake, and the ripple effect of bobbing boats and docks around the lake's perimeter. Smaller movements can come about either naturally or from alterations we make in the details of the situation. Using shih is working directly with the world on this level.

Specifically, the text tells us that shih is about power and strategic advantage, joined with the critical moment of application or release, called the *node*. "Node" refers to the very small connection that separates segments of bamboo, essentially a moment of transition from one phase to the next.

Chapter five of the *Sun Tzu* introduces us to shih in three ways: first as power-in-motion, where water, otherwise soft and harmless, can be amassed into a rushing force capable of tossing huge rocks about; next as shape, where shih is described as steep, evoking the power of troops taking the higher ground in a mountain ravine; and finally as accumulation, like the drawing back of a crossbow and the power released at the pulling of the trigger (the node).

The text summarizes all these three in the last lines of the chapter:

One who uses shih sets people to battle as if rolling trees and rocks.

> *As for the nature of trees and rocks—*
> *When still, they are at rest.*
> *When agitated, they move.*
> *When square, they stop.*
> *When round, they go.*

Thus the shih of one skilled at setting people to battle is like rolling round rocks from a mountain one thousand jen high.

It is important to note here that shih does not rely on changing the nature of things in the world, but on knowing how things are and how they work together, and on the right timing. For example, one habitual response to interpersonal conflict is to demand that the other party change his or her behavior in order to resolve the situation in our favor. By contrast, relying on shih involves awaiting the right moment to act, then nudging a "round rock" to trigger a pattern of action that leads to resolution. It's like eating a piece of fruit when it's ripe, not when you're hungry, in order to enjoy the greatest nourishment and fulfillment.

According to the *Sun Tzu*, appreciating the nature of shih and employing it well is what will help us most when we are faced with the need to apply force to move forward and when we want to attain our goal without engaging in a costly battle. Force is a natural human gesture. It is the power that moves things; breathing out is an example of its simplest form. But force becomes a problem when it is mixed with aggression and becomes the power to impose oneself upon others. At that point, it becomes an expression of frustration with our failure to attain our objective by other means, and it only engenders further conflict. When we align ourselves with the power of shih, things often seem to happen on their own, without a discernible actor applying causal force.

The ability to use shih begins with the simple act of enlarging one's perspective, taking a bigger view of the situation in either time or space. There are many common occurrences in our life where a bigger view explains something that, from a smaller reference point, seems like magic. Water comes out of a tap, a hulk of steel flies through the air, the words I type on a keyboard in my office are instantly communicated around the world—all these are commonplace to us but would be utterly magical to those from a time in the past. For us, the series of events preceding water coming out of the tap in our kitchen are known and obvious, and so it seems ordinary. And other many things we cannot understand now will be easily explained in the future as our collective view continues to get bigger. Even now, string theory, currently at the forefront of modern physics, is postulating the existence of unseen worlds to explain phenomena we now don't understand.

This points to a way of understanding shih as a kind of ordinary magic. Using shih arises from knowing the norms and patterns of things in a deeper way and being connected to the interdependent, changing world. This results in skillful action in the world that might be completely mysterious to those around us who aren't seeing those norms and patterns. Knowing how to fly an airplane is possible because we are in touch with how the world works in a deeper way than those from a previous time or those who have a smaller view of the world, and that makes the act seem like magic.

This view of shih implies an entirely different way of working with the world to accomplish a goal. Within the worldview of solid entities, fixed goals, and strategic plans, the leader regards the intelligence in any system—whether the system is a person, organization, or society—as centralized in the "I," or headquarters. Things are run from the corner office. Achieving one's goal is best accomplished through command and control, which necessarily results in a series of cascading effects, all directed by the central intelligence. But from the view of the *Sun Tzu*, the leader sees that intelligence is distributed throughout the system, and achieving one's goal comes about by disturbing rather than directing that system. Disturbing relies on the norms and patterns, and calls the intelligence of the system into action. This results in changing the ground to enable an unseen victory to be "known."

Working with the world in this way gives rise to a new, more demanding way of being. When employing shih to accomplish an objective, one is required to loosen one's grip on smaller objectives while at the same time opening up to a bigger view, which includes allowing even one's most cherished and hard-won views to be open to change and disintegration. It is not as simple as abandoning the objective in favor of the view. Both must be held in mind, firmly yet loosely, like a baby's grip on your finger, the model for how to properly hold a golf club or samurai sword. This allows a creative tension, holding open the space between one's vision and the reality of a situation until a resolution arises from the ever-shifting ground. Curiously, this is strikingly similar to how quantum mechanics describes working with reality: shih is about plucking victories out of the realm of possible results in much the same way that quantum physics describes a scientist pulling particular results out of the matrix of possible outcomes.

Working successfully in the world as the *Sun Tzu* text sees it, where interrelated parts interact in ever-shifting ways, relies upon knowing the world directly, being connected, and moving with the emerging shapes and conformations. Each piece affects all the others, and our awareness expands to see how altering a single piece moves the whole. We get a glimpse that acting in isolation is no longer an option. We have spontaneous experiences of the complete victories that come from taking whole, mixed with frustration and defeat. Yet, such complete and satisfying victories seem comparatively rare. What makes it so difficult to work with the world in this way?

The main obstacle to using shih is the fragmented view of the world that arises when we solidify and cling tenaciously to our separateness. This limits us to a partial view, habitually holding tight to smaller-minded agendas in a sea of change. The realization that the world is whole and interrelated only goes so far if one still clings to the view that this interconnected world still revolves around "me."

Many people are attracted to the *Sun Tzu* by its profound view, only to turn around and use its lessons to impose their smaller agendas onto the world more successfully. Using shih for this purpose can lead to success in the conventional sense if one is skillful. However, this approach reinforces and strengthens the sense of separateness, and while it indeed produces a "more successful" self, this inevitably leads to needless conflict that engenders battles that lead to more needless conflict. Using shih, or any skill, in order to sustain a sense of oneself as separate from the world only perpetuates the duality that is the root of conflict to begin with.

What safeguards, if any, does the *Sun Tzu* offer as protection against the use of its wisdom to attain smaller-minded victories? Ultimately, the safeguard arises from the profundity of the worldview that pervades the text.

Applying shih in discrete, focused settings is a powerful way of working with the world, but whatever we do always takes place within the larger framework of the interconnected world. And for all that the skillful use of shih can do to bring about favorable circumstances, that bigger, interconnected world is not ultimately subject to our control. Victory cannot be made.

The overwhelming power of the larger world is frequently demonstrated when humans try to rearrange the environment to their advantage. Take an example from the current debate on globalization. Stimulating economic development in order to address political or social problems can yield definite, measurable successes. But it may also give rise to potentially greater threats to social and political stability from the accelerated environmental degradation that accompanies development. The response of the greater whole—in this case the resulting environmental damage threatening continued human life on the planet—is an expression of its intelligence. The system as a whole is making the clear statement that smaller-minded solutions are not complete victories, and that conflict will not subside unless and until there is an approach based on taking whole.

The frustration that arises from applying smaller-minded solutions propels us to seek more profound ways of working with conflict. Then the wisdom of a deeper way of knowing and working with the world, such as the Sun Tzu presents, becomes more compelling. When knowing becomes an openness to how things fundamentally are in the world, we begin to suspend the habitual projections we impose upon the world. The grip of separateness is loosened and smaller agendas naturally give way to a bigger view.

Using shih to work with the phenomenal world arises from being woven into the interdependent and ever-changing whole, and going with it rather than controlling it from the outside. "Power over" becomes "tuned into." Skillful action comes from knowing, seeing, and catching the moment, rather than from practiced routines or "take-aways" gathered from corporate seminars or meditation weekends. Whether in our offices or at home, in a foreign war or neighborhood skirmish, the opportunity to work with the phenomenal world at a deeper level is always present. Using shih can be the gateway to ordinary magic in our lives.

The late Seung Sahn, a Korean Zen master who established an important Zen community in the United States, was a committed student-activist in his youth. In 1982, following the massacre of protesters in the city of Kwangju by South Korean forces, he wrote this letter to the then Korean military dictator, General Chun Du-Hwan. Undoubtedly the general, himself a Roman Catholic, was shocked to receive such blunt advice from a Zen master on how to govern his country, and when Seung Sahn later visited South Korea, he was interrogated about the letter by Korean CIA agents. This letter is extraordinary not only for its courage but for its profound statement that the only basis for good leadership is to go beyond dualistic thinking and discover one's true nature.

★ ★ ★

LETTER TO A DICTATOR

by Seung Sahn

Providence Zen Center
August 25, 1982

Dear President Chun,

Greeting you in the name of the Three Jewels—Buddha, Dharma, and Sangha.

Time flies swiftly as an arrow, and it is already more than two years since you became President of Korea. During that time, you have been working hard in the name of our country and our people. I send my concern that this has not been too hard on your health.

I am not writing in order to discuss whether or not your rule has been "good" or "bad." Nowadays in society we see so much fighting and quarreling over "right" and "wrong." In the world of human beings, this is an old and endless struggle. But if, instead of engaging in this sort of fighting, we were to ask ourselves, "What is the nature of 'good'?" and "What is the nature of 'evil'?" "What is the nature of this universe?" or "What is the nature of 'time' and 'space,' and do they really exist at all?" such petty arguing would immediately disappear and we would instantly begin to see the world of truth.

An eminent teacher once said,

> *Good and evil have no self-nature.*
> *"Enlightened" and "unenlightened" are empty names.*
> *In front of the doors [of sensory perception]*

is a land of perfect stillness and light:
Spring comes, and grass grows by itself.

So, "good" and "evil" do not possess any [self-existent] nature. It is merely our *thinking* that makes "good" or "evil." Then, if we cut off all thinking, where is the existence of good and bad, life and death, or upper-class and lower-class? If we find our original human face, which is present before thinking arises, we will be able to transform this world into a realm of freedom and equality.

This is why I do not wish to discuss here whether your rule has been just or unjust. Rather, I am writing this letter because tears well up in my eyes when I see our beloved country divided in two, and the needless suffering that this causes. [...]

It is not my wish to make this a long story, but I cannot help but point you to one thing: in our mind, there is no north or south, no life or death, no time or space. We are already perfectly complete.

But when thinking appears, mind appears. And when mind appears, all sorts of opinions appear, egoistic attachment appears, I-my-me. This is the reason for making "right-wing" and "left-wing," and judging them to be either "good" or "bad." Attachment to thinking is the cause of all this arguing and fighting over "good" and "bad." This is the cause of our attachment to life and death. Who could expect world peace to appear through such conditions?

The possibility of reunifying North and South Korea is intimately linked with the possibility of world peace. Yet how can we ever expect world peace when politicians, scholars, and religious leaders all claim that they and those who think like them are right, while others are all wrong? However, I beg you to imagine a world wherein anyone who aspires to be a politician, scholar, or religious teacher first makes effort to discover his true Self, and only then performs the role of politician, scholar, or religious teacher. World peace would spring out instantaneously! This is the goal to which I devote all of my meager efforts.

Thus I urge you, as president of our country, to lead a nationwide campaign to find our original human nature, our true Self. When many people accomplish this work, quarreling will cease, and not only will we attain an absolute world in which "right" and "wrong," and "good" and "evil" no longer exist, but your presidency could be said to have had some value, despite the many sufferings it has brought.

I am compelled to write to you with such urgency because great difficulties for every individual, every nation, and every people will intensify from now until Sakura flowers bloom in the spring of 1984. Unless you attain your true Self, you will face even greater personal sufferings, too.

So, it is important to keep this in mind, as an eminent teacher once said:

> *All formations are impermanent.*
> *This is the law of appearing and disappearing.*
> *When both appearing and disappearing disappear,*
> *Then this stillness is bliss.*

[...] Everything in this world is always changing, changing, changing, changing: that is the law of appearing and disappearing. But when mind disappears, our opinions and our attachment to I-my-me disappear. When we experience this state of perfect selflessness, or "no I," then everything that we see and hear is the truth. The sky is blue: that is truth. Trees are green: that is truth. Water is flowing: that is truth. A dog barks, "Woof! Woof!" Birds are singing, "Cheep, cheep, cheep!" Salt is salty, and sugar is sweet: this is the absolute truth. Right now we are all living in a world of truth. But because human beings do not know their true nature, they do not see and hear and smell the truth-world in which they live.

Sir, I am not interested in discussing your performance in office. Whether you are right or wrong in your policies or actions, you are still the president of the country. As president, you have a duty to lead and govern the Korean people well. Whatever may have been the past actions of your administration, that is all past and done. Rather, you should ask yourself now how you can improve the real lives of your countrymen. [...]

An eminent teacher once wrote,

Heaven is earth, earth is heaven:
   heaven and earth revolve.
Water is mountain, mountain is water:
   water and mountain are empty.
Heaven is heaven, earth is earth:
   when did they ever revolve?
Mountain is mountain, water is water:
   each is separate from the other.

This poem points directly to the human nature and universal substance that I am talking about. Human beings are very foolish, because while they claim to know many, many things, they do not have the faintest idea who they themselves really are!

So, if you attain your own self-nature, "north" and "south" will disappear from your mind, and the reunification of Korea will happen much sooner than you think. If all Koreans simply turned their attention to attaining their true mind, then the way to reunification would be an easy one.

The Great Way has no gate;
The tongue has no bone.
Spring sunlight fills everywhere.
Willow is green, and flowers are red.

[...] President Chun, I would like to ask you what your philosophy is? It is very, very hard for me to figure it out! You should live a philosophy that emphasizes filial duties and ethics. This is the only way the Korean people can survive. Our people can survive only if every one of us recovers our self-nature.

So, President Chun, if somebody asks you, "Who are you?" how would you answer?

When Socrates was teaching Athenians to find themselves, someone asked Socrates if he knew who he was. Socrates answered, "I don't know. But I know that I don't know." This is the famous "don't-know" philosophy of Socrates.

Sir, you must find a philosophy that will guide you. If you rule the country without a philosophy and without understanding your correct direction, relying instead on selfish, partisan instincts, too many Koreans will have to suffer. President Jimmy Carter used to advocate human rights, but he failed in his endeavors mainly because he could not take any actions to back up his words. Just you or someone else saying that we need human rights and ethics is not enough. An old saying goes, "There is virtue in action, and patience in virtue." Only when there is patience can you attain a correct direction. And the universe becomes yours only when you put your true words into *action.*

But intellectual knowledge alone is not the way. Having merely intellectual knowledge is like bank employees handling money: the amount of money may be great, but it does not belong to the employees. They are handling someone else's riches! The money becomes *theirs* only when they earn it through their labor.

In the same way, people everywhere are arguing endlessly about other peoples' understanding, without making that understanding theirs. This is why our world is divided into "right" and "left." When you cut off all thinking and return to your true Self, attaining your true self-nature, there is no longer any "right" or "left," no life or death, no upper-class or lower-class.

Buddhism has very basic teachings about how we create these distinctions in our minds. When "I" exists, then "that" object exists; and when "I" doesn't exist, "that" object also does not exist. Thus this illusory "I" is the most important problem. "Who are you?" Do you understand this "I" of yours, President Chun? What is it? Tell me! Tell me!

You do not truly know now, do you? Then I ask you, how can you suppose to rule a country when you do not even know what this "I" is? How can you rule a country of millions correctly when you do not even know who you are? [...]

President Chun, it is said that there are three dangerous tips: the tip of a sword, the tip of a tongue, and the tip of a pen. Thus it is taught that one should not surrender to the tip of a sword, one should not be conned by the tip of a tongue, and should not be deceived by the tip of a pen.

Sir, did you not stage a *coup d'etat* with the tip of a sword? Since you did, you must of course know that it is incumbent on you to use wisely this power that you captured. If you attain that, you will have attained your Great Function, which means keeping a mind that is clear like space, and using it meticulously for others. Although our true nature is absolute, and wide, when you attain your Great Function, then sky and earth, mountain and water, upper and lower are separate and clear. When you are hungry, you must eat; when you are thirsty, you drink: these are examples of the Great Function. When a true person wins, they receive a prize; and to one who does wrong action, a penalty is given. When you come to understand this dharma completely, you will see that actually true law contains the Great Way, justice, compassion, and ethical action. Attaining this, you will come to love and care for the whole nation as if its people were no different from your own children.

Sir, do you really think you know what ethics and morals are all about? We have an unlimited supply of them already inside our own minds. If you do not know this, I suggest that you go and seek out an enlightened teacher before you think of ruling a country. [...]

I must say to you: we must find our true nature so that we do not surrender to the tip of a sword, nor be fooled by the tip of a tongue, nor be deceived by the tip of a pen. For was it not the power of these "three tips" that created the existence of "communism" and "capitalism" in the first place, and then drew humanity into this war that threatens to destroy the world? So it must be clear that we must overcome the grave danger of these "three tips," and to do that we must return to our original nature.

But since you do not even know what your "I" is, Mr. President, I encourage you to seek out and question an enlightened person about the nature of ethical politics.

Yet you should not be fooled by mere intellectual knowledge of this matter: conceptual knowledge is still not true wisdom. When I was on the board of directors of Dongguk University, the largest Buddhist university in the country, I tried to locate for the university a person who had both scholarship and real virtue. I found many, many people who excelled in their scholastic fields, but could find no one in academia who combined great scholarship with true virtue and morals. My point is, we cannot expect scholars to guide the country well, since mere knowledge and learning do not have any real power. Most scholars are only filled with dry, empty cognition. You must understand that in school settings, we only accumulate more and more knowledge, whereas true wisdom comes from direct insight into our self-nature. Wisdom of this kind leads directly to moral behavior, and virtue.

Book knowledge is like having a tape recorder: everything recorded belongs to someone else. That is only someone else's ideas, which you have collected. But we can see clearly and live clearly only when we have wisdom, which leads to a compassion that saves all beings from suffering [....]

Don't you recognize that you live in a world that is constantly changing, changing, changing, changing, nonstop? This whole existence is fraught with change; it cannot be believed. So therefore you must attain your true root; you must attain the nature of the ground on which you now stand. Even a child knows that a tree without roots cannot stand! It will soon fall down.

You are president, yet you must also sense the mood of the people, and determine what they really want. This is your root, as president. You have to see the changing conditions in which your people live and work. You must use your ears to know the movement of their minds, and hear their complaints. You must use your nose to sense the direction of their mood, to perceive the winds of change blowing through our society and our world. You must use your tongue to know the taste of what you yourself are doing, from moment to moment. And you must use your body to act for them.

You can only last long as president if your body can find its roots, and then know the ground on which you stand. I ask you to please find these roots. You must ask yourself, "What are my roots?" "When were my roots made?" "Who made my roots?" You must ask yourself this, very deeply. Only then will you be able to perceive your direction and this whole society's correct direction. From this kind of study alone can Korea survive, and if through your example other leaders come to study like this, we will truly attain world peace. The point is that world peace appears when people in power lead the correct way.

Mr. President, it is said that blood is thicker than water. Though I have lived mostly outside Korea for the last twenty years, teaching in Japan and the West, the well-being of Korea and her people has always been paramount in my mind. Actually, it does not matter to me who or what party is in power, if you want to know the truth. My wish has always been and will always be that my homeland, Korea, be prosperous and strong.

Sir... [p]lease recover your human nature and become the guiding light of the Korean people. If Koreans have such a light to follow, can we doubt that the dawn of reunification is far away?

Wishing your continued health, and the realization of all your wishes,

The Han River's waters have been flowing for hundreds of years;
Sam Gak Sahn Mountain [a prominent peak on the outskirts of Seoul where Hwa Gye Sah Temple is located] *has watched us since time immemorial.*

In the Dharma,
Seung Sahn Haeng Won

Buddhism ascribes much of the suffering we cause ourselves and others to believing our own mental projections, to taking as true the labels our mind attaches to things and people. Racism is one of the most obvious examples of this, as we judge people by the mental construct of "race," and the fact that the problem is essentially cognitive doesn't make it any easier to uproot. Let's listen in on this dramatized phone conversation as Gaylon Ferguson, a well-known African-American Buddhist teacher and scholar, talks with a friend about the four noble truths and the politics of race.

★ ★ ★

NO COLOR, ALL COLORS

by Gaylon Ferguson

MY OLDEST FRIEND in the dharma, Al, has just returned from his annual solitary meditation retreat. We keep in touch sporadically, and when he calls to find out how I've been, he asks what I've been working on lately.

"An essay," I say, "trying to find something helpful to say about Buddhism and the politics of race."

"Really?" he says, with evident disbelief. "What does the pristine, holy Dharma have to do with something as sordid as contemporary politics?" There's a long pause and a loud silence on our cellphones—we've clearly boggled each other's minds, at least for the moment. Here we go again, I think to myself: the crisp mountain air of retreat meets the warm blast of city strife.

"I always thought Buddhism was primarily about waking up," Al continued, "you know, coming into a new state of consciousness, that sort of thing. 'Dharma politics?'—it sounds like an oxymoron! And more than a little scary with the rise of all these righteous fundamentalisms in the world today."

"One can find many statements by the Buddha in the early texts about how human beings might live together in sane, harmonious communities," I replied. "There's an interesting study from the 1970s; it's just called, simply, *The Buddha*, by Trevor Ling, a British scholar of religion. Ling insists that the Buddha intended his teaching primarily as a *social* revolution, not a religion in the narrow spiritual sense. That narrow sense of spirituality is a peculiarly modern invention, by the way, and goes hand in hand with the rise of materialism."

"It's just that I always thought that practicing sitting meditation and bringing about some change in my own state of mind was enough for one lifetime. Sure, I vote and send donations to worthy causes from time to time. But I never connected dharma, meditation, and awakening with issues like my neighborhood, or homelessness, or the national government, or war, or consumerism, or immigration policies, or for that matter, the tangle of issues around race. Everybody knows that discussing race and racism is like swatting at the proverbial 'tar-baby.' No one comes out of it clean."

"Well you're right about that—and isn't that a telling image to use for it? Back around the turn of the millennium, a group of *New York Times* correspondents did a series called 'How Race is Lived in America.' Both the journalists of color and the white writers acknowledged that, unlike most stories they cover, they had a feeling of inadequacy in dealing with race. As one of them candidly admitted: 'I can do a business story or a science story or a legal story and figure out right from wrong, up from down. With a race story, it's tougher because there are no absolute rights and wrongs.'"

"Yeah—we've all been there, but that can be a bit of a cop-out, too. As Katagiri Roshi used to say: 'You have to say *something!*'"

We both laughed, remembering the ruthless compassion of Katagiri's stern, Japanese face. And then Al pushed on:

"So—what do you have to say, or rather what does the Buddha's dharma have to tell us, about the politics of race?"

"Well, examining the politics of race begins with understanding racism, a social disease that still infects the body politic at large."

"Yes, I can see that. Just look at last year's riots in France: At first commentators said this was all part of the famous ongoing 'clash' between Islam and the West. When I got back from retreat and saw the photos online and in the magazines, I had to agree with Fareed Zakaria: 'The pictures looked more like those of America's race riots in the 1960s than of Fallujah or Ramallah.' And we don't have to look far for some of the sources of that pent-up frustration: 'A recent French study showed that job applicants with "French-sounding names" had 50 times the chance of being interviewed as those with Arab- or African-sounding names.' Fifty times!"

"So that's the starting point—the truth of racism. It's a little like those commentaries on the four noble truths, the original teachings of the Buddha: the truth of suffering, its origin, the truth of the stopping (or cessation) of suffering, and the path to that goal. Some commentators have noted that the structure of this teaching is a lot like a traditional medical diagnosis. The disease is called suffering. There is a cause for this disease: craving and greed and aggression based on ignorance. There is then—and this is the liberatory proclamation of all dharma—the third truth of the possibility of a return to health and basic sanity. But overcoming the disease and returning to good health doesn't happen automatically, just upon hearing the diagnosis. We have to take the medicine—the fourth truth of walking the 'eightfold path,' of which meditation practice, 'right mindfulness,' is one of the main 'folds.'"

"Yes, I've heard that model for understanding the path before. Sometimes they say we should regard our lives whirling around in conditioned existence (samsara) as a disease, the teacher as the physician, the dharma as the medicine, and practice as actually taking the medicine. Seems similar. So what's that got to do with racial politics?"

"Well, we've already started working our way through. The first step, the first truth so to speak, is acknowledging the existence of racism. As with suffering, things are only made worse by our denying this fact—pretending it didn't happen, that it doesn't continue to happen—bias, bigotry, racial discrimination, subtle and gross violence based on ethnic difference. It becomes an unmentionable presence in the room at certain moments. We perpetuate our imprisonment in neurotic suffering by ignoring it, by denial. Many people have mentioned the immense relief they felt upon first hearing the noble truth of suffering clearly and simply stated. Certainly that's what I felt when I first heard my own root teacher, Trungpa Rinpoche, teach on 'all-pervasive suffering.' It was painful and hilarious at once. Suddenly it was no longer this hideous little secret that everybody knows, yet we pretend isn't here with us constantly. So too with racism—

just acknowledging its prevalence and persistence is a step toward health. A necessary step—though not sufficient."

"I agree that it's a difficult topic even to look at—much less to actively engage in *changing*. Why do you think it's so hard just to acknowledge the existence of racism?"

"Well, several reasons. First, the topic makes us all uncomfortable because there's a feeling of powerlessness, often mixed with contrary impulses toward both guilt and blaming: 'I didn't start this, so what do you want me to do about it? I can't undo centuries of oppression. I'm sorry, truly I am. People have to help themselves; it's their own karma, their own fault for lacking discipline.' The insight buried among these conflicting emotions is that racism is much larger than any individual's *personal* goodwill!"

"Yes—it's daunting to face something so huge, with so much historical weight and momentum—from the genocide of indigenous peoples to the Final Solution, from internment camps during WWII to the continued exploitation of farm workers, from lynchings to the increase of racially segregated urban schools in America today. What's that old saying? 'History is a nightmare from which I am trying to awaken.'"

"You've got it. And the first step in 'awakening,' the goal of the Buddhist path, is recognizing that one is 'asleep.' If we don't acknowledge the prevalence of our habitual 'sleepwalking' state, how can we begin the path to waking up? Consider this: psychologist Beverly Tatum says that when she gives talks on 'the reality of racism in our society...in almost every audience I address, there is someone who will suggest that racism is a thing of the past. There is always someone who hasn't noticed the stereotypical images of people of color in the media, who hasn't observed the housing discrimination in their community, who hasn't read the newspaper articles about documented racial bias in lending practices among well-known banks, who isn't aware of the racial tracking pattern at the local high school, who hasn't seen the reports of rising incidents of racially motivated hate crimes in America—in short someone who hasn't been paying attention to issues of race. But if you are paying attention, the legacy of racism is not hard to see, and we are all affected by it.' Remember that story about how the media portrayed whites taking food and other necessities in the aftermath of Hurricane Katrina as stalwart 'survivors' and blacks doing the same thing as 'looters'?"

"So again, it's a matter of paying attention, being mindful and aware, not closing ourselves off in a little cocoon of denial."

"Yes—but some aspects of this first truth may not be directly visible to the naked eye; we may need to open the eye of insight to see them."

"Like what?"

"Like white privilege—the system of advantages that accrue to anyone with white skin. Tatum says, 'Most white people, if they are really being honest with themselves, can see that there are advantages to being White in the United States. Despite current rhetoric about affirmative action and "reverse racism," every social indicator, from salary to life expectancy, reveals the [socially conferred] advantages of being White.'"

"Hmm. Does she have any evidence of such honest self-reflection, in which whites actually become *conscious* of white privilege? Somehow I have my doubts."

"Well, yes, she cites an article by a Euro-American feminist scholar, Peggy McIntosh, called "White Privilege: Unpacking the Invisible Knapsack": 'McIntosh identified a long list of societal privileges she received just because she was White. She did not ask for them, and it is important to note that she hadn't always noticed that she was receiving them.'"

"I suppose that accounts for the sense of unconscious, taken-for-granted entitlement we see so much of today—sort of 'Isn't everyone like we are?'"

"Exactly. Theater critic John Lahr wrote recently: 'As the federal government's response to the hurricane in Louisiana showed the world, institutional racism is a concept that white America has yet to acknowledge.'"

"Not just white America. When secretary of state Rice, a prominent African American indeed, visited her hometown of Birmingham, Alabama soon after the hurricane, she assiduously assured local reporters that President Bush hasn't, as the saying goes, a racist bone in his body. This is precisely beside the point. It's like people who insist that they aren't *personally* racist. That's not the issue. Structural racism, systemic white supremacy, does not mean that Bush minds shaking hands with Colin

Powell or Secretary Rice or U.N. secretary-general Kofi Annan. It means
that when he nominates someone to the federal judiciary, that nominee
will show certain biases, a pattern of sensitivities and insensitivities."

"Like what?"

"Well, take Judge Alito, one of Geroge W. Bush's choices for the
Supreme Court. During the nomination process, no one questioned his
judicial experience and intelligence. But as the *New York Times* editorial
page noted: 'Judge Alito has favored an inflated standard of evidence for
racial- and sex-discrimination cases that would make it very hard even to
bring them to court, much less win…. When lawyers for a black death-
row inmate sought to demonstrate bias in jury selection by using statistics, Judge Alito dismissed that as akin to arguing that Americans were
biased toward left-handers because left-handed men had won five out of
six of the preceding presidential elections.' This is, to say the least, sadly
out of touch with the harsh realities of gender and racial bias historically
and as they continue to operate in our societies today. By the way, is it true
that, while in Birmingham, Secretary Rice compared the U.S. invasion of
Iraq to the Civil Rights struggle?"

"Yes, indeed. I guess we should begin to worry that she's in trouble."

"What do you mean?"

"Well, after rap artist Kanye West's remark on national television that
George W. Bush doesn't care about black people, cartoonist Aaron
McGruder said: 'If you're black and you don't know that by now, you're
in trouble,' adding, 'I think it's time that poor whites start realizing that
George Bush doesn't care about them either, and he will let them die too.'
But we must move on now to the second truth—racism has an origin.
That is to say, racial prejudice and the system of white privilege arise from
causes and conditions. They aren't decreed by a supernatural being; it
isn't simply a matter of fate. Racism is a learned mental model!"

"Is that the bad news or the good news?"

"Well, it's both, my friend. Because racism is a set of learned attitudes
and behaviors (just as no child is born speaking Italian, no infant is born
racist), that means that it could be 'unlearned,' systematically and personally undone."

"Sort of like the Buddha's twelve 'links' of dependent arising, the *nidanas*—where you work backwards from effect to cause and so undo your confusion? Working backwards, from grasping to craving to feeling to basic ignorance. Then, working forwards, if we eliminate ignorance, eventually we get to no grasping?"

"Yes, remarkably similar. Tatum notes that, growing up in more or less homogeneous, racially segregated neighborhoods, as most of us do, means that we gain little direct experience and information about those who are different from us—whether that difference is ethnic, religious, or economic. And the information we do receive is often biased and distorted, exaggerating negative traits and omitting positive achievements—or the reverse! This suggests that ignorance is a prime cause of racism."

"What about the third truth—the truth of liberation, the truth of stopping the madness? Is it really possible to awaken from the nightmare of human history?"

"Well, we aspire to that. As Zen master Suzuki Roshi used to say, in Mahayana Buddhism we aspire to save *all* sentient beings not because we think that's going to happen at some time we can foresee, but *because* it is beyond all our concepts of what's possible and impossible. We make the aspiration to step *beyond* the petty dualistic mind that tells us what can and cannot happen. Who believed that the Berlin Wall would come down in our lifetime? Who believed, when Rosa Parks refused to stand up, that the era of segregated bus rides would come falling down?"

"So...it's more like a vision, a vision of a truly egalitarian community—not based on gender or racial or class domination."

"Yes, the third truth is like a true vision. It inspires us, like the brilliant warmth of the sun, to walk toward it: *that's* where we'd like to live, in a sane society. That's what we'd like for our children, and our children's children, all of them. When we say, in the contemplation of loving-kindness: 'May all beings be happy,' there's an implied universality: 'all beings.' It's not, "May all the beings who look like me be happy." From the point of view of this contemplation, racism is a form of xenophobia; we've been trained, badly trained, to fear and distrust those beings who are not like us. It's inspiring to me personally that many people have entered into meaningful conversations and transformative disciplines to counter that training, to 'unlearn racism,' or to re-consider, as men, our deeply internalized sexism. There are some really moving moments in Lee Mun Wah's documentary, *The Color of Fear*, showing men of diverse racial backgrounds in honest and revealing dialogue with each other."

"Right—a bigger vision of compassion is built right into the teachings: 'May *all* beings be free from suffering.' That reminds me of a saying from Sakyong Mipham: 'The dharma is all colors and no color. The dharma is all truth and no truth.'"

"Yes, that could be one description of liberation—beyond fixation, all colors and no color, welcoming everyone and not fixating on color. In King's still ringing words, we aspire to a world in which we would be judged by 'the content of our character, rather than the color of our skin.'"

"So is that one description of this healing journey, from colorism to no color to all colors?"

"Possibly. This gets a little tricky. Some people use 'no color' to mean 'our color'—you're welcome here as long as you act, dress, and pretend to look like everyone else here—but we don't have any 'color consciousness,' so you shouldn't bring that up, okay? Whiteness is often invisible. Law professor Harlon Dalton compares it to 'the tick of a familiar clock,' easily tuned out: 'In settings where whites dominate, being white is not noteworthy.... The challenge for white folk is to realize, even when they are not in the minority, that *their* race matters too. It establishes their place in the social pecking order. It hangs over the relationships they establish with people of color.'"

"That's very similar to when the word 'mankind' was used to mean 'humankind.' If you asked someone, particularly a person of the male persuasion, about this unmarked gender bias, they would probably have said, 'No, no! When we say "he," it means "he" *and* "she."' After you stopped laughing, you would have noted that, in the same way, some people feel that 'white' means everyone is included. It's a curious version of universalism. We're all one, so don't rock the boat by mentioning any differences. I've often heard a related question—why the need for people of color retreats? Isn't that self-segregation? Isn't it against the teachings of the Buddha to have retreats that exclude white participants?"

"Yes, I was part of a People of Color Retreat at Spirit Rock Meditation Center—and afterwards heard that same question several times from some well-meaning Euro-American Buddhist practitioners. (We are touching on aspects of the path here.) The spiritual journeys of people who have been wounded by white supremacy may usefully include times of retreat with others of similar backgrounds and experience. There have now been Asian-American and Pacific Islanders dharma retreats, African-American retreats, People-of-Color retreats, and Gay/Lesbian retreats—at least in some of the more progressive sanghas. This is not unlike women's retreats and men's retreats, is it? This can all be part of establish-ing a 'safe container'—temporarily free from unintended or unthinking harassment. In such settings, meditators are often able to open to them-selves in new ways, freed for the moment from the chronic need to defend and be on guard from the next attack. Then, as with retreats from time immemorial, practitioners can return strengthened to the challenges of daily life with work and family."

"So are you going to suggest that Buddhist practice in itself frees one from racism and all other social ills—classism, sexism, homophobia? Is that the fourth truth here, the truth of the Buddhist path?"

"Definitely not. As they say, most definitely not. It seems quite clear that, whatever the brilliance of the teachings of the buddhadharma, indi-vidual practitioners can continue for years, perhaps lifetimes, with these prejudices left largely untouched by meditation practice. One may even learn to use dharmic concepts like 'karma' to reinforce separatism and indifference to the suffering around us. Why engage in outreach efforts, since, if those people had a 'karmic connection' with the dharma, they would already be living in the same neighborhoods we do?"

"Yes. The white supremacist thinking in my own sangha and commu-nity is so deeply entrenched that it does not see itself. 'What, we racist? Surely you're kidding?' Yet—what of the path, the fourth truth, in this case, the way of undoing racism. What do you recommend?"

"Well, there's no generic prescription here. We enter this work from very different identities and locations and histories. The path to undoing will be different for descendants of immigrants and those of us whose ancestors arrived here enslaved, for those of us who grew up materially comfortable and those who grew up impoverished, different for historically privileged WASPs from the Upper East Side than for a straight Latina from Spanish Harlem, for middle-class Midwesterners from the suburbs than for a working-class, Irish Catholic gay man from Dublin. We all have different entry points, different sets of insights and blinders to our own internalized oppression and privilege. Different paths for different folks. According to some traditions, these were the Buddha's last words: 'Work out your liberation with diligence!' Or as another, more recent buddha put it, 'Jolly good luck!'"

"And the politics part? Do we work with other people to engage the dharma politically—and in particular the politics of race?"

"Yes—and that's the other part of the fourth truth of the path. Since 'race' is largely a *cultural* construction, a matter of *social* definitions, we cannot undo racism alone. The word 'politics' is from *polis*, the ancient Greek city-state. Politics has to do with our lives together, in cities and communities and societies. It's where we get the word 'polite'—how we can live together with decency and gentleness. So a cultural politics of race needs to involve group work, community activities. It cannot be a matter of an isolated individual's practice and exploration alone. Bondage and collective liberation are both born in social life, our humanly vibrant, lived experience with others.

An example is Bhimrao Ambedkar, born an 'untouchable' or *dalit*, in the caste system of India. To read his experiences growing up—when he was beaten for drinking water from a well and thus 'polluting' it—reminded me of the many brutal stories of segregated life in the pre-Civil Rights era South. Later, Ambedkar was educated at the London School of Economics and Columbia University, where he studied with John Dewey. Ambedkar had many energetic exchanges with Gandhi and helped draft the constitution of modern India. In 1950, he resigned from his position as the country's first minister of law when President Nehru's cabinet refused to pass the Women's Rights Bill. In 1956, renouncing the caste system that had abused him for his dark skin for decades, he 'went for refuge,' in a large public ceremony, committing himself to the 'three jewels' of Buddha, Dharma, and Sangha. Joining him, in a great gesture of collective liberation, were 380,000 dalits, women, men, and children, who also formally became Buddhist."

"Wow, that's an amazing story; I'd never even heard of him. Still, as inspiring as Ambedkar's life and journey were, I'm left wondering: what's that got to do with you and me and the situations we find ourselves in today?"

"Yes, you're right. As 'words don't cook rice,' there's much good work remaining to be done. Shall we continue our dialogue another time?"

Spiritual people are often seen as naïve and "idealistic." Here, Thich Nhat Hanh argues that spirituality is actually the most practical and effective approach to defense and foreign policy. Thich Nhat Hanh combines deep realization with a serious understanding of world affairs. He shows his compassion in criticizing conventional military thinking, not the soldiers who are its victims too.

★ ★ ★

COMPASSION IS OUR BEST PROTECTION

by Thich Nhat Hanh

THE REVELATION of the abuse of prisoners of war in Iraq, Afghanistan, and Guantánamo Bay provides us with the opportunity to look deeply into the nature of war. This is an opportunity for us to be more aware, for these abuses reveal the truth about what actually goes on during military conflict. This isn't new—everywhere that there is war, there is abuse and torture of prisoners.

Soldiers are trained to kill as many of the enemy as possible and as quickly as possible. Soldiers are told that if they don't kill, they will be killed. They're taught that killing is good because the people they are trying to kill are dangerous to society; that the others are demons and our nation would be better off without them. Soldiers are trained to believe they must kill the other group because these others aren't human beings. If soldiers see their "enemies" as human beings just like themselves, they would have no courage to kill them. Every one of us should be aware of how soldiers are trained, whether or not we think we agree with the fighting. It is important not to blame and single out any country. The situation is more a consequence of our way of fighting rather than something particular to the United States. During the Vietnam War, atrocities were committed by both sides.

When the torture was revealed, President Bush responded by saying that the U.S. had sent dedicated young soldiers, not abusers, to Iraq. This statement showed a lack of understanding of war that shocked me, because the torture and abuse these soldiers engaged in was the direct result of the training they had undergone. The training had already made them lose their humanity.

The young men going to Iraq arrive there already full of fear, wanting to protect themselves at all costs, pressured by their superiors to be aggressive, act quickly, and be ready to kill at any moment.

When you are engaged in the act of killing, aware that fellow soldiers on your side are dying every day and that it is possible for you to be killed at any moment, you are filled with fear, anger, and despair. In this state, you can become extremely cruel. You may pour all of your hate and anger onto prisoners of war by torturing and abusing them. The purpose of your violence is not primarily to extract information from them, but to express your hate and fear. The prisoners of war are the victims, but the abusers, the torturers, are also the victims. Their actions will continue to disturb them long after the abuse has ended.

Even if the superiors of the individual soldiers have not directly given orders to mistreat, abuse, or torture, they are still responsible for what happened. Preparing for war and fighting a war means allowing our human nature to die.

There are many other ways to defend ourselves: through diplomatic foreign policy, forming alliances with other countries, humanitarian assistance. These are all approaches motivated by the wisdom of *interbeing*. When we use these approaches to resolve conflicts, the army doesn't have to do much. They can serve the people by building bridges and roads and mediating small conflicts. This is not idealistic thinking; armies have worked this way in the past. With good foreign policy, the army will not have to fight.

Of course, when a country is invaded, the army should resist and defend the people. It is also sometimes necessary for other countries to help a country that is being invaded. But that is quite different from attacking other countries out of national interest. The only really necessary and appropriate circumstance under which an army should resort to violence is to physically defend itself or an ally from a direct invasion. And even in this case, much suffering will result.

Military action can be compassionate, but the compassion must be real compassion. If compassion is only a screen masking anger and fear, it is useless. It upsets me that former generations have committed the same mistakes and yet we don't learn from them. We haven't learned enough from the war in Vietnam. There were so many atrocities committed there. So many innocent people were tortured and killed because they were perceived as either "communist" or "anticommunist."

Mindfulness has so many layers. When we kill because we think that the other person is evil and killing them will bring peace, we are not practicing Right Mindfulness. If we are mindful, we will see beyond the present situation to the root and the future consequences of our act in that moment. If we are truly mindful, other insights will arise: "This person I want to kill is a living being. Is there any chance for him to behave better and change his present, harmful state of mind? Maybe I have a wrong perception and one day I will see that he is just a victim of misunderstanding, and not really the evil person I think he is." Mindfulness can help a soldier to see that he may just be an instrument for killing being used by his government.

A general who is mindful of his actions is capable of looking deeply. He may not need to use weapons. He will see that there are many ways to deter the opposite side and he will exhaust all other means before resorting to violence. When nothing else works, he may use violence, but out of compassion, not out of anger.

Some soldiers are able to remain compassionate, treating prisoners and others kindly, despite their military training. These individuals are lucky enough to have received a spiritual heritage of kindness and goodness that stays at least partially intact, even through their training. This heritage is transmitted by parents, teachers, and community. Their humanity is preserved to some extent even if they have been damaged during their training. So they are still able to be shocked by their fellow soldiers' acts of torture and perhaps to practice Right Action and alert the world to the torture that is being committed. But many soldiers don't have this spiritual heritage. They come from families with much suffering and have already experienced violence and oppression before entering the army. For most people, it is possible to lose all their humanity in the process of military training.

Compassionate killing can only be done by bodhisattvas, awakened and compassionate beings. In combat situations, the majority of us kill because we are afraid of being killed. So most of us are not capable of killing out of love. When our dog or horse that we love very much is suffering from a terminal sickness, we are capable of killing it to stop it from suffering. We are motivated by love. But most people in our army aren't motivated in this way. The best is to not kill at all. When you kill for your country, to defend your fellow citizens, it isn't good, but still it is better than invading other countries in the name of democracy and freedom. History has shown us that the countries the U.S. has invaded to "help" have not become more democratic and free. Prime Minister Tony Blair said that the UK is committed to democracy and freedom in Iraq. If we use this kind of justification, we could invade many countries because there are many that do not have enough freedom and democracy, including our own.

TORTURE IS NEVER JUSTIFIED

There is no "good cause" for torture. As a torturer, you are the first to be a victim because you do harm to yourself in the act of harming another. If you had a good cause to begin with, it is lost when you torture another human being. No cause can justify this kind of violence.

When we imagine situations where torture could be justified, we jump to conclusions too quickly and too easily; it is not so simple. Torturing someone will not always give us the result we wish for. If prisoners in custody do not tell us the information we want, it is because they don't want their people, their fellow soldiers, to be killed. They withhold information out of compassion, out of faithfulness to their cause. Sometimes they give out wrong information and sometimes they really don't know anything. And there are those who prefer to die rather than give in to the torture.

I am absolutely against torture. Other forms of pressure or firmness may be acceptable, but not torture. When we have fear and anger in us, it is very easy to create a pretext for torturing a prisoner. When we have compassion, we can always find another way. When you torture a living being, you die as a human being because their suffering is your own suffering. When you perform surgery on someone, you know the surgery will help him and that is why you can cut into his body. But when you cut into someone's body and mind to get information, you cut into your own life; you kill yourself. We must look at why we are engaged in war and how we have become involved in things like this. So the problem is long-term, not just looking at the immediate situation of torture.

We have to learn how to prevent situations from escalating to this point. We can do things every day to create more peaceful and harmonious relations with other countries and other peoples. Why do we wait until the situation is so bad, and then say we have to resort to the most atrocious means to stop it? We can do much better by taking care of the conflict compassionately from the very beginning.

People usually think in extreme terms of absolute nonviolence and violence, but there are many shades of gray in between. The way we talk, eat, walk can be violent. We are not dogmatic, worshiping the idea of nonviolence, because absolute nonviolence is impossible. But it is always possible to be less violent. When we have understanding and compassion in us, we have a good chance. When we are motivated by fear and anger, we are already victims. No cause is worthy enough to be served by this state of being. A truly good cause is always motivated by compassion.

OUR COLLECTIVE KARMA

An act of cruelty is born of many conditions coming together, not by any separate, individual actor. When we hold retreats for war veterans, I tell them they are the flame at the tip of the candle—they are the ones who feel the heat, but the whole candle is burning, not only the flame. All of us are responsible.

The very ideas of terrorism and imagined weapons of mass destruction are already the result of a collective mentality, a collective way of thinking and speaking. The media helped the war happen by supporting these ideas through speech and writing. Thought, speech, and action are all collective karma.

No one can say they are not responsible for this current situation, even if we oppose our country's actions. We are still members of our community, citizens of our country. Maybe we have not done enough. We must ally ourselves with the bodhisattvas, the great awakened beings, who are around us in order to transform our way of thinking and that of our society. Because wrong thinking is at the base of our present situation, thinking that has no wisdom or compassion. And we can do things every day, in every moment of our daily life, to nourish the seeds of peace, compassion, and understanding in us and in those around us. We can live in a way that can heal our collective karma and ensure that these atrocities will not happen again in the future.

Don't be tempted to use the army to solve conflicts. The only situation in which we use the army is to defend our country during an invasion. But even in this circumstance we should not rely heavily on the army; we must find other ways to protect ourselves. In the past, the U.S. was loved by many of us in the world because the U.S. represented freedom, democracy, peace, and care for other countries. The U.S. has lost this image and must rebuild it. In the past, when I would go to the U.S. Embassy for a visa, it was not heavily guarded. But now, all over the world, American embassies are surrounded by tight security and heavily armed guards. Fear has overtaken us. It's the primary motivation for many of the U.S. government's actions, because we don't know how to protect ourselves with compassion. Students of political science must learn this in university so that they can bring real wisdom into politics. Compassion is not naïve or stupid; it goes hand-in-hand with our intelligence.

Love is the same; real love is born from understanding.

A KNIFE TO KILL OR CHOP VEGETABLES

Soldiers from armies around the world have asked me how to reconcile their desire for mindfulness and peace with their occupations as soldiers. If, as a soldier, you have understanding and compassion in you, then military force may help prevent something or achieve something. But that shouldn't keep us from seeing that there are other kinds of force that may be even more powerful. We don't know how to recognize and make use of these methods so we always have cause to resort to military force. The spiritual force is also very powerful. It is much safer to use the powerful spiritual, social, and educational forces. Because we have not been trained to use these forces, we only think of using military force.

Suppose there are two people, both of them full of anger, misunderstanding, and hatred. How can these two people talk to each other, and how can they negotiate for peace? That is the main problem: you cannot bring people together to sit around a table and discuss peace if there is no peace inside of them. You have to first help them to calm down and begin to see clearly that we and the other people suffer. We should have compassion for ourselves and for them and their children. This is possible. As human beings we have suffered, so we have the capacity to understand the suffering of other people.

The spiritual and educational dimensions can be very powerful, and we should use them as instruments, tools for peace. For example, suppose you live in a quarter or a village where Palestinians live peacefully with Israelis. You don't have any problems. You share the same environment, you go shopping in the same place, you ride on the same bus. You don't see your differences as obstacles, but as enriching. You are an Israeli and she is a Palestinian, and you meet each other in the marketplace and you smile to each other. How beautiful, how wonderful. You help her and she helps you. Such places exist, and such images should be seen by other Palestinians and Israelis. The same thing is true with Iraqis and Americans, with Pakistanis and Indians.

If you are a writer, you can bring that image to many people outside of your group. If you are a filmmaker, why don't you offer an image of peaceful coexistence to the world? You can televise it to demonstrate that it is possible for two groups who have fought to live peacefully and happily together. That is the work of education. There are a lot of people in the mass media who are ready to help you bring that image, that message to the world. That is very powerful—more powerful than a bomb, a rocket, or a gun—and it makes people believe that peace is possible.

If you have enough energy of understanding and peace inside of you, then this kind of educational work can be very powerful, and you won't have to think of the army and of guns anymore. If the army knows how to practice, it will know how to act in such a way as to not cause harm. The army can rescue people; the army can guarantee peace and order. It is like a knife. You can use a knife to kill or you can use a knife to chop vegetables. It is possible for soldiers to practice nonviolence and understanding. We don't exclude them from our practice, from our sangha. We don't say, "You are a soldier, you cannot come into our meditation hall." In fact, you need to come into the meditation hall in order to know how to better use the army, how to better be in the army. So, please don't limit your question to such a small area. Make your question broad—embrace the whole situation—because everything is linked to everything else.

Every bit of our understanding, compassion, and peace is useful; it is gold. There are many things we can do today to increase these capacities in ourselves. When you take a step, if you can enjoy that step, if your step can bring you more stability and freedom, then you are serving the world. It is with that kind of peace and stability that you can serve. If you don't have the qualities of stability, peace, and freedom inside of you, then no matter what you do, you cannot help the world. It is not about "doing" something; it's about "being" something—being peace, being hope, being solid. Then every action will come out of that, because peace, stability, and freedom always seek a way to express themselves in action.

That is the spiritual dimension of our reality. We need that spiritual dimension to rescue us so that we don't think only in terms of military force as a means to solve the problem and uproot terrorism. How can you uproot terrorism with military force? The military doesn't know where terrorism is. They cannot locate terrorism—it is in the heart. The more military force you use, the more terrorists you create, in your own country and in other countries as well.

The basic issue is our practice of peace, our practice of looking deeply. First of all, we need to allow ourselves to calm down. Without tranquility and serenity, our emotions, anger, and despair will not go away, and we will not be able to look and see the nature of reality. Calming down, becoming serene, is the first step of meditation. The second step is to look deeply to understand. Out of understanding comes compassion. And from this foundation of understanding and compassion you will be able to see what you can do and what you should refrain from doing. This is meditation. Every one of us has to practice meditation—the politicians, the military, the businessmen. All of us have to practice calming down and looking deeply. You have the support of all of us in doing this.

Of course it is very difficult to not get angry when they are killing your wife, your husband, or your children. It is very difficult to not get angry. That person is acting out of anger, and we are retaliating also out of anger. So there is not much difference between the two of us. That is the first element.

The second element is, why do we have to wait until the situation presents itself to us as an emergency before we act, dealing only with the immediate circumstance? Of course you have to act rapidly in such an emergency situation. But what if we are not in an emergency situation? We can wait for an emergency situation to arise or we can do something in order to prevent such a thing from happening. Our tendency is not to do anything until the worst happens. While we have the time, we do not know how to use that time to practice peace and prevent war. We just allow ourselves to indulge in forgetfulness and sense pleasures. We do not do the things that have the power to prevent such emergency situations from happening.

The third element is that when things like this happen, it is because there is a deep-seated cause, not only in the present moment but also in the past. *This* is because *that* is. Nothing happens without a cause. You harm me, I harm you. But the fact that you are harming me and I am harming you has its roots in the past and will have an effect on the future. Our children will say, "You killed my grandfather, now I have to kill you." That can go on for a long time. When you get angry, when you have so much hatred toward the person who has made you suffer, and when you are willing to use any means to destroy him, you are acting out of anger just like he is. And anger is not the only cause. There are also misunderstandings, wrong perceptions about each other, and there are people who urge us to kill the other side because otherwise we will not be safe. There are many causes.

In the past our fathers and our grandfathers may not have been very mindful and may have said things and done things that have sown seeds of war. And their grandfathers also said things and did things, planting seeds of war. And now our generation has a choice. Do we want to do better than our grandfathers, or do we want to repeat exactly what they did? That is the legacy we will leave for our children and grandchildren.

Of course in a situation of great emergency you have to do everything you can to prevent killing. And yet, there are ways to do it that will cause less harm. If you have some compassion and understanding, the way you do it can be very different. Bring the dimension of the human heart into it; help the military strategists to have a human heart. It's the least we can do. Do we teach the military to conduct a military operation with a human heart? Is that a reality in the army, in military schools?

In one of his past lives, it seems that the Buddha was a passenger on a boat that was overtaken by pirates, and he killed one of them while trying to protect the people on the boat. But that was in an earlier life of the Buddha, before he was an awakened being. If awakened Buddha were there he may have had other means; he may have had enough wisdom to find a better way so that the life of the pirate could have been spared. Because in life after life, the Buddha made progress. You are the afterlife of your grandfather; you must have learned something over the past three generations. If you don't have more compassion and understanding than he did, then you have not properly continued your grandfather. Because with compassion and understanding we can do better; we can cause less harm, and create more peace.

We cannot expect to achieve one hundred percent peace right away—our degree of understanding and love is not yet deep enough. But in every situation, urgent or not, the elements of understanding and compassion can play a role. When a gangster is trying to beat and kill, of course you have to lock him up so he will not cause more harm. But you can lock him up angrily, with a lot of hate, or you can lock him up with compassion and with the idea that we should do something to help him. In that case, prison becomes a place where there is love and help. You have to teach the prison guards how to look at the prisoners with compassionate eyes. Teach the guards how to treat the prisoners with tenderness so they will suffer less in prison, so we can better help them.

Do we train them to look at prisoners with eyes of compassion? Perhaps a prisoner has killed, has destroyed. Maybe he was raised in such a way that killing and destruction were natural for him, and so he is a victim of society, of his family, and his education. If, as a prison guard, you look and see him in that way, then you will have compassion and understanding, and treat your prisoner with more gentleness. When you help this person to become a better person, you help yourself to be happy.

We should not focus only on short-term action. Again, we have to look with the eyes of the Buddha. We must train ourselves to look at things with a broad perspective and not just concentrate on the immediacy of the problem. That is what our lives are for, and so are the lives of our children. We are a continuation of each other. We build synagogues, churches, and mosques in order to have a place to sit down and do that— to look deeply, so that our actions will not only be motivated by desire, greed, or anger. We have a chance to sit in the mosque, the church, or the synagogue for a long time, and in that time our compassion and understanding should grow. And then we will know how to act in the world in a better way, for the cause of peace.

As a soldier you can be compassionate. You can be loving and your gun can be helpful. There are times you may not have to use your gun. It is like that knife that is used to cut vegetables. You can be a bodhisattva as a soldier or as a commander of the army. The question is whether you have understanding and compassion in your heart.

Sulak Sivaraksa, one of Asia's most important progressive voices, is watching with concern the effects of unfettered capitalism on developing countries. In response to globalization's environmental and cultural destructiveness—and the encouragement of materialism on which it depends—he offers the practices of mindfulness and interdependence. These alone are the antidote to individualism run wild.

★ ★ ★

A BUDDHIST RESPONSE TO GLOBALIZATION

by Sulak Sivaraksa

SOMETIMES I FEEL that *globalization* is not really an accurate descriptor of the age we are said to be living in. The word is at best too socially neutral, at worse highly misleading and deceptive. Sometimes I prefer the terms *free market fundamentalism* or *extreme modernism* to *globalization*.

Free market fundamentalism is a more accurate descriptor because globalization, which preaches the interdependence of nations, the mutuality of their interests, and the shared benefits of their interactions, has triggered the very opposite consequences; namely, increasing dependence of "developing" states on "developed" states; increasing inequalities between the North and the South, investors and workers, agro-businesses and peasants; and widening income inequalities within and between states. As a result of the free market system, the natural environment in large parts of the world is also in ruins beyond repair, threatening ecological equilibrium and human survival in general. And despite these obvious consequences, we are told that the free market system is still not free *enough*: there are still barriers to trade, economies have to be further deregulated or restructured at almost all costs, and so on. All these must be done in the name of progress, prosperity, development. Surely this faith in the emancipatory power of the free market system is akin to any other kind of fundamentalism!

Extreme modernism is also a more accurate descriptor because we are living in a world characterized by the intensification, radicalization, and universal spread of "modernity." One Thai scholar has called this age one in which "modernity now relies simply on its own justification and devours all other forms of actualization of human beings." Other forms of human aspirations are degraded as inferior—the products of weak and abnormal minds—and the implication is clear: there is only one way to be sane and normal. This is understandable, as the development concept of modernization is racially coded. Its intellectual precursor is none other than "Europeanization." *New York Times* columnist Thomas Friedman has even labeled critics of globalization "advocates of a flat earth." According to Friedman, these critics are locked in the abnormal past, refusing to accept the unilinearity of time.

If my criticism of globalization makes me a flat-earther, so be it. For all of us who are interested in freedom, justice, non-violence, democracy, and environmental sustainability, we should intensify our activism, criticisms, and analyses—not seal our lips, refuse to think, and disengage ourselves from the sufferings in the world. Luckily, and here I may be overly optimistic, the term *globalization* may overstate its case, inviting resignation or fatalism. We are in a *globalizing* world as opposed to a *globalized* one. As such, we still have a chance to define its contours and contents before the "center" is occupied without our participation. It is indeed empowering to feel that we can still make a difference.

I turn to the teachings of the Buddha in order to responsibly engage with the sufferings in the world. Throughout the decades of my activism, I am sustained and rejuvenated by a very simple magic the Buddha had to offer. I shall share it with you and hope that you too will be nurtured.

Let me begin with the story of a monk who went to see the Buddha and who told the Awakened One that he had meditated for many years before he could obtain a magical power to walk on water across the river. The Buddha commented on how silly that monk was to waste so much time to achieve something that is not at all useful. If the monk wished to cross the river, the best way to do so was to get a boatman and pay him to take him across.

In Buddhism, magic is not walking on water or flying in the air. It is indeed miraculous to walk on earth mindfully and to attribute what mother earth contributes to the welfare of all. When we look at a flower mindfully, we will realize that it is indeed a very simple magic: the flower also has non-flower elements. Right now it is fresh and beautiful, but soon it will decay and die. Yet it will become compost and will be reborn as a plant, which will again produce flowers for all those who appreciate beauty and goodness.

Likewise, each of us too will one day die, and our dead bodies will unite with the earth, and rebirth will take place miraculously or magically for those who wish to understand the interconnectedness of all things or the inter-being of all.

Without you, I could not be me. You and I *inter-are*, as Thich Nhat Hanh puts it. In each of us, there are also non-human elements. We are the sun, the moon, the earth, the river, the ocean, the trees, and everything else. Without trees, we human beings cannot survive.

Scientific knowledge conditions humans to be like machines, and we perceive the world and the universe as merely composed of matter. Matter is merely things, and things have no life or feeling. Hence we destroy Mother Earth and cut down trees merely for financial gain or in the name of economic development.

If we adopt the Cartesian "I think therefore I am," then any being which cannot think is regarded as inferior and can therefore be exploited by those who can think. Even among thinking beings, the clever ones who can think better are in a position to exploit the weaker ones—in accordance with the Darwinian notion of survival of the fittest.

The more we concentrate on thinking, the more our thought becomes compartmentalized. The deeper we think, the more we can bury our thoughts and ourselves. We cannot see the wood for the trees. We are unable to perceive the world holistically. Hence the products of this thinking and our experiments with matter, scientism, and technology, are unable to be questioned.

An even greater problem is that when we reach the age of economism and consumerism, which goes by the name of globalization, we change the phrase "I think therefore I am" into "I *buy* therefore I am." Hence human beings on the whole have only two aspects in life: to earn money in order to consume whatever advertisers brainwash us to purchase.

Advertisers are on the whole controlled by transnational corporations, which have become more influential than any nation-state, and their main objective is to exploit natural resources and human beings in the relentless pursuit of economic gain.

The heart of Buddhist teaching has much to do with social ills. The crux of the Buddha's teachings transcends the notion of individual salvation and is concerned with the whole realm of sentient beings. The inescapable conclusion is that Buddhism requires an engagement in social, economic, and political affairs. One cannot overcome the limits of the individual self in a selfish and hermetically sealed manner.

The four noble truths—suffering, the causes of suffering, the cessation of suffering, and the path to that cessation—can be skillfully applied to social activism. This is indeed a very simple magic. Moreover, through deep breathing one can see the roots of social suffering on a basis of Buddhism's three main root causes of evil, namely greed, hatred, and ignorance.

In narrow terms of interpretation, understanding these three root causes can help us to get rid of pains and disturbance in our personal lives. But in broader terms, or in the social context, they can really help us to envisage the causes and give us hints about the ways the causes can be ceased.

In my view, consumerism and capitalism can be explained as the most important damaging modern form of greed. With them, our values are geared toward satisfying the gaps in our life by ever-increasing consumption and accumulation. By failing to understand the magic of advertising we are at its mercy. This inevitably leads to conflicts of interests, and more importantly, exploitations are justified by the concept of the "invisible hand."

Militarism embodies hatred as its core basis. The lust for power, which leads to widespread human rights abuses, is a prime example of how hatred can manipulate individual minds and lure them to install unjust social structures in order to uphold their power.

The last main root cause, ignorance, is caused mainly by centralized education. Students are taught not to think holistically, but to compartmentalize their thinking, to memorize, and to abide by the existing norms. This can help explain much of the weakening in the mobilization of student movements, as well as other social movements. Often times, students are trained and equipped just with the skills to become employees for multinational companies, to exploit their own fellow nationals and nature. Children also get exposed to detrimental values through television, computer games, etc., which have been replacing, to a certain unknown degree, the traditional roles played by teachers.

Buddhism is unique in that its approach is not reinforced by faith, but rather by practice. Thus, to attain understanding, one has to really experiment with the truths themselves. Aloofness is never a value praised by Buddhists. Buddhism also gives us a sense of inter-belonging. With this view, we feel the inter-relatedness of all beings. It helps to internally affirm a common phrase among Buddhists that we all are "friends in common suffering."

Thus, the Buddhist model of development must begin with everyone truly practicing to understand himself or herself. In the Buddhist tradition, we call it *citta sikkha*, or the contemplation on mind. Meditation is important for us to attain insight, which includes the qualities of alertness and criticality. Critical self-awareness is important for us, and from the critical understanding of our self, we can begin to critically understand our community, society, nation, and eventually our world. From criticizing ourselves, we hold the critical awareness toward society, the government, and all the establishments, in order to understand how these mechanisms of greed, hatred, and ignorance operate and manipulate people at the structural levels. Bearing in mind the solutions, we can use all non-violent means to achieve a peaceful end.

Buddhist tenets also help us feel closer to and eventually be one with the people. In our tradition, it is believed that every being embodies a buddha nature, or the potential to attain the highest understanding. Thinking this way, we feel the equality among all of us, regardless of rank and status. We feel that the poor are entitled to the same dignity as us to struggle for what they should be given.

For me, activism grows out of a very simple magic offered by the Buddha. Our formula for it could go like this:

Let us pray for world peace, social justice, and environmental balance, which begin with our own breathing.

I breathe in calmly and breathe out mindfully.

Once I have seeds of peace and happiness within me, I try to reduce my selfish desire and reconstitute my consciousness.

With less attachment to myself, I try to understand the structural violence in the world.

Linking my heart with my head, I perceive the world holistically, a sphere full of living beings who are all related to me.

I try to expand my understanding with love to help build a more nonviolent world.

I vow to live simply and offer myself to the oppressed.

By the grace of the Compassionate Ones and with the help of good friends, may I be a partner in lessening the suffering of the world so that it may be a proper habitat for all sentient beings to live in harmony during this millennium.

Sam Harris' book *The End of Faith* was an impassioned polemic against the threat of literalist religion in a heavily armed world. Harris believes deeply that the wisdom, ethics, and practices of Buddhism are precisely what the world needs—but he believes they'd be more effectively offered in a universal, secular context. He argues that presenting Buddhism as a religion limits its benefit and legitimizes the religious divisions that are the greatest danger of the twenty-first century.

★ ★ ★

KILLING THE BUDDHA

by Sam Harris

THE NINTH-CENTURY BUDDHIST MASTER LINJI is supposed to have said, "If you meet the Buddha on the road, kill him." Like much of Zen teaching, this seems too cute by half, but it makes a valuable point: to turn the Buddha into a religious fetish is to miss the essence of what he taught. In considering what Buddhism can offer the world in the twenty-first century, I propose that we take Linji's admonishment rather seriously: as students of the Buddha, we should dispense with Buddhism.

This is not to say that Buddhism has nothing to offer the world. One could surely argue that the Buddhist tradition, taken as a whole, represents the richest source of contemplative wisdom that any civilization has produced. In a world that has long been terrorized by fundamentalist religion, the ascendance of Buddhism would surely be a welcome development. But this will not happen. There is no reason whatsoever to think that Buddhism can compete successfully with the relentless evangelizing of Christianity and Islam. Nor should it try to.

The wisdom of the Buddha is currently trapped within the religion of Buddhism. Even in the West, where scientists and Buddhist contemplatives now collaborate in studying the effects of meditation on the brain, Buddhism remains an utterly parochial concern. While it may be true enough to say (as many Buddhist practitioners allege) that "Buddhism is not a religion," most Buddhists worldwide practice it as such, in many of the naïve, petitionary, and superstitious ways in which all religions are practiced. And, needless to say, all non-Buddhists believe Buddhism to be a religion—and, what is more, they are quite certain that it is the *wrong* religion.

To talk about "Buddhism," therefore, inevitably imparts a false sense of the Buddha's teaching to others. So insofar as we maintain a discourse as "Buddhists," we ensure that the wisdom of the Buddha will do little to inform the development of civilization in the twenty-first century.

Worse still, the continued identification of Buddhists with Buddhism lends tacit support to the religious differences in our world. At this point in history, this is both morally and intellectually indefensible—especially among affluent, well-educated Westerners who bear the greatest responsibility for the spread of ideas. It does not seem much of an exaggeration to say that if you are reading this article, you are in better position to influence the course of history than almost any person *in* history. Given the degree to which religion still inspires human conflict, and impedes genuine inquiry, I believe that merely being a self-described "Buddhist" is to be complicit in the world's violence and ignorance to an unacceptable degree.

It is true that many exponents of Buddhism, most notably the Dalai Lama, have been remarkably willing to enrich (and even alter) their view of the world through dialogue with modern science. But the fact that the Dalai Lama regularly meets with Western scientists to discuss the nature of the mind does not mean that Buddhism, or Tibetan Buddhism, or even the Dalai Lama's own lineage, is uncontaminated by religious dogmatism. Indeed, there are ideas within Buddhism that are so incredible as to render the dogma of virgin birth plausible by comparison. No one is served by a mode of discourse that treats such pre-literate notions as integral to our evolving discourse about the nature of the human mind. Among Western Buddhists, there are college-educated men and women who apparently believe that Guru Rinpoche was actually born from a *lotus*. This is not the spiritual breakthrough that civilization has been waiting for these many centuries.

For the fact is that a person can embrace the Buddha's teaching, and even become a genuine Buddhist contemplative (and, one must presume, a Buddha) without believing anything on insufficient evidence. The same cannot be said of the teachings for faith-based religion. In many respects, Buddhism is very much like science. One starts with the hypothesis that using attention in the prescribed way (meditation), and engaging in or avoiding certain behaviors (ethics), will bear the promised result (wisdom and psychological well-being). This spirit of empiricism animates Buddhism to a unique degree. For this reason, the methodology of Buddhism, if shorn of its religious encumbrances, could be one of our greatest resources as we struggle to develop our scientific understanding of human subjectivity.

THE PROBLEM OF RELIGION

Incompatible religious doctrines have Balkanized our world into separate moral communities, and these divisions have become a continuous source of bloodshed. Indeed, religion is as much a living spring of violence today as it has been at any time in the past. The recent conflicts in Palestine (Jews vs. Muslims), the Balkans (Orthodox Serbians vs. Catholic Croatians; Orthodox Serbians vs. Bosnian and Albanian Muslims), Northern Ireland (Protestants vs. Catholics), Kashmir (Muslims vs. Hindus), Sudan (Muslims vs. Christians and animists), Nigeria (Muslims vs. Christians), Ethiopia and Eritrea (Muslims vs. Christians), Sri Lanka (Sinhalese Buddhists vs. Tamil Hindus), Indonesia (Muslims vs. Timorese Christians), Iran and Iraq (Shiite vs. Sunni Muslims), and the Caucasus (Orthodox Russians vs. Chechen Muslims; Muslim Azerbaijanis vs. Catholic and Orthodox Armenians) are merely a few cases in point. These are places where religion has been the *explicit* cause of literally millions of deaths in recent decades.

If you think that religious conflict is reducible to lack of education, poverty, or politics, it is worth reflecting on the fact that the September 11th hijackers were college-educated, middle class, and had no discernable political grievances. Our situation, astonishingly enough, is this: a person can be so well-educated that he can build a nuclear bomb, while still believing that he will get seventy-two virgins in Paradise following his martyrdom. Such is the ease with which the human mind can be partitioned by faith, and such is the manner in which our intellectual discourse still patiently accommodates religious fantasy. If we want to uproot the causes of religious violence we must uproot the false certainties of religion.

WHY IS RELIGION SUCH A POTENT SOURCE OF HUMAN VIOLENCE?

First, our religions are intrinsically incompatible with one another. Either Jesus rose from the dead and will be returning to earth like a superhero, or not; either the Koran is the infallible word of God, or it isn't. Every religion makes explicit claims about the way the world is, and the sheer profusion of these incompatible claims creates an enduring basis for conflict.

Second, there is no other sphere of discourse in which human beings so fully articulate their differences from one another, or cast these differences in terms of everlasting rewards and punishments. Religion is the one endeavor in which us-them thinking achieves a transcendent significance. If you really believe that calling God by the right name can spell the difference between eternal happiness and eternal suffering, then it becomes quite reasonable to treat heretics and unbelievers rather badly. It may be quite reasonable to kill them, if you really think this is the way the universe is structured. If you think there is something that your neighbor can say to your children that could put their souls in jeopardy for all eternity, then the heretic next door is actually far more dangerous than the child molester. The stakes of our religious differences are immeasurably higher than those born of mere tribalism, racism, or politics.

Third, religious faith is a conversation-stopper. When was the last time anyone was admonished to respect another person's beliefs about physics or medicine? Religion is the only area of our discourse in which people are systematically protected from the demand to give evidence in defense of their strongly held beliefs. And yet these beliefs often determine what they live for, what they will die for, and all too often what they will kill for.

This is a problem, because when the stakes are high, human beings have a simple choice between conversation and violence. At the level of societies, the choice is between conversation and war. There is nothing apart from a fundamental willingness to be reasonable—to have one's beliefs about the world revised by new evidence and new arguments—

that can guarantee we will keep talking to one another. Certainty without evidence, therefore, is necessarily divisive and dehumanizing.

One of the greatest challenges facing civilization in the twenty-first century is for human beings to learn to speak about their deepest personal concerns—about ethics, spiritual experience, and the inevitability of human suffering—in ways that are not flagrantly irrational. Nothing stands in the way of this project more than the respect we accord religious faith. While there is no guarantee that rational people will always agree, the irrational are certain to be divided by their dogmas.

Finally, it seems profoundly unlikely that we will heal the divisions in our world simply by multiplying the occasions for inter-faith dialogue. The end game for civilization cannot be mutual tolerance of patent irrationality. Generally, parties to ecumenical discourse have agreed to tread lightly over those points where their worldviews would otherwise collide, while these very points remain perpetual sources of fascination and violence for their coreligionists. Such political correctness does not offer an enduring basis for human cooperation.

If religious war is ever to become unthinkable for us, in the way that slavery and cannibalism are, it will be a matter of our having dispensed with the dogma of faith—the idea that beliefs can be sanctified by something other than evidence and rational argument. If our tribalism is ever to give way to an extended moral identity, our religious beliefs can no longer be sheltered from the tides of genuine inquiry and criticism. Where we have reasons for what we believe, we have no need of faith; where we have no reasons, we have lost both our connection to the world and to one another. It is time we realized that the only thing we should respect in a person's faith is his desire for a better life in *this* world; we need not respect his certainty that one awaits him in the next.

A CONTEMPLATIVE SCIENCE

What the world most needs at this moment is a means of convincing human beings to embrace the whole of the species as their moral community. For this we need to develop an utterly non-sectarian way of talking about the full spectrum of human experience and human aspiration. We need a discourse on ethics and spirituality that is every bit as unconstrained by dogma and cultural prejudice as the discourse of science is. What we need, in fact, is a *contemplative science,* a modern approach to exploring the furthest reaches of psychological well-being. It should go without saying that we will not develop such a science by attempting to spread "American Buddhism," or "Western Buddhism," or "Engaged Buddhism."

If the methodology of Buddhism (ethical precepts and meditation) uncovers genuine truths about the mind and the phenomenal world— truths like emptiness, selflessness, and impermanence—these truths are not in the least "Buddhist." No doubt, most serious practitioners of meditation realize this, but most Buddhists do not. Consequently, even if a person is aware of the timeless and non-contingent nature of the meditative insights described in the Buddhist literature, his identity as a Buddhist will tend to confuse the matter for others.

There is a reason that we don't talk about "Christian physics" or "Muslim algebra," though the Christians invented physics as we know it, and the Muslims invented algebra. Today, anyone who emphasizes the Christian roots of physics or the Muslim roots of algebra would stand convicted of not understanding these disciplines at all. In the same way, once we develop a scientific account of the contemplative path, it will utterly transcend its religious associations. Once such a conceptual revolution has taken place, speaking of "Buddhist" meditation will be synonymous with a failure to assimilate the changes that have occurred in our understanding of the human mind.

It is as yet undetermined what it means to be human, because every facet of our culture—and even our biology itself—remains open to innovation and insight. We do not know what we will be a thousand years from now—or indeed *that* we will be, given the lethal absurdity of many of our beliefs—but whatever changes await us, one thing seems unlikely to change: as long as experience endures, the difference between happiness and suffering will remain our paramount concern. We will therefore want to understand those processes—biochemical, behavioral, ethical, political, economic, and spiritual—that account for this difference. We do not yet have anything like a final understanding of such processes, but we know enough to rule out many false understandings.

There is much more to be discovered about the nature of the human mind. In particular, there is much more for us to understand about how the mind can transform itself from a mere reservoir of greed, hatred, and delusion into an instrument of wisdom and compassion. Students of the Buddha are very well placed to further our understanding on this front, but the religion of Buddhism currently stands in their way.

TO CONCLUDE, here are some pithy statements by the Zen teacher, translator, and renowned calligrapher Kaz Tanahashi on principles of mindful citizenship and strategies to achieve the breakthroughs our world so badly needs.

★ ★ ★

FOUR TRUTHS & TEN LAWS

by Kazuaki Tanahashi

FOUR COMMONPLACE TRUTHS

1. No situation is impossible to change.
2. A communal vision, outstanding strategy, and sustained effort can bring forth positive changes.
3. Everyone can help make a difference.
4. No one is free of responsibility.

TEN LAWS OF BREAKTHROUGH

1. Breakthrough may or may not occur. The result is unpredictable and how it happens is mysterious. All we can do is to work toward breakthrough.
2. Some breakthroughs are life-affirming and others destructive.
3. The chance for breakthrough increases when the objective and the process are clearly stated.
4. The chance for breakthrough increases when the blocks are clearly identified.
5. The smaller the objective is, the greater is the chance for breakthrough.
6. An effective, intense, and continuous effort builds a foundation for breakthrough.
7. The more forces combine, the greater is the chance for breakthrough.

8. The greater the objective is, the easier it is to bring together force for breakthrough.

9. The chance for breakthrough increases when more attention is directed to the process than to the goal.

10. Nonattachment is a crucial element for breakthrough.

CONTRIBUTORS

Ezra Bayda teaches Zen at the Zen Center of San Diego. He is the author of *Being Zen, At Home in Muddy Water,* and, most recently, *Saying Yes to Life (Even the Hard Parts),* with Josh Bartok.

Jerry Brown is mayor of Oakland, California. He served as governor of California for eight years and was a three-time presidential candidate. He has a strong spiritual and philosophical background as a student of Zen and as a former Jesuit seminarian.

Pema Chödrön is an American Buddhist nun and resident teacher at Gampo Abbey in Cape Breton, Nova Scotia. Her many best-selling books include *The Places that Scare You, When Things Fall Apart,* and, most recently, *No Time to Lose: A Timely Guide to the Way of the Bodhisattva.*

Gaylon Ferguson is an *acharya* (senior teacher) in the Shambhala Buddhist tradition and has taught Buddhist studies at Naropa University. He has a doctorate in cultural anthropology from Stanford and was a contributor to *Dharma, Color, and Culture: New Voices in Western Buddhism.*

Gehlek Rinpoche is the founder and president of Jewel Heart, based in Ann Arbor, Michigan with chapters in the United States, Singapore, Malaysia, and the Netherlands. He is the author of *Good Life, Good Death: Tibetan Wisdom on Reincarnation.*

James Gimian has been studying and teaching the *Sun Tzu* text for more than twenty-five years. He served as general editor for *The Art of War: The Denma Translation* and conducts seminars on the text's strategies and practices. He is publisher of the *Shambhala Sun* magazine.

Roshi Bernie Glassman is a Zen teacher and was first dharma successor of Taizan Maezumi Roshi. He founded the Greyston Mandala of community development organizations in Yonkers, New York, and was cofounder of the Zen Peacemaker Order. He recently established the Maezumi Institute in Montague, Massachusetts.

Joseph Goldstein is a cofounder of the Insight Meditation Society in Barre, Massachusetts, where he is one of the resident guiding teachers. He is also a founder of the Forest Refuge, a center for long-term meditation practice. Goldstein is the author of several books, including the influential *One Dharma: The Emerging Western Buddhism*.

Rita M. Gross is a scholar-practitioner who has written extensively on Buddhism and gender. She teaches Buddhism in a wide variety of academic and dharmic contexts. Her best-known book is the influential *Buddhism after Patriarchy: A Feminist History, Analysis, and Reconstruction of Buddhism*.

Tenzin Gyatso, the 14th Dalai Lama, is the spiritual and temporal leader of the Tibetan people and winner of the Nobel Peace Prize. Unique in the world today, he is a statesman, national leader, spiritual teacher, and deeply learned theologian. He advocates a universal "religion of human kindness" that transcends sectarian differences.

Thich Nhat Hanh is a Zen master, poet, and founder of the Engaged Buddhist movement. A well-known antiwar activist in his native Vietnam, he was nominated for the Nobel Peace Prize by Martin Luther King, Jr. In 2005 he returned to Vietnam for the first time since his exile in 1966. Among his recent books on political themes are *Calming the Fearful Mind: A Zen Response to Terrorism* and *Peace Begins Here: Palestinians and Israelis Listen to Each Other.*

Sam Harris is author of the controversial bestseller, *The End of Faith: Religion, Terror, and the Future of Reason*. Currently completing his doctorate in neuroscience, he is a graduate in philosophy from Stanford University. He spent many years practicing Vipassana meditation and later studied Dzogchen under Tulku Urgyen Rinpoche and Nyoshul Khen Rinpoche.

bell hooks is one of America's most versatile and prolific social critics. Best known for her ground-breaking book on feminism and race, *Ain't I a Woman?*, she is a leading thinker on the search for love and community in a society marked by power imbalances in many forms. She is currently Distinguished Professor in Residence at Berea College in Berea, Kentucky.

Charles R. Johnson is a novelist, scholar, and essayist who combines his study of Buddhism with a deep knowledge of the African-American struggle for liberation. Johnson holds the S. Wilson and Grace M. Pollock Professorship for Excellence in English at the University of Washington in Seattle. He has been the recipient of many prestigious awards, including a Guggenheim Fellowship and a MacArthur Foundation grant. His novels include *Dreamer* and *Middle Passage*, for which he won a National Book Award.

Ken Jones is secretary of the UK Network of Engaged Buddhists and author of *The New Social Face of Buddhism: An Alternative Sociopolitical Perspective.*

Stephanie Kaza is an associate professor of environmental studies at the University of Vermont, where she teaches on religion and ecology, ecofeminism, and unlearning consumerism. A long-time student of Zen, she is coeditor of *Dharma Rain: Sources of Buddhist Environmentalism*, and editor of *Hooked: Buddhist Writings on Greed, Desire, and the Urge to Consume.*

David Loy is Besl Professor of Religion and Ethics at Xavier University in Cincinnati. His books include *A Buddhist History of the West: A Study in Lack,*

The Great Awakening: A Buddhist Social Theory, and, most recently, *The Dharma of Dragons and Daemons: Buddhist Themes in Modern Fantasy,* with Linda Goodhew. He has been a Zen student for many years.

Melvin McLeod attended the National Defense College of Canada, the country's highest institution for the study of domestic and international affairs. He is the Editor-in-Chief of *Shambhala Sun* magazine and *Buddhadharma: The Practitioner's Journal.* He is also the editor of the *Best Buddhist Writing* collections. He has spent his life studying politics: he took a degree in political science, including a period of study in Washington, and has covered political stories in his capacity as a journalist. He lives in Halifax, Nova Scotia.

Fabrice Midal is professor of philosophy at the University of Paris. He is the author of *Chögyam Trungpa: His Life and Vision* and *Recalling Chögyam Trungpa.*

Reginald A. Ray is professor of Buddhist studies at Naropa University and president of the Dharma Ocean Foundation in Crestone, Colorado, where he teaches Buddhist programs. His books include *Indestructable Truth, Secret of the Vajra World,* and *In the Presence of Masters.*

Seung Sahn was the first Korean Zen master to live and teach in the West. He was founding teacher of the Kwan Um School of Zen, an international organization of more than one hundred centers and groups. Seung Sahn died in 2005. The most recent book of his teachings to be published is *Wanting Enlightenment Is a Big Mistake.*

Sulak Sivaraksa is founder of the International Network of Engaged Buddhists. An outspoken activist and social critic in his native Thailand, he has published more than one hundred books, including *Seeds of Peace* and *Socially Engaged Buddhism.* In 1995, he won the Right Livelihood Award, also known as the Alternative Nobel Prize.

Kazuaki Tanahashi is a Zen teacher, author, translator, and renowned calligrapher. Among his books are *Brush Mind, Endless Vow,* and *Enlightenment Unfolds.* He recently collaborated with John Daido Loori, on *The True Dharma Eye: Zen Master Dogen's Three Hundred Koans.*

Thanissaro Bhikkhu (Geoffrey DeGraff) is abbot of Metta Forest Monastery in Valley Center, California. He also teaches at the Barre Center for Buddhist Studies and at the Sati Center for Buddhist Studies in Palo Alto. He has translated a four-volume anthology of Pali suttas, *Handful of Leaves;* many of his writings and teachings are available at www.accesstoinsight.org.

Jigmi Thinley is Home Minister of Bhutan, where he has also served as Prime Minister. He is president of the Council of the Centre for Bhutan Studies.

Chögyam Trungpa Rinpoche (1937–87) was a pivotal figure in the transmission of Buddhism to the West. His best-known books are *Cutting Through Spiritual Materialism* and *Shambhala: The Sacred Path of the Warrior.* The eight-volume *Collected Works of Chögyam Trungpa* was published in 2003.

Margaret Wheatley is president of the Berkana Institute and an internationally recognized authority on leadership and organization. She is the author of the ground-breaking book *Leadership and the New Science;* her most recent book is *Finding Our Way: Leadership for an Uncertain Time.*

CREDITS

INDEX

ABOUT WISDOM

Wisdom Publications, a nonprofit publisher, is dedicated to making available authentic works relating to Buddhism for the benefit of all. We publish books by ancient and modern masters in all traditions of Buddhism, translations of important texts, and original scholarship. Additionally, we offer books that explore East-West themes unfolding as traditional Buddhism encounters our modern culture in all its aspects. Our titles are published with the appreciation of Buddhism as a living philosophy, and with the special commitment to preserve and transmit important works from Buddhism's many traditions.

To learn more about Wisdom, or to browse books online, visit our website at www.wisdompubs.org.

You may request a copy of our catalog online or by writing to this address:

Wisdom Publications
199 Elm Street
Somerville, Massachusetts 02144 USA
Telephone: 617-776-7416
Fax: 617-776-7841
Email: info@wisdompubs.org
www.wisdompubs.org

THE WISDOM TRUST

As a nonprofit publisher, Wisdom is dedicated to the publication of Dharma books for the benefit of all sentient beings and dependent upon the kindness and generosity of sponsors in order to do so. If you would like to make a donation to Wisdom, you may do so through our website or our Somerville office. If you would like to help sponsor the publication of a book, please write or email us at the address above.

Thank you.

Wisdom is a nonprofit, charitable 501(c)(3) organization affiliated with the Foundation for the Preservation of the Mahayana Tradition (FPMT).